THE
ROOTS
OF
LIBERALISM

PRAISE FOR F. H. BUCKLEY

His prose explodes with energy.

—James Ceasar

FOR CURIOSITY:

You are our Montaigne!

—Christopher DeMuth

FOR THE REPUBLIC OF VIRTUE:

This is Buckley at his colorful, muckraking best—an intelligent, powerful, but depressing argument laced with humor.

—Gordon S. Wood

FOR THE WAY BACK:

Frank Buckley marshals tremendous data and insight in a compelling study.

—Francis Fukuyama

FOR THE ONCE AND FUTURE KING:

Penetrating, . . . iconoclastic. No U.S. political scientist has achieved what F. H. Buckley does in this ambitious book.

—Times Literary Supplement

THE ROOTS OF LIBERALISM

*What Faithful Knights
and the
Little Match Girl
Taught Us about
Civic Virtue*

F. H. BUCKLEY

Encounter
BOOKS

New York • London

First American edition published in 2024 by Encounter Books, an activity of Encounter for Culture and Education, Inc., a nonprofit, tax exempt corporation. Encounter Books website address: www.encounterbooks.com

Manufactured in the United States and printed on acid-free paper. The paper used in this publication meets the minimum requirements of ANSI/NISO Z39.48–1992 (R 1997) (*Permanence of Paper*).

FIRST AMERICAN EDITION

LIBRARY OF CONGRESS CATALOGING-IN-PUBLICATION DATA IS AVAILABLE

Information for this title can be found at the Library of Congress website under the following ISBN 2024026700 and LCCN 9781641774031.

TABLE OF CONTENTS

So there is in us a world of love to somewhat,
though we know not what in the world that should be.

—THOMAS TRAHERNE

For Esther, Sarah, Nick, Ben, and Max.

1

THE CRISIS OF LIBERALISM

In today's politics, there is a growing sense that liberalism has been tried and failed. Illiberal ideas we had thought long buried—the belief that inconvenient constitutional guardrails can be ignored and that democracy doesn't matter unless our side wins—are now commonly accepted. We judge others solely by their politics and preen in our hatred of ideological enemies.

This is true of both sides, but it's especially true of the left, which has come to dominate our culture and finds that liberalism gets in its way. Free-speech rights were all very well when the left was the dissenter, but not after it ascended to power. Then the dissenters were on the right, and the left became the censors. At one time a patriotic respect for our founding principles might have restrained leftists, but such impediments were removed when the Founders were revealed to be evil racists. In the riots and looting, something had snapped, and in place of liberalism the left adopted an explicitly illiberal ideology called Critical Race Theory.

While CRT describes itself as progressive, it's really a regressive movement that spurns Christian and Enlightenment virtues. Nothing new there. It's what the deconstructionists were peddling fifty years ago. This time it's different, however. CRT doesn't come to us from incomprehensible French intellectuals. Instead, it's a cult of resentment that rejects the norms of a color-blind society and preaches that liberalism is a fraud which masks the structural racism of an historically unjust nation. It tells us that America was founded on slavery and that we're a police state that continues to hold people of color in involuntary servitude. Crude and degraded as this is, it has become the official ideology at our best universities, and that also is new.

Immanuel Kant said that rules aren't moral unless they can be applied universally, and Jeremy Bentham thought that everyone should count as one and no one as more than one. This comes down to saying that all lives matter, but that phrase has become toxic and taken as an assertion that black lives don't matter. To be on the right side of these issues is to be a friend. To be on the wrong side is to be an enemy and unworthy of ordinary civility.

The abandonment of universal moral norms represents a return to the darker illiberal politics of Carl Schmitt and Germany in the 1930s. Schmitt was a German philosopher and jurist whose *Concept of the Political* (1932) argued that every question of politics must come down to a choice between friends and enemies.[1] Those who fail to recognize this are at best naïve and at worst hypocritical. Behind their pose of fairness, they provide aid and comfort to the enemy. Like Martin Heidegger, Schmitt became a member of the Nazi Party.

A Schmittian Moment

We are now at a Schmittian moment in our politics, in which everything comes down to a struggle between friends and enemies who are long past talking to each other. Those lighthearted moments when we chose novels to read, movies to watch, or people to befriend for the sheer pleasure of doing so are things of the past.

Instead, we're first to ask whether they're political enemies. If a woke establishment finds that they are, observe how quickly it turns on them, how rage becomes a sign of virtue, and how moral grandstanding takes the place of reasoned argument. In a twinkling of an eye and across the entire culture, an Elon Musk or J. K. Rowling metamorphosizes from hero to villain.

Read the bitter comments to stories in the *Washington Post* and you'll encounter moral nullities craving their anger high. They could avoid it by turning to the sports section, but instead they search for rage-inducing provocations to trigger the dopamine reward receptors in their brains. And like a pusher at the corner, the *Post* is happy to give them their fix. The paper should be delivered in a brown paper bag, like the smut magazines of the 1950s.

The mainstream media, which catered to a woke readership during the Trump years, now finds itself a prisoner of the emotions it had inflamed. At left-wing CNN, CEO Chris Licht was fired after he tried to make the network more balanced. He had sought the middle of the road and found there was no one there. Pre-Licht, viewers had tuned into CNN to get their shot of ire and then went into withdrawal when this was denied them. Walt Kelly's *Pogo* understood what had happened. "We have met the enemy and he is us."

In our maddened debates, the rituals and practices devised to protect liberal constitutionalism have been tossed out the window, and in their place the left has adopted three Schmittian principles. First, Schmitt thought that the state needn't respect individual rights. These included economic rights, which Schmitt thought hypocritical since the purportedly universal principles masked the dominance of a plutocratic elite. Today's left has the same problems with free markets, as well as First Amendment rights of free speech, except when these are employed to defend Hamas apologists.

Second, Schmitt rejected the legitimacy of political disagreement. As the Schmittian state asserts a monopoly on power, it regards all dissent as wrongful and has no curiosity about the defeated. "The adversary is thus no longer called an enemy but a disturber of peace and is thereby designated to be an outlaw of humanity."[2] To the extent that Schmitt supported democracy, it was based upon the homogeneity of the collective unity of a people, which the anti-Semitic Schmitt thought excluded Jews in the Third Reich. Similarly, the woke left refuses to acknowledge the legitimacy of dissent, and calls its opponents fascists.

Third, Schmitt was impatient with the procedural norms of constitutional democracies that get in the way of its substantive goals. So too, the woke left wants to eliminate the Electoral College, stack the Supreme Court, restrict free speech, ban voter ID, and jail a Republican presidential candidate.

The U.S. Constitution, with its checks and balances, was designed to tame Leviathan by requiring the assent of different bodies before a law could be enacted. The separation of powers was meant to serve as a barrier against an all-powerful sovereign, but Schmitt denied that it would do so. In every constitution, he said, there are gaps or exceptional circumstances in which the constitution may be suspended, and in his famous definition the sovereign is he who can invoke the exception.[3] That would make the president what the Framers most feared, an elective tyrant who could set aside the legal and constitutional order whenever he wants.

The illiberal state that Schmitt supported, one that crushed dissent and persecuted minorities, was so repellent that only intellectuals could find his ideas attractive. Surprisingly, this includes some conservatives, for Schmitt had given his anti-liberalism a far-right countenance by linking it to the ideas of nineteenth-century Catholic absolutists. What liberalism lacked, said Schmitt, was an explanation of why the state legitimately commands our obedience; and to explain the foundation for political obligation he turned to nineteenth-century arch-reactionaries such as Juan Donoso Cortés (1809–53). Since only the Catholic Church could ground an obligation of support, Cortés argued, "it follows . . . that the Church alone has the right to affirm and deny, and that there is no right outside her to affirm what she denies, or to deny what she affirms."[4]

Such ideas provided Schmitt with a similar explanation for political obligations, where the state assumes the right to command our loyalty just as the Church had done for Cortés. Schmitt's political sovereign took a handoff from the Church, in a transfer of the moral and political imperium to a sacralized state. Similarly, today's left sees itself as a Schmittian sovereign, composed of every thought leader and moral authority in the country, from the media to Wall Street to the academy to the bureaucrats of an overregulated economy. These are exceptional times, the left says, and it asserts the power to decide what is an exception and to sweep away the Constitution's procedural barriers.

For older Democrats, this represents a radical change. The Democratic Party had formerly embraced American ideals of liberal constitutionalism, but it now found them dated. They were like a jacket a person once had loved but which no longer was in style. It was perfectly serviceable, and there was a time when its cut was the height of fashion, but his new radical friends scorned it. "How can you go on wearing that thing?" they said. And so the Democrats cast it off, and took on the garb of the censors and racists.

For Republicans, the intelligent thing to do is to pick up the jacket and claim it for their party. Republicans who fondly recall an older set of GOP conservatives will recognize that they were really liberals. Abraham Lincoln, Theodore Roosevelt, and Dwight Eisenhower would all have been appalled at the thought that left illiberalism might provoke right illiberalism. That would be un-American, they would have said, and they would have been right.

Not so long ago we all felt this way, and when in 1955 Clinton Rossiter struggled to define conservatism, he had to admit that "the American political tradition is basically a Liberal tradition."[5] That apart, Rossiter's conservatism came down to a sense of fallen humanity and a list of Boy Scout virtues (a conservative will respect tradition, display loyalty, etc.). And while this might usefully repress a too-giddy leftism, American conservatism is vapid and lacking in substance. Conservatives might think they have exclusive rights to the defense of religion, families, and patriotism. But they don't. In addition, conservatism fails to explain why autonomy and individualism are good, why we prize our privacy, and why we owe obligations to others. It's on the wrong side of aristocracy and of American nationalism. That was why Lionel Trilling could say in 1950 that "liberalism is not only the dominant but even the sole intellectual tradition" in America.[6]

The long 1950s were a time when Daniel Bell could speak of "The End of Ideology." Since then, however, the left has become ideological and illiberal, and it's up to conservatives to pick up the mantle of a non-ideological liberalism. When a woke culture seeks to suppress dissent, it's conservatives who will defend liberal free-speech norms. When the left turns politics into a racial spoils system, it's the conservative who will seek the common good without discriminating. It's also the conservative who recognizes that free bargaining and free markets explain our prosperity. Conservatives have everything to gain from recognizing that, apart for some aging Democrats, they're the only liberals left in town.

Forget labels. The wokerati call themselves liberals but are anything but that, if there's any content to the word. They decry prejudice but perpetuate stereotypes about white males and evangelical Christians. They tell us that you have to become a racist to oppose racism. They imagine themselves standing up to Joe McCarthy but practice McCarthyism when they call millions of Republicans fascists and demand that they be silenced. They tell us that they value free speech but deny it to conservative speakers on college campuses. Older liberals, such as the Free Speech Movement's Mario Savio, would have felt betrayed by them.

Their liberalism is performative and made complete with the expression of the right set of pious utterances, without the need for anything more to be done. In the post–George Floyd era, they proudly confessed their racial guilt in yard signs that blacks would never see, simply to assert their superiority over their benighted neighbors. Their privileged institutions issued land-acknowledgement statements about how their property had unjustly been taken from Native Americans, but none of them offered to give it back.

For them, liberalism requires nothing more onerous than a knowledge of the current cultural signifiers. They instruct everyone on how to employ terms like Latinx and TERF and announce that it's offensive to refer to "the French." There are sixty-two genders, they say, and one of them isn't "women." They tell us that they want a more inclusive America, but they lie. They deploy their signifiers to exclude everyone but themselves.

They belong to what John McWhorter calls "the Elect," the priests of a religion of wokeness who enforce an ever-shifting catalogue of sins. Several years ago, they discovered cultural appropriation, a crime unheard of before then. Then they told us about unconscious racism. Today it's people who object to drag queen story hours for eight-year-olds. Like Savonarola, they have an insatiable desire to denounce other people.

The Elect tell us they seek justice, but what they really want is power. That's why we're asked to believe that biological men can get pregnant. They can't, and everyone knows this. But you don't exercise power when you require people to believe things that are true. The only power that counts is when people are made to think that two plus two equals five.

They say they're the party of humanity, but they're really misanthropes. They tell us we live in an overpopulated world, and that it's morally wrong to have children, who will consume resources, emit carbon dioxide, and harm the climate. In the name of sexual freedom, they encourage the sterilization of minors. They hate right-to-lifers and have made a sacrament of euthanasia. They were given a choice between life and death, and they chose death.

The right accuses them of communism, as though that is the worst thing there is. It's not. During the Soviet Era, the Russians had scholars, poets, classical musicians, and a high culture, and they lost twenty-seven million people fighting real fascism. The communists also had an ethos that, however oppressive and wasteful and however much they betrayed it, at least purported to offer a vision of the common good. The *nekulturny* Woko Haram are so much worse than the communists. Without learning, without cultural attainments, without a universal moral code, they are a stain upon our history and when they've departed will leave no greater trace than the froth left by a polluted wave as it sinks into the sand.

Despite this, far-right "Integralists" also reject liberalism. They include the intellectuals who admire Carl Schmitt and Donoso Cortés. Others of them think that liberalism lacks a moral code other than the satisfaction of personal preferences and the sacralization of individual choice, and they blame liberalism for the way the left has won the culture wars. They're right to find the decline in standards troubling, but so great is their revulsion at the banal and unimaginative ways in which we all offend God that it's not hard to see an element of misanthropy in their Integralism.

There was a similar sense of despair on the fall of France in 1940. After the Germans marched down the Champs-Elysées, people accused André Gide of having corrupted the youth of France. Even Gide—the Immoralist—came to agree with this. "Softness, surrender, relaxation in grace and ease, so many charming qualities that were to lead us, blindfolded, to defeat. And, most often, a simple ignoble, spineless permission slip."[7] If Gide could become a Pétainist,[8] perhaps we shouldn't be surprised to see Integralists turn antiliberal today.

Improbably, they seek to turn America (23 percent Catholic) into a Catholic confessional state. That's political lunacy, of course, and recalls Marx's comment on Young England's feudal socialism—half lamentation, half lampoon. Even majoritarian Catholic societies, such as Quebec and Ireland, would reject Integralism.

It would also be self-defeating, since Catholics have been and are a principal beneficiary of the ways in which liberalism has checked anti-Catholic bigotry. Émile Combes (1835–1921), the anti-clerical prime minister of France, employed the logic of Integralist absolutism to justify the suppression of Catholic schools in 1905, saying that "there can be no rights except the right of the State . . . and there can be no other authority other than the authority of the Republic."[9] On the left, many agree with this, and condemn Catholic hospitals that refuse on religious grounds to perform abortions.

Integralism's caricature grossly misrepresents what liberalism has meant in the past. Lincoln was as different from Gide as any two men could be, and no one mistook Dwight Eisenhower for *Playboy*'s Hugh Hefner. The Integralist's idea of liberalism is what you get when it's wholly detached from the idea of virtue. What is needed, then, is a better understanding of liberalism and its relation to virtue.

LIBERALISM BEFORE LOCKE

Anti-liberalism has obscured the story of how liberalism arose in the West. It began not with political philosophers such as John Locke but centuries before, in our culture's institutions and longings. It's not an ideology that stands above our practices and judges them, but a practice itself, and its content is found in the adventures of moral heroes and a literature about kindness. Nor is it buried in an irretrievable past. Rather, it's embedded in the present, in actively remembered heroes such as the Black Prince and in the modern superheroes who are their embodiments.

Until very recently, liberalism was the wellspring of our political culture. To call someone illiberal is to rule him out of bounds, to think him morally debased. On one side were the Founders, the Framers of the Constitution, and Abraham Lincoln. On the other were the communists, the conservative apologists for Jim Crow, and Joe McCarthy. On one side the pro-Dreyfusards, on the other the anti-Dreyfusards. Liberalism was a faith that mainstream Republicans and Democrats both shared, however much they might quarrel about smaller issues.

Most obviously, the liberal is on the side of free choice and opposed to paternalism and state interference with personal preferences. Free choices ordinarily lead to better consequences, says the liberal, since individuals know better than the state what they need in order to flourish. "The strongest of all the arguments against the interference of the public with purely personal conduct," said John Stuart Mill (1806–73), "is that when [the state] does interfere, the odds are that it interferes wrongly, and in the wrong place."[10] That's a prudential argument about the clumsiness of legislation and the limits of rulemaking, known all too well by anyone who's had dealings with City Hall. The state should hesitate before it plays the paternalist and second-guesses an individual's idea of the good. It lacks the information to do so intelligently.

A second defense of liberty is rooted in the value of personal autonomy, the idea that self-rule is desirable in itself and not only for what is chosen. We take joy in self-mastery, and it is good that we should do so. Through personal autonomy we take control of our lives and achieve the moral freedom of an adult, free from the tutelage of parents and the state. We feel what a child does when he assumes control of his destiny.

The grinches who take choices away tell us they're simply pushing us toward the good. You want a Big Gulp? You can't have that. You want a Jeep? You can't have that. You want a gas stove? You can't have that. Sometimes they're right, and sometimes they're just joyless Savonarolas, but in either case they forget that how we get to the good matters. Autonomy is a means of doing so, and as Derek Parfit noted, "mattering as a means is a way of mattering."[11] The freely chosen ice cream tastes better than the one forced on us, even if it's the same flavor in the end.

That won't satisfy philosopher John Kekes. Liberals have an "evil problem," he says, because they believe that personal autonomy trumps virtue. We get to do what we want, however nasty that might be. Alternatively, liberals might naively think that we'll always choose to act morally. But liberals needn't believe either of these things. The most famous liberal, John Stuart Mill, explicitly denied them. Like him, liberals will think that some choices are morally wrong and that evildoers should be prosecuted if their actions are crimes and shamed if they're not. Some choices are noble, some ignoble. The liberal can say all this because he does not identify his creed with autonomy or think that the answer to evil is more autonomy.

The overarching desideratum for liberals like Mill is not autonomy but the common good. They know that this includes other things that Kekes lists as important: peace, prosperity, civility, a high culture, and a healthy environment. Liberals also know that, to promote the good, the autonomy of murderers and rapists must be abridged. They might not think the free-speech rights of pornographers worthy of respect, but they will think that autonomy matters. What makes them liberals is their belief that personal autonomy is one element of the common good. As such, they are not required to answer the anti-liberal's charge of immoralism. Rather, the onus of explanation lies with the anti-liberal to tell us why he objects to totalitarianism, if autonomy isn't a good.

Liberals don't think that the good life can always be defined in a single manner, that there's always a single right thing to do and that we all know what it is.[12] Instead, liberals are *pluralists* who think that there is a diversity of goods from which individuals must choose, and that one can't always say which is best.[13] But that doesn't mean that liberals can be charged with moral skepticism. While there is a diversity of goods, that doesn't exclude the possibility of absolute goods, like life and the value of love and friendship, or absolute bads, prompted by envy, malice, or an indifference to another's pain. Severe evils might warrant a civil or criminal penalty, while less serious harms might be policed by society's signal of moral opprobrium without the need for legal sanctions.

We can therefore reject the Integralist's claim that liberal pluralists lack a moral vision and a set of ends to pursue. Virtue might firstly be supplied from the outside. A good society might fly on two wings and incorporate both a set of virtues and constraining liberal principles, with virtue supplying the moral requirements that liberalism lacks, and liberalism protecting individuals from the crushing illiberalism of Grand Inquisitors who'd impose their oppressive ideas of virtue on unwilling individuals.

Liberalism and the virtues don't belong in separate categories, however. Instead, liberalism arose from within the virtues themselves, and thus does not threaten them. From benevolence, we learned to promote the common good. From knightly magnanimity, we adopted the Geneva Convention's duties to prisoners of war. By rubbing shoulders with our neighbors at the market, we cultivated a sense of republican virtue. From nationalists, we were shown the requirements of fraternity and the duty to attend to the worst-off of our fellow citizens. From the self-effacing virtues of modesty and humility, we learned to mistrust the morally arrogant and to respect the individuality of others. Through our admiration for virtuous people, we were taught liberalism.

In today's vain and furious politics, it's easy to forget the virtues of liberalism. That is why it's good to recall that we're members of a liberal culture and that membership in a culture erases differences in time. The dead don't go anywhere. They're all here, said Isaac

Bashevis Singer. And so we live in a country populated by the liberal heroes we bring to mind, Washington and Lincoln, Eisenhower and John Kennedy. They're real presences, and still with us.

In Chapter Two I explain why liberalism cannot be justified on philosophic theories. Instead, liberalism is grounded in a general virtue of benevolence, a Moral Sense that can either be embraced as a matter of choice or recognized as inherent, but which cannot be subjected to proof or required belief. These are the subjects of Chapters Three and Four. The more specific virtues and instincts of liberalism are discussed in Chapters Five though Twenty, and if he wishes the reader may turn to them directly.

Liberalism did not originate from a set of abstract theories, but from the adventures of faithful knights, the reports of Jesuit missionaries, and the tales of wanderers. It came from Hans Christian Andersen's story about the *Little Match Girl*, and from joyous people who turn aside scowls with a jest. Curiously, however, few have bothered to examine how this taught us to seek the common good and to prize individualism and equality. And that is the subject of this book.

2.

THE POVERTY OF PHILOSOPHY

There's an extensive literature on what a state must do if it wishes to be called liberal. Left unexplained, however, is why a state should care or want to do so. Political philosophers begin by assuming that everyone is equal and that we're all endowed with a right to respect and say that liberalism follows from this. But where did the egalitarianism and rights come from? We're more intelligent than animals, but then some of us are more intelligent than others and that points to inequalities rather than to equality. On any metric one can think of, what we'll observe are differences and not similarities. Nor is it an answer to say, as Ronald Dworkin does, that the ascription of rights is a precondition for a liberal, democratic order. That assumes that this is an incontestable good, but the goodness of liberalism and democracy is precisely what Carl Schmitt contested.

If we're looking for explanations why equality and human rights matter, we might find them in the sense of benevolence seen in Chapter Three or in the religious traditions discussed in Chapter Seven. But we can't prove that we ought to be benevolent, and religions are accepted as a matter of faith and not reason. So that gets us no further.

Besides, one might rationally prefer to live in a relatively benign, autocratic state than in a democracy. That was called Josephism, after Austria's Joseph II (r. 1780–90), an absolute ruler who imposed Enlightenment principles upon an unwilling nobility. Granted, autocratic rule usually ends up badly, but sometimes democracy does too. Schmitt wasn't entirely wrong to despise Germany's Weimar Republic, even if what replaced it was immeasurably worse. Wanting to live in an autocratic regime might be ill-advised, but it's not necessarily irrational.

Moreover, even if we could somehow show why a state should be liberal, we'd still have the problem of showing why it should exist and why a person is bound to support it. What makes me a citizen of *this* state, as opposed to any other or to no state? Liberal philosophers have offered four explanations, none of which avails.

The first is a *contractarian* theory under which a government derives its authority from the implied promises or consent of the governed. Second, we might consent to be governed by a state because it is in our *rational self-interest* to do so. Under the third, the state's legitimate authority arises as a matter of *natural law*. Because we are naturally sociable, we seek to live with other people, and to be fully human is to live under a government in a political society, and a liberal one at that. Finally, *utilitarianism* would justify liberal constitutionalism because this would make for a happier society, but that won't do the trick unless we could first prove that we owe duties to other people, and that's not something Schmitt would concede.

CONTRACTARIANISM

Contractarianism purports to derive legal and political obligations to support the state from a hypothetical bargain people are deemed to make in a pre-political state of nature. Such theories are most closely identified with John Locke's *Second Treatise on Government* (1690) and are called Lockean.

Contractarians assume, reasonably, that we'd be better off if we surrendered the freedom anarchy would give us. We'd want a state to be created to enforce our property rights, for example, because we'd want to see our goods protected from lawless thieves. So that would explain both why the state would exist, and why the constitution would be liberal, since we'd not consent to be ruled by an illiberal government. It would also explain why we're required to support a particular state, having agreed to do so.

Contractarianism might take several different forms, but whichever it might take, David Hume (1711–76) exposed its weaknesses. Search though the history books, he said, and you'll never find any state emerging from a social contract. Instead, you'll find rulers who simply seized power. That's not all, said Hume. Contractarianism assumes that one's hypothetical promise or consent to the state grounds an obligation of loyalty. However, the promise to support the state is circular because it assumes the existence of a prior convention that promising creates morally binding obligations. A promise to perform promises obviously won't do the trick, for where did the obligation to perform the first promise come from? What makes promises binding must come from outside promising, and this must be the existence of linguistic or legal conventions which themselves require a non-promissory justification.[1] They might arise from a duty to promote the common good on utilitarian theories of ethics, but it's circular to argue that it comes from promising itself. The promissory argument for political obligations therefore collapses into something like utilitarianism.

Consent explanations don't face the same problem since consent doesn't assume a background convention of promising. If I consent to your entry on my land, I can't afterwards sue you in trespass. That doesn't require a promise or anything more than a nod of one's head. But if my consent to a past trespass binds me, it doesn't require me to consent to future trespasses. Consent obligations are defeasible and cannot explain why I should continue to be bound to a state after my initial consent. I have the right to say, "thus far and no more."

Moreover, one can't be said to have consented to anything unless one had a real choice in the matter. In contract law, bargains tainted by duress ("Your money or your life!") are unenforceable since they lack the badge of consent that signals that one has been made better off. Similarly, a social contract would not bind people who are forced to accept it. And that is the kind of choice we'd be given in Locke's social contract, argued Hume.[2] When we are born, we find ourselves embedded in a state, with no possibility of rejecting this unless we move to another country, an option which would be closed to all but the wealthy.

This is also a fatal objection to benefits explanations for the duty of loyalty to the state. John Rawls argued that such duties arise on a principle of fairness, under which those who have availed themselves of the state's benefits are bound to support it.[3] The problem is seeing how the benefits might ground a duty where we don't have the option to reject them.

Rational Choice

In economics, the rational-choice hypothesis posits that we'll always seek to maximize our well-being. That's called *psychological egoism*, and it would turn our choices into a matter of calculating costs and benefits. For example, the rational and risk-neutral thief will commit a crime when his benefit from the anticipated loot exceeds his cost as measured by the probability of detection and sentencing times the penalty.

Rational choice is merely an explanatory hypothesis, and behavioral economists report that there's a great deal of experimental evidence that people don't always act rationally. Those thieves are often pretty irrational. In addition, rational choice is a positive and not a normative theory. It doesn't argue that people *ought* to act rationally. But two related theories argue that rational choice explains moral requirements to support the state. First, the rational egoist might argue that we ought to do so in our own self-interest; and second, John Rawls derives political duties from the rational choices we'd make about what justice requires of us.

I. RATIONAL EGOISM

Rational egoism is a normative theory that argues that we should always act in such a way as to advance our self-interest. To choose rationally one must choose morally, and moral choices are always rational choices.[4] That's what the followers of Ayn Rand think. It's a theory that appeals to limited-government libertarians. At most, they'd have us live in a minimal, night-watchman state.

As an account of political obligation, this avoids some of the weaknesses of Lockean contractarianism. It doesn't assume that we'd bargain ourselves into a state. However, rational egoism is no better able to explain one's obligation to support the state because it cannot account for anything more than the thinnest moral code. What makes it attractive at all is that its thin code is better than no moral code at all.

Montesquieu observed that commercial societies soften our selfish interests and make us more agreeable to each other. "Happily, men are in a situation such that, though their passions inspire in them the thought of being wicked, they nevertheless have an interest in not being so."[5] So while the rational egoist might be entirely selfish, he'll not descend into complete immoralism. He won't want to lie, cheat, or steal if word would get out and this would ruin his reputation. No one would want to bargain with him, and he'd lose the gains to be derived from future bargains. When Montesquieu contrasted commercial societies with the martial values that had previously prevailed, he labeled the new ethic one of *doux commerce*—sweet commerce.

That's an advance over Schmitt's categories of friends and enemies. A Schmittian individual would cooperate with his friends and refuse to truck with his enemies. But the rational egoist will recognize that he might enter into mutually beneficial agreements with his enemies, and for Jews in Schmitt's Nazi Germany that would have been a vast improvement. The rational egoist wouldn't value the Jews for themselves, but only for the benefits to be derived in dealing with them. Still, that's better than nothing.

That doesn't take one very far, however. Rational egoism is the morality of clever sociopaths. As David Gauthier noted, it won't help the "animals, the unborn, the congenitally handicapped and defective [who] fall beyond the pale of a morality tied to mutuality."[6] It would seem to exclude Good Samaritan duties to rescue unconscious people on the side of the road or to care for people we'll never meet. If this seems unsatisfactory, it's because we think that moral imperatives are strongest when we're asked to ignore self-interest and do the right thing.

This doesn't mean that rational egoists will be entirely indifferent to the welfare of other people. To their friends they might be altruists, for there is nothing irrational about promoting their welfare. We are social creatures and made happier through our friendships with others, and with friendship comes a sense of empathy for the other person.[7] Aristotle said that friends are like another self (*heteron auton*), whose happiness one desires as much as one's own.[8] Out of self-interest, the rational egoist might therefore want to make his friends better off.

The rational egoist's bonds of affection might even extend beyond friends to strangers, people he'll never meet but about whom he nevertheless does care. For example, he might want to support the poor in other countries—or save the whales—because he'd be pained if he thought they were suffering. But what matters in such cases is the egoist's pain, and not that of the objects of his benevolence. If he felt nothing for them, he couldn't be faulted for his lack of empathy, from the perspective of rational egoism.

In sum, the failure of rational egoism to account for duties to others is a fatal flaw. It assumes that rationality means that, in deciding what one ought to do, only self-interest matters. To be moral, however, a theory must include an impartial and disinterested concern for other people. That's why Derek Parfit thought that rational egoism doesn't even count as a moral theory. If we want to use the languages of should and ought, we're required to take the interests of others into account even if we lack any economic or emotional ties with them. For that, however, we'd have to move beyond rational choice and cut directly to altruism or some form of utilitarianism.

II. RAWLS'S THEORY OF JUSTICE

Like rational egoists, John Rawls assumed that people are necessarily self-interested. He departed from mere egoism, however, by imposing a veil-of-ignorance constraint in which the parties bargain into a hypothetical social contract without knowing who they are and where they find themselves. Since he wouldn't know how wealthy he is or what he possesses by way of human capital, the rational bargainer's risk aversion would make him want to redress extreme inequalities, said Rawls.

That's a form of prioritarianism, the idea that welfare programs should give a priority to the worse-off.[9] It's a thought that informs the utilitarian's intuition about progressive taxation schemes (given diminishing marginal utility) and the Catholic Church's preferential option for the poor. In Rawls's case, however, this was taken to impossible lengths. Rawls assumed extreme risk aversion, where all we care about is the worst-off possibility.

Rawls thought that, in doing so, he was reporting a fact about human psychology. There are two problems with this, however. First, we're not really like that. In weighing the possible outcomes we face, we'll often want to maximize our mean welfare. For a very high payoff at the top end, we might be willing to take some risks at the bottom end.[10] Second, even if Rawls were right, this doesn't provide the template for a theory of justice, as compared to a utilitarianism that takes everyone's welfare into account and not just the worst-off class.

Rawls's book was called *A Theory of Justice*. However, his extreme prioritarianism would excuse economic policies that many would think unjust.[11] It told the super wealthy that they could keep their money, provided they supported a political party that transferred wealth to the very poorest of Americans. As for the people in between, their welfare could be ignored. In the table below, the move from Economy A to B would promote justice, even though middle-class wealth has cratered.

Table A *Picking the Best World*

ECONOMY	WORST-OFF CLASS	MIDDLE CLASS	HIGHEST CLASS
A	18,000	100,000	500,000
B	20,000	30,000	500,000

If ostensibly revolutionary, the book was thus a very complacent one, so far as the 1 percent is concerned. With their contempt for middle-class deplorables, it's the unofficial ideology of America's elites and a Hillary Clinton Democratic Party, but that doesn't make it morally attractive.[12]

Natural Law

Many of the Integralists are natural lawyers who think that our nature informs us about the good. Contractarianism may also overlap with natural-law theories, and Locke was both a contractarian and a natural lawyer. He was a contractarian in his explanation of obligations to support the state, and a natural lawyer in his account of an individual's moral obligations to other people. That is, he argued that our obligation to support the state arose from a hypothetical bargain but thought that we owe moral duties in a pre-political state of nature as a matter of natural law. For Locke, natural duties included importantly the right to preserve one's property, a right prior to and independent of the existence of civil society and government.

It would seem a short step to employ Locke's natural-law duties to ground a duty to support a just state. If we have natural duties in a pre-political state of nature, and these include a duty to make others better off, and people are better off living in a just state, then why not let this serve as a foundation for political obligations?

But has the natural lawyer really added anything to our understanding of right and wrong? We don't need him to tell us that murder is wrong, and he hasn't moved the ball when he informs us that it's also contrary to nature. If we begin with a knowledge of murder's badness, natural law is a wheel that turns nothing.

There are, in addition, several well-known difficulties with natural-law theories. They assume that, as a matter of human nature, we have a sense of benevolence and that from this we can derive a duty of benevolence. The problem is that, along with benevolence, we have a good many beastly preferences as well. We're a bit of a mess, neither wholly good nor bad, and if the natural lawyer identifies nature with the good, he's cherry-picking.

Even our dark side might not matter if, among our instincts, we could always distinguish the good from the bad. And so we can, claims the natural lawyer. We might have immoral desires, but it's enough if by nature we always know the right thing to do. But what exactly that might be won't be clear to anyone who is self-deceived about his goodness.

With self-delusion, we too easily think ourselves virtuous. We're all guilty of that, and the people with the greatest sense of self-worth are often the nastiest people we know. "There are only two kinds of men," wrote Pascal. "The just who think themselves sinners and the sinners who think themselves just."[13] Self-deception is a difficulty that every moral theory faces, but it's especially problematical for natural lawyers who tell us that knowledge of the good is written on our hearts.

Natural-law theories suffer from a further weakness that David Hume identified in his *Treatise of Human Nature*. We might feel a sense of benevolence to others, but that doesn't prove that we ought to feel that way. A moral "ought" cannot be derived from an existential "is" statement of fact. An "is" statement describes how things are, while a normative "ought" statement tells us how they should be, and the second doesn't follow from the first.[14]

More recently, natural lawyers such as Germain Grisez have come to accept that Hume's No-Ought-From-Is principle represents a fatal objection to natural-law theories of this kind.[15] Grisez then went on to develop a different natural-law theory that he said would avoid the fallacy, which has come to be called "New Natural Law" (NNL). However, NNL is simply a theory of rational egoism under which we ought to make our choices based on rational calculations about how to achieve the greatest benefits and satisfactions. "All these things to which man has a natural inclination, are naturally apprehended by reason as being good," said Aquinas, "and consequently as objects of pursuit."[16] People who chose badly are both morally at fault and foolish, for they have not understood their proper ends. As Grisez puts it, "one must do something good if he is to act intelligently at all."[17]

As such, the self-referential and insular NNL literature suffers from the same difficulties as rational egoism. It cannot explain duties to promote the common good where this requires self-sacrifice and doesn't even count as a moral theory. NNL's Catholic thinkers might have had second thoughts had they gotten out more often and recognized the overlap between their ideas and those of the followers of Ayn Rand.

Utilitarianism

Utilitarianism is a form of consequentialism, under which the rightness of a rule or act depends on what follows when it is adopted or made. For utilitarians, good consequences are those which make people better off and which would promote the common good. There is a lengthy philosophical literature on utilitarianism, for and against, but those who defend it include some of the leading moral philosophers, and it's a perfectly good ethical theory. If you want a theory of ethics, that is.

Utilitarianism is preferable to Rawls's theory of justice since it doesn't ignore the weakened middle class. That's not enough to prove that we should be utilitarians, however. The utilitarian can tell us what to do if we'd like to promote the common good. What he can't tell us, however, is why we should want to do so. That would require a demonstration that we should be altruists and care about other people as something more than a means to maximize our own self-interest. And here we run into the same problems we saw with rational egoism. There might be prudential reasons to make nice to others, as a way to make ourselves better off, but utilitarianism and altruism require something more than that. They ask us to take the interests of strangers into account, even if we'll never meet or interact with them. They begin by assuming we want to act morally, and then fill in the blanks.

Against this, Thomas Nagel argues in *The Possibility of Altruism* that altruism is a rational requirement for action. Words like "should" and "ought" imply that one has adopted a neutral and objective stance that takes everyone's interest into account. This bears a family resemblance to the Kantian criterion of universalizability, the idea that to count as a moral imperative a rule should govern everyone in the same way. As a defense of altruism, however, this assumes away the possibility of abandoning our moral language, and it's not irrational for the rational egoist to say, "Fine. I won't be moral then." I won't take an impersonal or universal standpoint, even if that means I must give up my moral language or mentally apply an asterisk when I use words like should and ought.

We might all prefer to live in a society guided by a utilitarian code of morality, as opposed to one of complete immoralism. We'd be happier in the first than the second society, but that doesn't prove that we ought to be utilitarians. That was a mistake that John Stuart Mill made. Happiness, and only happiness, is desirable, said Mill, and then he said that the only evidence that something is desirable is that people really do desire it. But saying that people desire happiness is an empirical claim, while the claim that they ought to do so is logically quite different, and one can't move from one statement to the other without committing the No-Ought-From-Is fallacy.[18]

* * *

In sum, philosophical theories that purport to justify liberal constitutionalism fail to rise to Schmitt's challenge. We can't prove that we ought to support a liberal state because we can't prove that we're morally required to care about other people. Nor can we derive such duties from within liberalism if this is defined as a regime that permits a person to satisfy all his desires, since this is nothing better than rational egoism. If we seek a justification for liberalism, we must do so from outside abstract philosophic theories.

23

But if we can't explain just why liberalism deserves our support, does that really matter? There is another way to understand moral imperatives, which Charles Taylor calls the ethics of inarticulacy.[19] We have understandings, hunches, and intuitions about how we should act, and, while we can't link them to a deeper touchstone of the good or place them in the philosophic literature, they inform our ideas about the common good, kindness, and fraternity, as well as our sense of risible illiberalism. They come from a variety of sources: a general instinct of benevolence, religious belief, the way in which commerce softens our morals, nationalism, and many more. It's not necessary to pick one of them as determinative or even to rank them. As one goes through them, however, one recognizes how profoundly our culture is liberal and how much illiberalism cuts against the grain.

3.

BENEVOLENCE

The thinkers in Chapter Two failed to answer Carl Schmitt's challenge to liberal constitutionalism. But then Schmitt failed to prove the converse and show why illiberalism trumps liberalism. Which is only to say that it's a matter of experience and not of proof, of moral sentiments and not of philosophic theories.

A liberal might thus concede the need to grant the government exceptional powers in times of emergency without concluding, as Schmitt did, that a sovereign tyrant could invoke an emergency whenever he wanted. Civil liberties were suspended for a time during the Civil War, but, when it was over, we snapped back to a being a democratic country with a separation of powers. As we'll see in Chapter Nine, something like this happened during the War on Terror when the Supreme Court reined in the George W. Bush administration.

If we can't prove the necessity of liberalism, we can at least say something about its origins. Its appeal is to our emotions, and many more people became liberals by reading *The Little Match Girl* than by studying Locke's *Second Treatise*. One thing that is central to liberalism is a feeling of benevolence, an altruistic desire to look beyond self-interest and take the interests of others into account. During the eighteenth century, the philosophers and armchair psychologists of the Scottish Enlightenment said that this arose from an innate Moral Sense. Others might think that benevolence is something we're taught as children.

However it arises, I take benevolence to be a virtue, and indeed the fount of virtues. Benevolence prompts the gift-giver's charity, the knight's magnanimity, and the gentleman's civility. It's what is behind the sense of fraternity with fellow citizens and the instinct to tolerate harmless eccentricities. It's the impulse behind the desire to help strangers who lie injured on the side of the road, and the sorrow felt at their distress.

The benevolent will want to share with you the things that brought them joy, a piece by Bach on YouTube and even the much-derided photos of their dinners on Facebook. They won't complain about their misfortunes, lest this pain their listeners. They're not self-assertive narcissists and don't think self-esteem a virtue. They are rebels against the morals of modernity.

Does benevolence supply the foundation for American liberalism? Not if the Declaration of Independence and the break with Great Britain were really inspired by ideas in Locke's *Second Treatise*, and not by a Moral Sense. "Most Americans had absorbed Locke's works as a kind of political gospel," wrote Carl Becker, "and the Declaration, in its form, in its phraseology, follows closely certain sentences in Locke's second treatise on government."[1] Becker's book appeared in 1922 and became the standard interpretation of the logic of the Declaration. Beginning in the 1960s, however, several historians whom we'll see in Chapter Twelve argued that the Revolution was prompted by virtue politics and the rediscovery of a civic-humanist tradition. Then, in 1978, Gary Wills argued that the Declaration should be understood by the way in which Jefferson had channeled the ideas of Moral Sense thinkers.

Did Jefferson read Locke's *Second Treatise*? We can't be sure. Wills noted that he had bought a copy of it in 1769, but then his entire library perished in a fire the next year and he doesn't seem to have repurchased it. Of course, he might have been influenced by its ideas because they were simply in the air. Such claims are impossible to falsify, but Becker had seemingly overstated the influence of Locke's theory of government in America. The *Second Treatise* was known less here than in England and did not figure on the syllabus of American colleges before the Revolution.[2] The few, mostly perfunctory references Jefferson made to Locke don't tell us much one way or the other.

As an alternative to Locke, Wills pointed to the then-dominant Moral Sense school and to writers such as the Earl of Shaftesbury (*The Characteristics of Men, Manners, Opinions, Times*, 1711), Francis Hutcheson (*Theory of Human Nature*, 1740), Joseph Butler (*Six Sermons*, 1749), Adam Smith (*The Theory of Moral Sentiments*, 1759), Thomas Reid (*Inquiry Into the Human Mind on the Principles of Common Sense*, 1764), and Adam Ferguson (*Essay on the History of Civil Society*, 1767). All were known in America, and Ferguson was the secretary of the 1778 Carlisle Commission, which the British sent to America in the vain hope of negotiating a peace with the Americans.

Moral Sense writers thought that we have an instinct to benevolence, in which we seek the happiness of others. Because we take pleasure in doing so, we serve ourselves by serving others.[3] That was how Pope explained the Moral Sense in *An Essay on Man* (1733).

> Thus God and Nature link'd the gen'ral frame
> And bade Self-love and Social be the same. (317–18)

That was also how Jefferson understood how "the Laws of Nature and of Nature's God" had prompted us to serve the common good. In his *Dialogue between Head and Heart*, in a 1786 letter to Maria Cosway, he wrote:

> Morals were too essential to the happiness of man to be risked
> on the uncertain combinations of the head. [Nature] laid their
> foundation therefore in sentiment, not in science.

The heart concludes the debate by telling the head, "I do not know that I ever did a good thing on your suggestion, or a dirty one without it."[4]

The Common Good

As we saw, the rational egoist is not an immoralist. But that doesn't make him willing to help others when this requires something above and beyond self-interest. That would require benevolence, and with benevolence comes a desire to promote the welfare of others.[5] That was how Cicero understood the common good.

> We are not born simply for ourselves alone, but our country claims a share of our being, and our friends a share . . . and as men, too, are born for the sake of men, that they may be able mutually to help one another; in this direction we ought to follow nature as our guide, to contribute to the general good by an interchange of acts of kindness, by giving and receiving, and thus by our skill, or industry, and our talents to cement human society more closely together, man to man.[6]

Because we're better off living under a government than in a state of anarchy, we serve the common good by recognizing our political obligations to the state in which we find ourselves. We can't prove that we owe such duties, as we saw in the previous chapter, any more than we can prove that we ought to show benevolence. But that takes nothing away from the sense that benevolence is a virtue and that supporting a just state promotes the common good.

The wasteful partiality shown for special interests is a betrayal of the common good. For example, the trade barriers sought by America's sugar producers raise sugar prices 64 to 92 percent above the world average. They don't create jobs, and the burden lies heaviest upon poorer Americans, who spend a higher proportion of their earnings on food. The sugar cartel has nothing going for it, except interest-group clout.

Public-choice economists such as Mancur Olson tell us that's to be expected when there's a competition for government largesse. The system favors concentrated interest groups that impose costs on a dispersed group, be it sugar consumers or taxpayers. Both concentrated and dispersed groups face a collective-action problem in

28

getting organized, hiring lobbyists, billing their members, and over-coming the temptation to free ride, but the smaller group can over-come this more easily than the larger group. On one side it's a hun-dred sugar companies. On the other it's 330 million consumers. In addition, it's big bucks for the smaller group, and small pennies for the members of the larger group. It's corrupt and wasteful, but the structure of government tends to shift wealth from dispersed losers to concentrated interest-group winners.

Benevolence imposes a duty to support the common good by op-posing corrupt interest-group bargains. It might also require per-sonal sacrifices, such as those made by the Founders in 1776. Their pledge in the Declaration of their lives, fortunes, and sacred honor was not an idle promise but an undertaking to risk all in a war against the most powerful country in the world, and many of them paid for it through imprisonment or the destruction of their property. If cor-ruption represents a departure from the common good, so too does pusillanimity or an indifference to causes greater than oneself.

The Degrees of Good and Evil

Not everyone feels the same sense of benevolence. Some people are mean and selfish, while others are moral saints. In *The Science of Evil*, psychologist Simon Baron-Cohen (a cousin of Sacha Baron-Cohen of *Borat* fame) studied empathy and reported that it wasn't binary and a matter of having it or not. Rather, there's an Empathy Quotient, which sorts people out along a bell curve, from selfish people on the left to benevolent empaths on the right.

What Baron-Cohen calls empathy is composed of two elements: (1) Cognitive Empathy (the intellectual ability to recognize the need for a benevolent response) and (2) Affective Empathy (the ability to respond with an appropriate emotion). People on the autistic spec-trum have a form of moral blindness and might lack Cognitive Em-pathy. While they are faulted for their lack of emotional response, this is a genetically based disorder and beyond praise or blame. At the more normal edge of the spectrum, which used to be called the

Asperger syndrome, people can seem almost normal and don't lack the ability to feel an appropriate emotion. They might have a problem reading faces, but when they're told that someone is in pain, they'll have Affective Empathy and feel sorry for him.

A lot of ordinary people seem to have moral blinders, even if they're not Aspies. They're the people who hog the left lane in traffic and are oblivious to the people behind them wanting to pass. Or else they mechanically follow a rule without recognizing the harm that results. Hannah Arendt attended Eichmann's trial in Jerusalem, where she found a soulless bureaucrat in place of the moral monster she expected to see. She came across something new in the moral lexicon and called it the banality of evil. These were people who had shut down their Cognitive Empathy to excuse themselves from Affective Empathy.

It's hard to say how much of moral blindness is an intellectual and how much a purely moral error. Socrates thought it was all mental. In the *Protagoras*, he argued that, although there is evil in the world, one never consciously chooses to do wrong. Knowledge "will not allow a man, if only he knows the good and the evil, to do anything which is contrary to what his knowledge bids him do."[7] When you know what's good for you, that's just what you'll do, and when you see someone doing something wrong, he's really trying to do good and simply doesn't know that it's bad for him. So ignorance is the root of all evil.

Sometimes the ignorance looks strategic, however. Without giving it much thought we avert our gaze from the man lying in the road, while the more alert Samaritan has trained himself to see people in need. "Oh, I didn't notice him," says the passerby, truthfully. Thomas Merton wrote about people like that in *Confessions of a Guilty Bystander* (1968). He thought this included all of us.

The experiments conducted by psychologist Stanley Milgram demonstrate that the lack of Cognitive Empathy is a very human failing. The subjects were required by an authority figure to administer electric shocks to an unseen person, and most of them cranked up the dial to levels that would have been fatal had they been real. They did what they were told and shut off the recognition of the pain that would result. Skeptics have scoffed at Milgram's findings, but the evidence has held up.[8]

Deeper forms of evil lie on the far edge of the left-handed tail of Baron-Cohen's bell curve, people whose empathy circuit has entirely shut down. They might have a borderline personality disorder and simmer with hatred for anyone they think disrespects them. Then there are the psychopaths, people incapable of feeling guilt, who constitute about 1 percent of the male population and 15 percent of those in prison. Without emotional affect, they can commit what they know to be the most hard-hearted crimes. Evidently, not everyone shares in the sense of benevolence that Moral Sense thinkers thought was part of everyone's human nature.

At the other end of Baron-Cohen's bell curve are the superempaths, the people who possess an exceptional level of Cognitive and Affective Empathy. They include some of the people we'll see in the following chapters, saints, missionaries, and rescuers. They have a heightened ability to pick up on cues that signal another's distress and an exceptional willingness to do something about it, even at a great personal cost. They'll gravitate to the caring and service professions.

The empath has a heightened moral alertness. He'll look past the people who howl their resentments in his face and see things that others miss. He'll recognize the abandoned lover in the memories of the elderly woman and see the pain in the worker's stooped shoulders. He'll pick out the lonely girl who's been mocked by her peers and the boy who's been separated from his parents. In the casual cruelty of a heartless world, he'll throw his arms around a horse to prevent it from being whipped.

Few people displayed greater empathy than Simone Weil (1909–43), a French philosopher and religious thinker. She was educated in France's elite École normale supérieure and became a teacher. She was reasonably well-off, but during the Great Depression she identified with the unemployed and kept no more of her salary than they had received on the dole. The rest she handed out to them. To better understand the workers, she worked on a Renault assembly line during a sabbatical. Then, when the war began, she joined the Free French in London, where she wrote *The Need for Roots* about the very human desire to be connected to other people. She had always been sickly but nevertheless restricted her diet to the rations her countrymen lived on under the German Occupation. She died in 1943, apparently a suicide by starvation.

Baron-Cohen's median Empathy Quotient, the sense of benevolence felt by the average person, the man at the check-out counter or the Clapham omnibus, oscillates between the two extremes. He observes the moral slug and prides himself that he's better than that, but lest he become too vain the comparison with the empath reveals his failures. Out of self-love we're apt to be self-deceived about our moral worth, which is why the empath's corrective tug is so important.

THE CLOUDINESS OF BENEVOLENCE

Benevolence excludes short cuts. Everyone counts, and over-simple rules necessarily scant some people's claims. A one-sentence definition of justice will always lead to injustice, and if pushed too far a right will result in a wrong. With all its murkiness, the sense of benevolence is a better guide than brittle rules derived from abstract theories.

Rules are mental shortcuts that are meant to economize on the costs of search and investigation. They're the first cut at a moral answer, and in many cases that's all you need. "Thou shalt not kill" doesn't admit of too many exceptions. But rules fail to capture all that's required of us. You can follow all of them and be mean-spirted, insensitive, and cold-hearted. It's what's outside of the rules that matters more, and recognizing this requires the emotional engagement provided by a Moral Sense.

Kant thought that rules about truth-telling were so absolute that one should never lie. When a would-be murderer knocks on your door and asks whether his intended victim is within, you're not permitted to lie and say no. Victor Hugo disagreed. In *Les Misérables* (1862), the heroes are the rule-breakers. The merciless Inspector Javert corners the virtuous Jean Valjean and asks Sister Simplice if she is hiding him. "Are you alone in the room?" Yes, says the nun— even though Valjean is hiding within. "Have you seen Valjean?" No, says Sister Simplice. Two quick lies, one after the other, from one who had never lied before. "O holy maiden," writes Hugo. "May this falsehood be remembered to thee in Paradise."

We'd not want to do without rules, however. Without stiff rules, it would be too tempting to think they didn't apply to one. No one can serve as an impartial judge in his own cause because he'd always be biased in his favor. It's all too easy to come up with a fanciful reason why I'm permitted to lie, cheat or steal. Any theory of the common good must therefore incorporate both a set of rules and a willingness in rare cases to permit exceptions. The rules are presumptively binding, but not absolutely so. A strong onus of explanation would lie on the person who claims an exemption, but one that is not irrebuttable.

In a good society, individuals are endowed with stiff rules about their rights, since doing without them would open the door to totalitarian rulers. But the common good can't be defined solely through a set of rights. It's not only that rights can collide, like the right to safe streets and the rights of the accused, or that a pure theory of rights lacks stopping points like the privacy rights that are thought to ground a right to late-term abortions. It's not even that a strict insistence on one's rights encourages the selfishness that disregards the superior claims of other people. The greater problem with rights theories is that only the common good explains why rights should exist in the first place and why there should be rights-bearers.

That's not to deny the need for legal rights, but rather to assert, with John Stuart Mill, that the reason to ascribe them is because this serves the common good. Without a set of rights, the state might make excessive demands on a person in the name of the greater good. But then the good will trump individual rights where their strict observance would impose a wasteful burden on everyone else. While rights and the common good exist in tension, the common good is fundamental.

Without a sense of benevolence and the common good, there would be no reason to respect another person's rights. Before the duty to do so arises, it must be shown that he is entitled to my consideration, and that requires an overarching commitment to benevolence that can be found in the Moral Sense.

4.

THE MORAL SENSE

The feeling of benevolence might have religious roots, which we'll examine in Chapter Seven. Jefferson's "Nature's God" doesn't much sound like the God of the Christian Bible, but he was raised as a Christian, as were all the Moral Sense thinkers. Shaftesbury's first work was an edited collection of sermons. Butler was an Anglican bishop. Thomas Reid began his career as a Church of Scotland minister, and Francis Hutcheson and Adam Ferguson had sought church appointments. Adam Smith referred to God often in his *Theory of Moral Sentiments*.

The Moral Sense writers didn't think that their ideas were specifically Christian, however. Instead, they believed that the Moral Sense was natural to everyone. Smith's *Theory of Moral Sentiments* began with the observation that, "how selfish soever man may be supposed, there are evidently some principles in his nature, which interest him in the fortunes of others, and render their happiness necessary to him, though he derives nothing from it except the pleasure of seeing it."[1] After reading Baron-Cohen, however, one can be a little skeptical about the idea of a universal and uniform Moral Sense. Genetics and culture must have something to do with it as well.

However derived, the Moral Sense is the primary source of our moral knowledge, the touchstone against which we distinguish good from evil. When moral philosophers debate among themselves, they'll base their arguments on commonsense moral beliefs, which themselves are derived from our instinct of benevolence. Like Derek Parfit, they'll pose a thought experiment and tell you that they've disproven a moral claim when all they've done is appealed to our Moral Sense. "The quick sensibility, on this head, is so universal among mankind," said Hume, that it "gives a philosopher sufficient assurance, that he can never be considerably mistaken."[2]

If we have a Moral Sense, it doesn't follow that we ought to have it. Drawing that inference would violate Hume's No-Ought-From-Is principle. Nor can we attribute inerrancy to our emotions. Some of them rest on blind prejudice, after all. You might say that the Moral Sense tells you that x is good, but it's nevertheless meaningful to ask, "Is x really good?" It's what philosopher G. E. Moore called an open question.

ALTRUISM, EMPATHY, AND SYMPATHY

Benevolence is related to several other emotions or instincts: altruism, empathy, and sympathy. The *altruist* feels that he owes moral duties to others, and when called on will aid a victim out of a sense of duty. That distinguishes him from a person who helps another, not out of a sense of duty to the victim but purely out of self-interest because the victim's pain triggers his own pain. He'll share the victim's distress and will be personally relieved if it goes away. Like Bill Clinton, he "feels your pain."

A person like Clinton who feels another's pain *empathizes* with him. Empathy is a moral emotion if it prompts one to help another, whether out of an altruistic sense of duty or out of Clintonian self-interest. But that's better than nothing. If I'm not even aware of the other's distress, I'll pass him by and may be accounted a moral slug.

Empathy isn't the same thing as *sympathy*. Empathy requires shared emotions, while sympathy doesn't. If I'm on a plane and find myself sitting next to a person who is frightened of flying, I can sympathize with him without feeling afraid myself. I can also sympathize with someone who is deeply depressed without feeling depressed myself. In addition, the sympathetic person must care for the victim's well-being for the victim's sake, and not merely out of Clintonian self-love. [3]

The benevolent are altruists who sympathize with the victim. But Moral Sense writers thought that benevolence differs from empathy. The benefactor takes satisfaction from performing a virtuous act and not from sharing in the beneficiary's pleasure. In doing good, the benefactor observes his action like an impartial observer and takes pleasure in the thought that he has acted morally.

Empathy, sympathy, and benevolence are all emotional states. Moral theories that don't require personal affect miss a crucial element of our understanding of virtue. Utilitarianism might thus be faulted if it praises a person who maximizes desired consequences but who feels nothing when he does so. Kant also dispensed with the element of inward awareness so long as a person obeyed the categorical imperative.[4] By contrast, the liberal virtues discussed here assume a subject whose feelings prompt him to act altruistically for the common good. Feelings alone won't cut it if a person is too easily satisfied with himself and does nothing to help others. But while the required inner state is not a sufficient condition for virtuous behavior, it is a necessary condition.

MIMICRY, RECIPROCITY, AND FAIRNESS

We have a natural instinct to mimic others, from which benevolence breeds benevolence. We learn how to reciprocate favors, and even to anticipate them by adopting a cooperative attitude to others. Our natural acquisitiveness is also tempered by an innate sense of fairness. Given all that, is there an evolutionary explanation for our sense of benevolence? If so, there might be little need to cultivate our Moral Sense.

Mimicry is natural to us. Even newborn infants will imitate facial and hand gestures within two weeks of birth. Stick out your tongue, rotate your head, and wiggle your fingers, and they'll copy you. Those aren't things they'd do unless they were prompted by an instinct to imitate others.[5]

As with infants, so too with adults. We see a person we admire and copy his style and mannerisms, along with his ideas. If he's got something, we'll want it too, and René Girard made an entire philosophy out of the resulting competition for scarce resources. More benignly, when we see someone in pain we're pained too, and might want to help him. Similarly, we have an instinct of reciprocity, where we mimic the kindness another shows us by repaying him in kind. That's why the rational egoist will want to gain the reputation of a person with whom people can profitably bargain. He won't be an altruist but might be willing to help others in what amounts to an efficient insurance contract. After a snowfall, I might shovel your driveway if I think that you'll return the favor someday.

That doesn't count as a moral theory, but it can come close to the simulacrum of benevolence shown by the rational egoist in Chapter Two. Through repeated interactions with others, a pattern of *reciprocal altruism* might easily emerge. I'll scratch your back in the expectation that you'll do the same for me. That's especially likely to happen when the parties deal with each other repeatedly, as the snow-shoveling neighbors do. In such cases, the parties can signal their openness to this through a form of constrained altruism, where they begin with a cooperative first move. That's what a famous round-robin showed forty years ago, when people were invited to submit their strategies in a repeated prisoner's dilemma game.

In a PD game, the parties are put to an election between cooperating and defecting. In bargaining, cooperating means performing one's promises and defecting means breaking them. The parties are better off when they both cooperate, but the problem is that, while it is collectively rational to cooperate, it is individually rational to defect and treat the cooperating party as a patsy. The seller will get paid and then omit to deliver the goods. Or vice versa. Knowing this, both parties will defect. They'll not trust each other, and the gains of cooperation will be lost. When ecologist Garrett Hardin recognized this, he called it the tragedy of the commons. We'll pollute and not pick up after ourselves, overfish a lake, and welch on our promises, even though that's the worst result for everyone collectively.

But what if the game isn't one-shot, and the players are told they'd be playing against each other through several iterations? They'd also be matched up against different opponents, each with his own strategy. That's what Robert Axelrod tested, when he asked a group of eminent economists and game theorists to give him their strategies for a repeated PD game. When the results were in, the winner was a strategy called tit-for-tat (TFT). In it, a party begins with a cooperative first move and thereafter mimics the other player's previous move. If the second party always defects, the first party will cooperate on his first move and defect thereafter. If both parties adopt TFT, they'll cooperate on every move. When the total scores were added up, TFT was the overall winner.

TFT has several things going for it. It is easily communicated to the other party and, by signaling a willingness to cooperate, invites a cooperative response in turn. While not excessively forgiving, it does not carry a grudge. After the results were in from the first round, the participants were invited to participate in a second round-robin. Before doing so, they were told that TFT had been the overall winner the first time. They were invited to try to beat it, but in the second round TFT again emerged as the overall winner.

What the experiment showed is that, without enforcement mechanisms, the prudently cooperative TFT strategy encourages the development of trust when a PD game is repeated numerous times. Each party will realize that the other's gain from continued future cooperation will exceed his gain from defection at every step along the way, and a benign relationship might become self-enforcing, without the need for legal enforcement.

The reciprocal altruism generated in iterated games shows how Schmitt's categories of friends and enemies may be transcended. Nothing is due a Schmittian enemy, but TFT tells us that it's irrational to treat him as such to the extent that this fails to capture the gains from self-interested patterns of cooperation. Axelrod's results were exciting because they showed how rational egoism explained why it made sense to cooperate initially, even with strangers, and to continue to cooperate with fellow cooperators.

We also have fairness instincts when it comes to cutting a deal with others, and they constrain how we divide up a pie.[6] When asked in experiments to allocate a set of valuable lottery tickets, the parties bargain for an equal split where the cash payoffs are the same. But when they're told the value of each ticket, they will bargain for equal expected values and divide the tickets unequally to produce the same expected value (probability times cash outcome) for each.[7]

Further evidence of fairness instincts is provided by ultimatum games, where bargainers are willing to bear a personal loss to punish another party for unfairness. One party (the "sender") divides up a fixed amount of money, and the other (the "receiver") must accept or reject his share. If he rejects it, neither party receives anything. The sender will therefore be tempted to offer a very one-sided split, such as $99 for himself and $1 for the receiver, thinking the latter will accept it since the alternative is to receive nothing at all. But that's not what happens in bargaining experiments. Most receivers reject sharply unequal splits, even when this means giving up large offers.[8] Even in one-shot experiments, they'll incur a penalty to enforce a sense of fairness and, knowing this, future senders are more likely to propose an equal split.

There is additional evidence of fairness constraints in the way in which stores refuse to increase prices in emergencies. For example, drugstores often refuse to mark up shovels during snowstorms or flashlights during power outages. That might seem puzzling to an economist, who would expect that prices will go up with increased demand. What seems to be behind the apparent generosity are fairness norms and the risk that a "price-gouging" merchant will be punished by outraged consumers once the emergency is over.[9]

What this shows is that, as a moral theory, rational egoism is more attractive than one might have supposed. But as we saw in Chapter Two, it can't explain why moral duties are owed to people we'll never encounter or who could never help us, and therefore it fails as a moral theory. For that we'd need the sense of general benevolence that Moral Sense philosophers proposed.

A Gene for Benevolence?

Moral Sense writers thought that the instinct of benevolence was deep-rooted in our psyche. Today we might wonder whether we're hard wired for it and look for an explanation from the perspective of evolutionary biology, as Matt Ridley did in *The Origins of Virtue.*

Evolutionary theories have been used to explain cooperative animal behavior, and the idea of reciprocal altruism came to us from biologist Robert Trivers.[10] For example, large fish permit smaller "feeder fish" to pick food particles from their teeth without defecting and eating them. The feeder fish get the food, and the large fish get free teeth-cleaning services. This can't have been a result of a TFT bargain between them, and so Trivers suggested the possibility that natural selection might account for a cooperative gene in their DNA.

In theory, evolutionary processes might help account for the instinct of reciprocal altruism in humans, just as in animals, and more generally for the traits of sociability and altruism.[11] However, no evolutionary biologist subscribes to a hard determinism that attributes all our behavior to genetics and that wholly discounts cultural and family influences. Were that the case, we'd not observe the differences that Simon Baron-Cohen identified with his Empathy Quotient. We'd not see the university presidents who've been educated into moral cretinism.

It took Judeo-Christian ethics to put an end to infanticide, which was commonly practiced in the classical periods of Greece and Rome.[12] In our own time, there's been a revolution in attitudes to same-sex attraction, and this can't be attributed to natural selection. More modestly, therefore, evolutionary biologist E. O. Wilson rejected hard genetic determinism in favor of a theory in which both genes and the human environment explain our behavior, and where social evolution is more cultural than genetic.[13] We might all share a general trait of sociability, but what matters more is how this is influenced by our family and culture.

5.

A TIME OF GIFTS

We each have our own story about the origins of benevolence, and in my case it goes back to a remote little village. When the American frontier closed in 1890, settlers moved to the "last, best West" in Canada, and they stopped at my Leoville. Three miles further north, the forest primeval began. We were North America's Scythians, at the outer limits of the world.

The village was almost entirely French-Canadian, as were the schoolteachers in its public school. They were nuns from Quebec and members of the Sisters of Charity. Americans might think it odd that nuns were permitted to teach in a public school, but then this wasn't America and as the village was almost entirely Catholic it seemed natural to us.

On feast days, Leoville was bedecked with papal flags. This wasn't *ancien régime* France, however. The Red Ensign was raised each morning in front of the school, and in each classroom a crucifix on one wall faced a portrait of the Queen on the other. We didn't think this exceptional, though the Integralists might have thought they had died and gone to Heaven. As for the Queen, she might have been Protestant, but we were assured that she was a Very Good Person.

The nuns wouldn't have called themselves liberals, but they had a liberalism of benevolence and empathy for others. One day in class a nun told us of how Joan of Arc had been burned at the stake by the English. Afterwards she took me aside. As I was the only person in the class with an English background, she wanted to make sure that I didn't feel hurt by the lesson. Had Joan not rallied the troops, France might have been conquered by England and in time become Protestant, and in that case we would be Protestants too. And so it had turned out well, I would agree, apart from that fifteenth-century unpleasantness.

Old men forget, but the incident sticks in my mind. And I don't think I'm alone in this. Unless they labor under a morally blinding sense of self-entitlement, I expect that most people can recall a similar moment when they received something to which they had no right. They had been given a gift by a benevolent person, in an epiphany that revealed a hidden world of unbought goodness.

One's life is told in three stories. The first is the one we tell about ourselves, a record of achievements, of ends pursued and goals attained. There's a second story, about the help we got along the way and the gifts we received. They might have made all the difference, but unless we have a strong sense of gratitude we might never have noticed them. The third story is of the gifts we made to others which made the crucial difference in their lives. That is the virtue without a name that describes the man who is unaware of the good he's done. It was the virtue of George Bailey in *It's a Wonderful Life*. All is gifts.

Once a year we were visited by a School Inspector from down south. Like the Queen, he was a Protestant, but we weren't as sure that he was a very good person, and the nuns asked us to pray that he wouldn't require them to remove the crucifixes from the school. We needn't have worried. He regarded us with the ironic detachment reserved for primitive people who in time would be civilized and for whom there was no need to hurry things along. We evidently amused him, and he thought he might have fun with us. You little French Canadians don't know how to say "the," he said. I'll tell you how. Stick your tongue out when you say it. "Do it," he insisted. "Do it!"

That was liberalism of a sort, but one devoid of the benevolence shown by the nuns. It was what happened when an elite liberalism became detached from virtue and contemptuous of benighted deplorables. It was the creed of the faux sophisticate and too often was taken to define twentieth-century liberalism, a triumphant creed in search of backward people to scorn, and wholly unlike the liberalism of the nuns.

For the nuns were true liberals. Unlike the school inspector, they didn't distinguish among people by race or ethnicity. Many of the people of Leoville were Native Canadians or Métis, the descendants of First Nation and European intermarriages, with Cree and French-Canadian roots, and one simply didn't know or care who was Cree and who European, who was Métis and who wasn't. In our (Catholics only) Religion classes, we were told not to look down on other religions. Anglicans, it was true, took communion under two species and passed around a cup of wine from which all were invited to drink. How unsanitary! That was the only criticism we heard of another religion.

In short, the holy ladies of whom I speak were at least as liberal as anyone was at the time. But where did that come from, and by whom? They hadn't studied Locke, and the Enlightenment had passed them by. When George-Étienne Cartier, a father of Canadian confederation, visited Paris in 1864 he was asked how it was that, separated from *la patrie*, the French Canadians had managed to maintain their identity. We did so precisely because we were cut off from France, he answered. Had Quebec gone through the convulsions of the French Revolution, we would have been improved out of existence.[1] The Revolutionary Declaration of the Rights of Man was no substitute for the free institutions the Quebecois had received from England, and the protection these offered their church, language, and schools.

So how did the nuns come by their liberalism? They didn't take in any of the newspapers or periodicals of the day. There was no television, perhaps not even a radio. Their days were spent in work and prayer. They never learned the language of rights, and, while they had a strong sense of things not to be done, that was the language of duties and not of rights.

45

The idea of duty doesn't capture the liberalism of the nuns either. When I was taken aside after the lesson on Joan of Arc, I had no right to the nun's solicitude, and she had no duty to attend to me. Rather, she had gone beyond her duties to the more interesting moral terrain of supererogatory virtues, where a person does more than what is required of him. These are the virtues of the super-empath who, like the Medal of Honor winner, has gone above and beyond the call of duty.

The nuns had sought perfection. That was the point of Christ's challenge to the rich young man in the Gospels. That's remembered as a condemnation of riches, but there was a deeper message about the complexity of moral life and the impossibility of reducing it down to a list of rules. The young man had followed all the commandments, but that didn't suffice. It never does. The moral life is more than the rule-driven life. There are no rules about how to how to be kind and benevolent. You can obey all the rules and still be cold-hearted.

The counsel of perfection can't be expressed in the language of rights and duties. Instead, it belongs to the vastly more important world of gifts, of things you're not required to do but which you should do anyway. What the nun had offered me was a gift, something to which I had had no claim whatsoever. She had bestowed on me the free blessing of her grace, and the choice was entirely hers to make.

GIFTS OF FAITH AND GOOD GOVERNMENT

The education I received was a gift from the nuns. But in their eyes the greater gift was the possibility of salvation through belief in Christ. It's the fashion to scorn religious missionaries, and people can deface their statues without being punished. If you believe in life after death, however, and think that Heaven represents eternal bliss, you'd be inhumanly selfish if you didn't want to share the possibility of salvation with others. That is what brought French missionaries to Quebec in the seventeenth century.

Many of them were Jesuits, an order founded in 1540 by an ex-soldier, Saint Ignatius of Loyola. Before turning to religion, Loyola had been an elegant man-at-arms, "given over to vanities of the world," who pursued the knight's "great and vain desire to win fame."[2] He enjoyed a courtier's amours and filled his head with tales of romantic chivalry. But in 1521 the twenty-nine-year-old Loyola was wounded in battle and when he recovered he was a changed man. He read the lives of the saints and sought to imitate them, spending his days in contemplation and prayer. As a mendicant, he made his way to Jerusalem, and in 1528 set out for Paris to continue his studies. There he gathered round him a group of followers, including Saint Francis Xavier, and with them he formed the Society of Jesus in 1539. The order was approved by the Pope the following year.

The Jesuits called themselves soldiers of Christ and upon ordination took the normal three vows of poverty, chastity, and obedience, as well as a fourth vow of special obedience to the pope. Well trained in dogmatics and Christian humanism, they quickly became one of the spearheads of the Catholic Counter-Reformation by founding the best schools in Europe, where they trained Descartes, Corneille, and de Gaulle, as well as less devout alumni such as Voltaire, Robespierre, and Fidel Castro. Like soldiers, they were willing to accept orders to go anywhere to spread the Gospel, and Saint Francis Xavier traveled to India and Japan. Their members also included Eusebio Kino, who founded the mission of St. Xavier del Bac near Tucson. The city of Los Angeles takes its name from Santa Maria de los Ángeles, a mission founded by the Jesuits in 1767.

We're apt to remember the Jesuits as the purveyors of cheap grace and painless penances mocked by Blaise Pascal in the *Provincial Letters* (1657). They were more than that. As missionaries, many of them mortified their bodies and courted capture and death. Saint Jean de Brébeuf wore a hairshirt and an iron-pointed belt and prayed for the martyrdom that would await him in Canada.[3] In England, Saints Robert Southwell and Edmund Campion won the martyr's crown in a country that, after Pope Pius V called for the overthrow of Elizabeth I, had made it a capital offense for Jesuits to minister to Catholics.

I. THE JESUIT RELATIONS

In the seventeenth century, the Canadian missionaries reported back to France in the *Jesuit Relations*, a series of annual chronicles.[4] They told of the progress of evangelization, the wars with the English, the epidemics, and the tortures. They are an ethnographic treasure, written by observant and highly educated men who had lived for years with the natives, and who did their best to win their respect and affection.

Brébeuf warned the missionaries that they'd have to leave behind the comfortable lives they had led in France and cheerfully accept extreme hardships and the possibility of martyrdom.

> You should try to eat their sagamité or salmagundi in the way they prepare it, although it may be dirty, half-cooked, and very tasteless. As to the other numerous things which may be unpleasant, they must be endured for the love of God, without saying anything or appearing to notice them.
>
> You must bear their imperfections without saying a word, yes, even without seeming to notice them. Even if it be necessary to criticize anything, it must be done modestly, and with words and signs which evince love and not aversion. In short, you must try to be, and also to appear, always cheerful.[5]

Paul Le Jeune, the first Jesuit superior of the missions, wrote that the natives were superior to Europeans in many ways.

> They are tall, erect, strong, well-proportioned, agile: there is nothing effeminate in their appearance. Those little fops that are seen elsewhere are only painted images of men, compared with our Indians. I was once inclined to believe that pictures of the Roman emperors represented the ideal of the painters rather than men who had ever existed, so strong and powerful are the heads; but I see here upon the shoulders of these people the heads of Julius Caesar, of Pompey, of Augustus.[6]

The physical attributes were matched by the Hurons' intellectual abilities. "As to the mind of the Indian, it is of good quality. I believe that souls are all made from the same stock and that they do not differ substantially."[7]

The stoic native virtues were also admired. Unlike the French, they never appeared to get angry and could accept suffering cheerfully, even laughing at pain and hardship. Family bonds were extremely strong, and they were greatly attached to each other. If one of them came upon an unusually great delicacy, he would offer it as a feast for his friends rather than eat it alone, and if anyone fell sick there was a rivalry as to who might help him most.[8] The idea of the noble savage in writers such as Fénelon was likely derived from the immensely popular accounts of the Hurons in the *Relations*.

The Jesuit mission in Huronia, the territory bounded by Lakes Huron, Erie, and Ontario, became a fortified village of eighteen priests and as many as forty-six lay assistants.[9] It could only be reached by canoe and backbreaking portages over the rapids of the St. Lawrence River. Getting there meant paddling upstream to the *pays d'en haut*, and the missionaries knew that, if they could not keep up, they might be left behind to perish.[10] Nor could they speak to anyone, except insofar as they had learned the native language. They might have been great scholars in France, but now they were exposed to everyone's laughter.[11]

In the exploration of North America, wrote the historian George Bancroft, "not a cape was turned, nor a river entered, but a Jesuit led the way."[12] To readers in France, they were heroes as brave as any knight in a chivalric romance. Lancelot and Amadís de Gaul were mythical figures, but Saint Isaac Jogues showed how the paths of glory lay open to those with courage and a spirit of adventure. The missionaries were celebrities, the astronauts and Medal of Honor winners of their day. As an exile in France, Richard Crashaw must have had them in mind when he wrote in his *Hymn to St. Teresa* about:

> Ripe men of martyrdom, that could reach down
> With strong arms their triumphant crown;
> Such as could with lusty breath
> Speak loud into the face of death
> Their great Lord's glorious name.

Instead of minimizing the hardships of missionary work, the Jesuits boasted of it. To the spirited youths of France, they said: We offer you the abandonment of every creature comfort, the likelihood of capture and torture, and unparalleled opportunities for perfection and union with Christ. Come join us!

Had Isaac Jogues remained in France, he might have won literary acclaim. Instead, he sought out a Huron mission and, en route, he and his party were captured by the Iroquois. Jogues hid in the bush, but then thought it dishonorable to hide and joined his companions in captivity. The Iroquois did not know what to make of his sang-froid and fell upon him. They stabbed and beat him and tore out his fingernails with their teeth until only the bones were left. The captives were brought on forced marches, where they encountered other Iroquois groups that wanted to share in the fun.

Jogues was brought to a scaffold, and a woman cut off his thumb. The children threw coals and burning cinders on him and took pleasure in watching him broil and roast. As this went on, Jogues saw his skin detaching from his body in several places. Throughout all this he baptized the natives, heard confession, and absolved other prisoners.[13]

Jogues finally escaped and made his way back to France. He arrived, penniless, at the Jesuit college in Rennes and begged admittance. The doorkeeper said that the rector was too busy to see him, and Jogues told him to say that a poor man from Canada wished to meet him. The Canadian missions were famous, and the rector hastened to him. Did the visitor know Father Jogues, he was asked? "I know him very well," was the answer. The Iroquois have taken him, said the rector. Have they murdered him? "No," said Jogues, "he is alive and at liberty, and I am he."[14]

Summoned to Paris, he was presented to the court, where Queen Anne kissed his mutilated fingers. Pope Urban VIII permitted him to consecrate the host, a necessary dispensation since church law required that it be held by the thumb and forefinger. Jogues stayed only a year and a half in France, however. Eager for martyrdom, he returned to Canada in 1646, and with Brébeuf was killed by the Iroquois a few months later.

If the *Jesuit Relations* are little known today, that's because they don't fit well with a dominant narrative about how the missionaries were colonialists who wrongfully suppressed native religions. At St. Xavier del Bac, a sign at the local museum blames them for converting the Tohono O'odham Nation. The sign is not without its own historical interest, and if it remains future generations will be able to learn something about the fashionable myths of today.

II. THE JESUIT REDUCTIONS

Jesuit missionaries were also sent to Latin America, where for more than 150 years (1609–1768) they organized and administered the Jesuit Republic of Paraguay, a series of missions for the Guaraní natives. At their peak, 140,000 Guaraní lived in thirty-one missions in an area twice the size of France. Until they were suppressed by the civil authorities, an event portrayed in the 1986 film *The Mission*, the Jesuits converted the natives and created cities with paved streets, orchestras, and printing presses. Their cathedrals, like the one in Córdoba, Argentina (where another Jesuit, Pope Francis, would make a spiritual retreat), were almost as impressive as the Jesuit Baroque churches of Spain and Italy.

The Jesuits sought to bring the Guaraní within the safe harbor of their settlements, which were called Reductions. Before this, the colonial authorities had created a form of de facto slavery called the *servicio*, in which the natives were bound to offer day labor in lieu of taxes. The governor would then grant the right to their labor to a colonist, who became an effective slaveowner. The Jesuits abolished the *servicio* and armed the Guaraní, who fought pitched battles with Portuguese slave-hunters. Spaniards were banned from visiting the Reductions, and, while this been condemned as paternalistic, the Reductions saved the natives from a far more troubling kind of paternalism.[15]

The Jesuits were faithful to Church doctrine, which held that the natives were entitled to salvation and could not be enslaved. In *Veritas Ipsa* (1537), Pope Paul III explicitly banned slavery in the Americas. "We . . . noting that the Indians themselves are true men . . .

declare . . . that the same Indians and all other peoples—even though they are outside the faith—. . . are not to be reduced to slavery, and that whatever happens to the contrary is to be considered null and void." That pronouncement was repeated by subsequent popes, and if slavery persisted in Brazil until 1888 it was because it was tolerated by the state and not the Church.

For good or ill, the Reductions have been described as a socialist utopia in which all property was held in common. To the extent this was true, it was a result of the lack of scarcity and the abundance of fruit and game all about the settlements. But it really wasn't true either. Each family had a house and a patio in which they kept hens and geese, as well as flocks of sheep and herds of cattle in the fields.[16] The natives were not permitted to sell their land without the approval of the Spanish governor, but that is no different from the restrictions on alienation in American reservations and Canadian reserves and like them was meant to prevent the property from falling into the hands of white purchasers.

The Guaraní were asked to work six hours a day, six days a week, but for four days they did so on their own farms. The Reductions traded with the outside world, selling yerba maté in Buenos Aires and Santa Fe and buying farm tools and kitchenware with the proceeds, but they were not run as business enterprises. The Jesuits' goal was not to make a profit but to earn just enough to keep the mission going. When they were expelled in 1768, no moneys were found in the till, all the revenues having been plowed back into the Reductions.

The Guaraní came of their own free will to the Reductions, which were largely self-governing. A native governor (*corregidor*) was appointed in each village, assisted by a deputy (*teniente*), three supervisors (*alcaldes*), several councilors (*rigadores*), a prefect of police, and a clerk (*secretario*), who together made up the town council (*cabildo*). Within each village, families were divided into *cliques* headed by chiefs (*caciques*), with thirty or forty families in each clique. Elections for office took place annually, from a list of candidates prepared by the retiring officials.[17] The priests had the right to challenge nominations, but apart from this the Jesuits had established a form of native self-government more democratic than almost anywhere else at the time, and moreover one made for people of color.

That did not save the Reductions from the ill will of anti-clerical Enlightenment figures such as Portugal's Marquis de Pombal, who as de facto ruler had the Jesuits expelled from his domains. Soon after, they were also expelled from Spain and France by rulers who resented the challenge the Jesuits posed to Bourbon absolutism. But if any evidence were needed of how benign the missions were, the Guaraní provided it when they rebelled against the expulsion of the Jesuits and began the Guaraní Wars against the civil authorities.

Gifts and Bargains

In 1633 the Hurons met with Samuel de Champlain, the governor of New France, to create a lasting alliance with the French. They presented Champlain with packages of beaver pelts, and in return he told them that the French greatly cherished their Huron friends and would honor their promises with them. The Jesuit missionaries would join them, and he asked the Hurons to receive them with love and honor. At this, Brébeuf told the Hurons that he would live and die with them, "that they would be our brothers, that hereafter we would be of their people."[18]

The exchange of presents was an example of how gift economies create bonds of affection. Before the missionaries began to evangelize the First Nation Hurons, there was nothing to indicate they were friends. Benevolence came first, then the gift, then friendship, and finally the requirements of liberalism.

The bonds formed by gifts are unlike the self-interested contracts made in market economies. Contracts create a legal relationship in which mutual promises are exchanged, and where what is given up is matched against what one gets. The give-up supplies the necessary element of consideration that makes the bargain legally enforceable. Without that, I'm getting something for nothing, and nothing for free is the rule in contract law. In gift economies, by contrast, the gift is freely given. There might be an instinct of reciprocity, but if return gifts are given the exchange is not to be confused with barter. The recipient is not required to reciprocate, and, if he does, the donor does not know what the return gift will be.

In gift economies, the willingness to create a bond arises from a general spirit of benevolence. In market economies there's also a desire to create a bond, but benevolence has nothing to do with it, said Adam Smith. Seventeen years after he described our sense of benevolence in *The Theory of Moral Sentiments*, Smith wrote in *The Wealth of Nations* that:

> It is not from the benevolence of the butcher, the brewer, or the baker, that we expect our dinner, but from their regard to their own interest. We address ourselves, not to their humanity but to their self-love, and never talk to them of our own necessities but of their advantages. Nobody but a beggar chuses to depend chiefly upon the benevolence of his fellow-citizens.[19]

Economists call the apparent change of heart the "Adam Smith Problem."[20] There really isn't a contradiction, however. Market and gift economies exist in separate spheres, and it's a mistake to think you can efface the barriers between them, as George Gilder tried to do in *Wealth and Poverty* (1981). Market economies began with barter, said Gilder, and barter began with the instinct of reciprocity in gift exchanges. There might be something to that, as a matter of market prehistory, but then Gilder argued that the sense of benevolence never disappeared and that the instinct to trade always arises from the desire to confer a gift on one's co-contractor. "Capitalism begins with giving."[21]

That's not without an element of truth. A sense of sharing does grease the negotiations between co-contractors. The hard bargainer who wants the entire contractual surplus for himself will do well against a weak bargainer, but when two hard bargainers face each other they're less likely to arrive at an agreement.[22] They'd be more likely to cut a deal if each were willing to sacrifice some of their gains and could persuade the other party that both will benefit from it.[23] The fairness norms we saw in the last chapter will therefore facilitate bargaining.[24]

Market economies are unlikely to develop when strangers are regarded as Schmittian enemies, as they were in the precapitalist society of southern Italy described by Edward C. Banfield in *The Moral Basis of a Backward Society* (1958). Banfield wrote of a society so riddled with envy—an Italian town he called Montegrano—that any form of economic progress was unthinkable. The Montegranese thought that every politician was on the take, that every priest was corrupt, that every employer cheated his employees. Only family members could be trusted. Banfield called this "amoral familism," and said that market economies could not arise in so selfish a society. Similarly, Max Weber said that "[t]he universal reign of absolute unscrupulousness in the pursuit of selfish interests by the making of money has been a specific characteristic of precisely those countries whose bourgeois-capitalistic development, measured according to Occidental standards, has remained backward."[25]

If market economies require some measure of fellow feeling, that's not the same thing as the disinterested desire to confer a gift. And in a commercial age, we can too easily ignore the role of gift economies. We forget how much in our society is contributed without the demand for anything in return. In 1993, when the Internet was still a far-off dream, Microsoft thought to create a digital, multimedia encyclopedia called Encarta. Its entries would be prepared by renowned experts, who'd be well-paid for their efforts. But Encarta is no longer around. It was pushed aside by another encyclopedia whose contributors were unpaid and who volunteered their labor. Before it went under in 2009, Encarta had 62,000 articles, mostly hidden behind a paywall. The upstart competitor, Wikipedia, has six million articles, all of which can be read without charge.

The difference between gift and market economies is reflected in the debate between heretical Pelagians and orthodox Augustinians, one that Eric Nelson says defines today's politics. Pelagians believe that salvation is like a contractual bargain, and that they can buy their way into Heaven by their good works without the need for the gift of God's grace. "Look, Big Fella," they say, "the deal is: I'll be good, and you'll take care of me when I die." But salvation isn't a market exchange, say the Augustinians. Rather, it's a free gift from

God, given *ex gratia* through His grace, and He can bestow it on whomever He wants.

You might be a perfect little saint, but He still might not care for you. That's what you get if, as Leszek Kołakowski put it, *God Owes Us Nothing* (1995). You might ask for mercy, Portia tells Shylock in *The Merchant of Venice*, but "in the course of justice none of us should see salvation."[26] All is grace, and the possibility of salvation the missionaries offered their converts is the greatest gift of all.

Gift economies will seem threatening to Pelagians, since they ask us to recognize our incompleteness and dependence on gifts and grace. They'll prefer market economies, where people are seen as Randian heroes, independent and self-sufficient, beholden to no one. They proudly make their own way. If instead they recognized their need for a gift economy, they'd reveal their beggary, their reliance upon the gratuitous kindness of others. Gift economies testify to wants that can't be met by contracts or lawsuits.

The failure to recognize our dependence on others is the welfare state's great failing, said Simone Weil. We're told we have rights to all sorts of things, but this excludes gifts given out of charity and the benevolence that creates bonds between strangers. Theories of rights permit us to think that any ties we might have to other people are fully requited by bargained-for exchanges or by the wealth transfers of state welfarism. Provided the state provides for food, housing, clothing, medical care, and whatnot, we can be entirely indifferent to the recipients. The elites would think it foolish to join them in their labors, as Weil had done at the Renault factory.

In the heartlessness of today's North America, whose generous welfare systems coexist with private contempt for an underclass, we've arrived at the peak rootlessness of a rights society. We were reminded of this when a British Columbia woman went to a Vancouver hospital because she felt suicidal. She had wanted a sympathetic ear, someone to talk her out of it, but sympathy wasn't on the cards. Instead she was told that she had a right to a medically assisted euthanasia. Afterwards the hospital said it had followed correct procedures. And they were right. She didn't have a right to sympathy. Just a right to die.

Sympathy is either a gift or it's nothing at all. Knowing this, we yearn for what Edmund Burke called the unbought grace of life. The proof is our sense of gratitude. We'll not say thank you when we merely get what we've paid for. We don't feel grateful to the garage mechanic who turned a simple tune-up into a $500 maintenance fee. Instead, we go to the cashier and pay our bill. And we'll not say thank you to the lawyer and accountant, except in the most perfunctory manner, because they carry on their practice in a market economy. Where we will say thanks is in a restaurant, in the form of a tip to our server. She also works in a market economy, but the practice of tipping permits us to imagine that the pleasureful experience of a restaurant meal has been removed from a commercial zone to the magic realm of a gift economy.

While we shouldn't want market economies to squeeze out gift economies, it's sometimes thought that they do just that and that the two are substitutes rather than complements. Introduce bargains and commercial exchange into gift relationships and they can decay. There is an example of this in blood drives. Richard Titmuss showed how blood clinics get their volunteers without having to pay them and that, if they did pay them, both the quality and quantity of the blood would decline. Similarly, the docents at the museum aren't paid. They are there simply because they want to share their joy in experiencing great art. In a singularly tone-deaf move, the Art Institute of Chicago replaced the lot of them with people of color, whom they put on salary. Not merely were the docents slapped in the face, but they were told that they had stood in the way of racial progress.

The tension between gift and market economies was explored in Shakespeare's reflection on usury, *The Merchant of Venice*. It's really the story of two cities. Belmont is where Portia will be given away as a bride and represents gift economies, while Venice is the city of usury, hard bargains, and market economies.[27] Gift economies are fecund and bring forth life, like the children that will be born from the union of Bassanio and Portia. Even without children, gifts add something through the new bonds of sympathy they create, which Lewis Hyde called the erotic life of property. By contrast, new life cannot be born from Shylock's "barren metal" of gold or his usury.[28]

57

Instead, usury kills life, as Shylock proposes to do in extracting his pound of flesh from Antonio, the childless merchant of Venice.

The message to be taken from the play, however, is that gift and market economies are meant to coexist. Belmont would not be able to sneer at wealth were it not produced from Venetian gold, like the money Bassanio borrows from Antonio to court Portia, a commercial transaction that drives all the play's action. Shakespeare himself was a savvy entrepreneur, as well as the greatest playwright in the English language.

The Obligations of Gift Economies

While gifts are free, Marcel Mauss identified three quasi-obligations in gift economies. In a market economy, no one is required to make a contractual offer, but in gift economies the donor ought to offer presents. Second, the recipient ought to accept them. Third, the recipient should make a return gift.[29] Put them together and they amount to a virtue, which if nameless is nevertheless one closest to our heart.

In market economies, there might be self-interested reasons to enter into a bargain, but that doesn't give rise to a moral requirement. In gift economies, on the other hand, we ought to make gifts because we value the bonds they create. They make our society more fraternal, and that's especially needed in today's America. Between 1985 and 2004, the number of Americans who told a friend something of personal importance during the prior six months fell from 73 to 51 percent, while the number of people who had no such confidants rose from 10 to 25 percent.[30] That is a staggering loss in social solidarity, and it's gotten worse. In the political animosities that divide us, the comforting belief that neighbors and strangers wish us well has been pitilessly shattered. In our loneliness, there has never been a greater need for fraternity.

There's another difference between market and gift economies. In sale-of-goods law, a seller's performance is complete when he tenders the goods, but in gift economies something more is needed. In addition to the property transfer, the donor must want to form a sympathetic bond with the recipient. That was the point of James Russell

Lowell's *The Vision of Sir Launfal* (1848), a poem every schoolchild was asked to memorize a hundred years ago ("And what is so rare as a day in June?"), but which is now unread.

In a dream, young Sir Launfal dons his armor and gaily rides forth from his castle in search of the Holy Grail. On crossing the drawbridge, however, he immediately encounters a foul-looking leper who begs for alms. Launfal shivers in horror and scornfully tosses the leper a piece of gold, which he refuses to pick up. He might have welcomed a bit of bread that affirmed the bond between them, but as for Launfal's coin, "He gives only the worthless gold / Who gives from a sense of duty."

Years pass, and the aged and frail Sir Launfal returns empty-handed. He never found the Grail, and now the castle is held by another. At its gate he sees the leper again, but this time a humbled Launfal gives the leper a crust of bread and water from a wooden bowl. At this the leper is revealed to be Christ, who tells Sir Launfal:

> The Holy Supper is kept, indeed,
> In whatso we share with another's need;
> Not what we give, but what we share,
> For the gift without the giver is bare.

From a purely economic perspective there was no difference between the two gifts, and indeed the first was more valuable than the second. But what was missing in the first gift, given in a spirit of condescension and out of a frigid sense of duty, was the sense of a solidarity with the beggar. It lacked what Mauss called the spiritual power of gift economies, where the point is to create a personal bond between two people.

Robert Frost reminded us that the giver must accompany the gift at John F. Kennedy's Inauguration. He had been asked to read a poem and produced a pompous one especially for the occasion. But on the windy steps of the Capitol the paper fluttered about and, as he couldn't read it, he stepped back and from memory recited another poem. It was "The Gift Outright," and it was about what makes us Americans. It's not about owning a piece of land, said Frost. Rather, we become Americans by giving of ourselves to the land:

Something we were withholding made us weak
Until we found out that it was ourselves
We were withholding from our land of living,
And forthwith found salvation in surrender.
Such as we were we gave ourselves outright.

Mauss's second obligation is imposed on the recipient and asks him to accept the gift. There's nothing like this in market economies, where there's never a duty to accept a contractual offer. But gifts are different. Inviting someone to dinner at one's house is an offer of friendship, and turning this down would amount to rejecting a relationship with the giver. Refusing to accept is "the equivalent of a declaration of war," said Mauss. "It is a refusal of friendship and intercourse."[31]

Mauss's third element in the gift economy is the instinct of reciprocity and the obligation to provide a return gift. The sense of reciprocity is ordinarily directed towards the giver, like the server at the restaurant, but it might also be more diffuse and become a generalized sentiment of benevolence. People who have received gifts are more likely to pay it forward. Blood-donation recipients will want to become blood donors themselves, for another set of recipients. The same is true of Alcoholics Anonymous, which runs on donations and whose twelve-step program asks the alcoholic to pass on his gift to other alcoholics. "Freely ye have received; freely give," the twelfth step commands, echoing Christ's command to his disciples.[32]

CIVILIZATION SEEN AS A GIFT

All that we value in our civilization—our family structure, high culture, religion, and political liberalism—can be seen to have begun as gifts. We didn't pay for them, and they came unbought.

I. MARRIAGE

Marriage is the greatest of gift exchanges, one in which kinship bonds are transcended and unrelated families united. The ceremony is a contract, made by parties who enter willingly into the matrimonial estate. Assets are shared, and it's a market exchange. Historically, it was also a gift exchange, in which fathers gave away brides, and there are still elements of this in our culture. In the Church of England's Book of Common Prayer, the minister asks the father of the bride, "Who giveth this Woman to be married to this Man?" That makes the woman seem like the gift, not the giver, a point made by Claude Lévi-Strauss. "The total relationship of exchange which constitutes marriage is not established between a man and a woman, ... but between two groups of men, and the woman figures only as one of the objects in the exchange, not as one of the partners between whom the exchange takes place."[33]

It is natural to see marriage as a gift because it unites people who, out of respect for the incest taboo, are genetically dissimilar. When the parties are genetically related, the instinct to reciprocate on receipt of a gift is weakest.[34] Within a family, people give gifts without keeping track of who gave to whom, since the natural love and affection does not need to be cemented by a gift economy. From the gene's-eye view of things, no reciprocity is required because the gene is simply giving to itself. But marriage is different and calls for the kind of gifts seen in O. Henry's "The Gift of the Magi" (1905).

Della and Jim are newlyweds and desperately poor. Della would dearly love to give Jim a Christmas present, but she has only $1.87 to her name. What she does have, however, is her gloriously long hair, which she sells to buy a chain for Jim's watch. He also wanted to buy her a Christmas present, and so he sold his watch to buy her a set of combs. The two gifts canceled each other out, but it didn't matter. Of all who give gifts, wrote O. Henry, they were the wisest, the Magi.

II. HIGH ART

High art has also been seen as a gift. Ezra Pound's Canto XLV, called the "Usura Canto" (which you can hear him recite on YouTube), raged against market economies because he thought that the true source of great art was gifts:

> Duccio came not by usura
> nor Pier della Francesca; Zuan Bellin' not by usura
> nor was "La Calunnia" painted.
> Came not by usura Angelico; came not Ambrogio Praedis,
> Came no church of cut stone signed: *Adamo me fecit.*

The art of a market economy is made for its time only, said Pound, and is not meant to last beyond that. "No picture is made to endure nor to live with, but it is made to sell and sell quickly." The impulse to create lasting art is different and comes from the desire to make a gift for all times, and not from an immediate bargain for money. Bach wrote for the ages, and not just for kings, princes, and margraves. These were gifts.

At a classical concert, the performers appear in formal dress as a mark of homage to the composer. The audience will share in the gift ceremony, through its applause. If the concert were nothing more than a market transaction, all this would be superfluous. The audience has already paid for the experience in the price of the ticket. We'd not even bother going to concerts. Glenn Gould was right to note that technology has made it unnecessary to listen to a live performance. We could enjoy the experience at home with a flawless recording, without having to get dressed up, drive to a concert hall, and spend money for the privilege. The performer would be spared the ordeal, which Gould thought a cruel spectacle. But instead, we'll insist on going to a concert, because this is a ceremony of thanksgiving, made complete through the applause.

Artists will ask for payment, but they're also impelled to create. Their talents themselves are like a gift that arrives unbidden, like the ideas or verses that come in dreamlike states, from a muse or some secret sharer. That was how Socrates thought poetry was written.

When he asked the poets to explain their verses, they couldn't do so, and he concluded that "it was not wisdom that enabled them to write poetry but a kind of instinct or inspiration, such as you find in seers and prophets."[35] Socrates described his own talent as a *daimonion*—an oracle or voice—that forbade him from doing wrong.[36] There was Socrates and there was the voice, and they seemed like two separate things. The artist exists in a market economy, but he also repays the gift from the muse by offering his creation as a gift.

Gifts and markets sustain each other, however, and there isn't a wall of separation between them. The great cathedrals would not have been built without an ecclesiastical entrepreneur like Abbot Suger to raise the money and pay the workmen. Pound's Renaissance artists weren't above hard bargaining for their services. If he had been right, musicians and authors wouldn't need copyright law. They'd release their work without looking for an economic reward. Tell that to Charles Dickens, who bitterly complained about the pirated editions of his novels.

III. RELIGIOUS CEREMONIES

Religious ceremonies arose from gift exchanges. In classical Greece, religion took the form of recognizing our dependence on the favor of the gods and expressing our thanks through sacrifices. The Minotaur was born from the union of a bull with King Minos's wife, whom Zeus made fall in love with the animal because Minos had refused to sacrifice for the god. Then, when Theseus killed the Minotaur, he sacrificed it to his protector, Athena. So, too, a crusading knight might vow to build a chapel for Our Lady, in thanks for her help in battle.

Christ's sacrifice on the Cross was also a gift, "for God so loved the world, as to give his only begotten Son" for our salvation.[37] Our worship for Him is an act of reciprocity, in response to the command to be thankful.[38] The logic of gifts calls forth our gratitude for what we have received. René Girard thought that worship began with sacrifice, from the Binding of Isaac to the Pascal Lamb and Christ on the Cross, but the true foundation of worship is the recipient's impulse to give thanks for a gift. Religions begin in benevolence, not in blood.

IV. LIBERALISM

Similarly, liberalism begins with a sense of benevolence for gifts offered and received. Before you tell me that you have rights I must respect, or that I am under any duty to you, you must explain why I should care about you. What makes you a friend rather than a Schmittian enemy to whom I owe nothing? If I'm not sure who you are, only a liberalism that begins with benevolence and the impulse to make a gift can ground rights and entitlements.

The liberalism of gifts is very different from the liberalism of what Thomas Carlyle (and later *The Communist Manifesto*) called "cash-payment."[39] Theories of self-interested bargains and market economies can't explain the instinct of benevolence in gift economies, or why the Jesuits should have risked martyrdom in Canada and created a Guaraní republic in South America. They also can't explain why, in addition to wanting to exploit a bargain opportunity, I might want to perform the works of corporal and spiritual mercy, to give shelter to strangers and forgive injuries. Abstract rights that are uncoupled from any sense of affection or fraternity are easily ignored, absent the liberalism of a gift economy that binds the parties together.

GIFTS THAT MISFIRE

Absent benevolence, gift giving can represent a nasty move in a status competition. Out of self-love we seek to show our superiority and will do so in a variety of ways, and one is by purchasing luxury goods. A Timex keeps time as well as a Rolex, but the latter tells one that its wearer is a top wage earner. Thorstein Veblen mocked this as conspicuous consumption, where the payoff from an otherwise wasteful purchase comes from parading one's wealth. Conspicuous donations are like conspicuous consumption, a showy way to signal one's superiority.

That was what the potlatch ceremony of the Kwakiutl and Haida natives of British Columbia became before it was suppressed. The potlatch was an all-day event in which gifts were passed from one tribe to another. A big gift revealed the donor's high status, and a failure to reciprocate was held to be shameful, since a tribe could not boast of its position unless it gave away property. Indeed, material goods were valued primarily for the status that accrued when the donor gave them away.[40] Sometimes, instead of doing so, the donor would simply burn them, since the point was to shame a rival tribe in a battle fought not with knives but with property. As Ruth Benedict noted, the tribes did not want wealth in order to better their economic conditions, but rather to use as counters in a zero-sum status competition.[41]

The potlach was an example of how an act that seems morally commendable—gift-giving—may nevertheless be questionable because it is tainted by an unworthy motive. The ceremonies continued until the Canadian government banned the potlach in 1885, at the prompting of Duncan Campbell Scott in the Indian Affairs department. Scott was a celebrated poet who regarded the natives as primitive wards of the state, and who sponsored the residential schools for native children that today are (rightly or wrongly) regarded as a national scandal. He thought the potlatches handicapped the natives, whom he wanted to see completely assimilated into white society. Today he's condemned for suppressing a native custom, but no one with the Kwakiutls' interests at heart would want to see the status competition revived.

Evolutionary biologists have identified the same kind of wealth-destroying competition in the animal kingdom. The competition for evolutionary fitness and the ability to pass on our genes comes at a cost, which the zoologist Amotz Zahavi labels a "handicap principle."[42] Among animals, competing males can handicap themselves to make themselves attractive to females, and the classic example is the peacock's tail. Peahens choose their mates by the size and color of their tails, preferring large to small tails, with lots of "eyespots" in the tail.[43] In this way, the genes of individual large-tailed birds are selected to survive. For the species, however, that's a handicap. The large, colorful tail makes birds more visible to predators, and as the tail is cumbersome it is harder for the bird to escape once it is noticed. But what's bad for the species is good for the individual, successful bird. The large-tailed male will seem a good genetic bet if it has escaped its predators notwithstanding its tail, since long-tailed birds with lower survivability will already have been eaten.[44] As a group, the males would be better off if they could sign and enforce a strategic tail-limitation agreement, but that's not about to happen. Similarly, the wealth-destroying potlach ceremony is good for individual tribes but bad for the Kwakiutl and Haida as a whole.

In addition, some gifts are meant to cement a corrupt relationship, and their acceptance might even be a criminal act. When he was Lord Chancellor, Francis Bacon had received "presents" from litigants, and, while he would plead that this was the way of the world, he was nevertheless convicted of bribery. "Thus you see *Corruption* laid to the Charge of a Judge too, a great Judge," concluded Bacon's prosecutor, "nay to the Great Keeper of the King's Conscience."[45]

When the United States broke with Britain, we meant to create a republic of virtue free of European corruption, but that's not how things turned out. We don't score highly on cross-country measures of corruption, and one reason for this is our practice of buying access to justice through gifts in the form of campaign contributions. Campaign donors will expect the politicians to return their calls and respect their views, and that's not illegal, ruled Justice Kennedy in *Citizens United v. FEC* (2010).[46] In *McCutcheon v. FEC* (2014),[47] Chief Justice Roberts took it one step further. Not merely will campaign donors gain access, but they can expect that the officials they support will respond to their interests. And there's nothing wrong with that, thought Roberts. Rather, it's a central feature of democracy. Still, it's another example of the dark side of gift-giving.

The gift will backfire if it's officious and unwanted. The recipient might think it presumptuous if he never wanted to treat you as a friend. Other gifts are insulting, like the tennis balls the Dauphin gave Henry V. Or inappropriate, like the Strip-O-Gram sent to the vicar. As for Greeks bearing gifts, consider yourself warned.

* * *

The dark side of gift-giving can't obscure the need for gift economies, however. They create the bonds of fraternity in a lonely society and are the cement of civilized life. Those who have benefited from them are more likely to yield the right of way, observe queues at the check-out counter, and perform the numberless acts of courtesy and kindness that together constitute a civilized society. It's when gift economies are weakest that we'll encounter road rage on the highways, the jerks at the grocery store, and the departures from liberalism that are so common today.

6.

THE SOCIAL CONTRACT

Intergenerational gifts represent the biggest wealth transfer in our economy. Over the next decade, $16 trillion will be left by the elderly (mostly Boomers) to their children and charities. That's the same size as the total wealth of Great Britain. Over the next twenty years, that number will grow to $84 trillion,[1] which is the size of China's total wealth. You can't take it with you.

The size of the wealth transfer puts the lie to economists who discount the bequest motive. Their life-cycle model assumes that individuals care only about themselves, and that any moneys they leave to their children would result from a miscalculation about how long they'll live. The goal is to spend one's last dollar at the moment of death and not to leave anything over. But that's not what the evidence shows. Laurence Kotlikoff and Larry Summers report that people save most of their money to pass it on as bequests and gifts rather than to consume in retirement.[2]

Life-cycle economists who fail to recognize the strength of the bequest motive, and extreme individualists who ignore family bonds, reveal their moral poverty. They have failed to recognize how the real social contract is not a hypothetical Lockean bargain but a set of felt duties that bind members of the same family. We are born into families and with this comes gifts and responsibilities. We take from our parents and repay them by giving to our children. The gift relationship, repeated over time, binds all of us who have children and persists through all generations and all time. Edmund Burke thought it a source of all that is great in our culture.[3] It is the begetter of desires to accumulate, to build, and to create.

We've allowed ourselves to forget this. Political philosophy myopically privileges individuals and scants the powerful impulse to provide for our children. In doing so it shortchanges the desire for a mobile society, which is a touchstone of liberalism. Because of the bequest motive, we'd like to see our children get ahead, and the true liberal will oppose an aristocracy of fixed classes, whether composed of a titled nobility or a twisted meritocracy in which meritocratic parents unjustly advantage their meritocratic children. That's a constant struggle, however, since neo-Darwinians will tell you that aristocracy is society's natural default, given our genetic predisposition to favor our children.

HAMILTON'S LAW

Religious conservatives are apt to scoff at evolutionary explanations of behavior, but they're wrong to think that evolutionary theorists are all village atheists. Pope Francis himself believes that evolution is not inconsistent with the idea of a Divine Creator. Further, the natural lawyer who thinks that we're hardwired with a knowledge of the good is taking a stand with genetics on the nature versus nurture debate. Finally, conservatives who tell us that the family is the bedrock of our civilization should recognize the genetic basis for the instinct to pass on wealth to our children.

The genetic explanation for intergenerational gift-giving is an application of "Hamilton's Law," from the work of W. D. Hamilton (1936–2000). We share genes with our relatives, and from this

Hamilton arrived at a theory to explain how we might sacrifice for them.[4] Darwinian natural selection shouldn't be seen at the level of individuals, he argued, but rather at that of our genes. On this hypothesis (which Richard Dawkins labeled "the selfish gene"), the gene is in charge. It's the decision-making principal, and the individual whose body the gene inhabits is merely its agent. The gene gives the command, and the individual follows it.

Hamilton's Law explains how we're biased in favor of our descendants and relatives. We share half our genes with our children and a quarter of them with our grandchildren. Between first cousins, the coefficient of relatedness is 0.125. From this, Hamilton arrived at Hamilton's Law, a theory that describes how a person might be expected to act altruistically for his relatives to enhance the survival of his genes and their copies. In one sense, that's a gift. In another, it's purely a self-interested act, since the gene is simply giving to itself or its copies.

Hamilton expressed his law as a cost-benefit rule about "inclusive fitness," with fitness referring to the gene's ability to maximize copies of itself. The cost arises when a person incurs risks that threaten his life or capacity to reproduce, and the benefit from the increased copies of the gene provided by children and other relatives. The decision-making gene will give the following order to its body when considering whether to bear a sacrifice in order to help a relative:

$$\text{Be altruistic if } rB > C$$

where r is the coefficient of relatedness, B is the relatives' fitness benefit (increased probability of the gene's reproductive success), and C is the donors' fitness cost (reduced probability of reproductive success). J. B. S. Haldane had earlier intuited the same idea by saying that he would lay down his life for two brothers or eight first cousins. For one brother, $r = 0.5$, and for two of them, $r = 1.0$. For one cousin, $r = 0.125$, and for eight of them, $r = 1.0$. When the donor sacrifices himself for either two brothers or eight cousins, it's an even trade.

Could it ever be more than an even trade? Yes, and this accounts for the intensity of the parent's willingness to sacrifice for his children. With one daughter he shares half of his genes, but then there's her children too. Suppose that the parent has two children (2*0.5), and they have two children themselves (4*0.25), and each of them has another two children (8*0.125), and so on ad infinitum. The co-efficient of relatedness for all the future generations is an infinitely large number.

ARISTOCRACY AND THE AMERICAN DREAM

Hamilton's Law explains why aristocracy is society's natural default position. To pass on our genes, we'd want our children to be attractive mates in marriage markets, and those in power have an enhanced ability to do so. They'll want to make sure their kids are rich and well-educated, and they'll provide them with the legacy-admissions programs that get them admitted to top schools. And that's what happens in America. Economist Raj Chetty found that students from families in the top 1 percent of earners were seventy-seven times as likely as poor students to be admitted to the Ivy League.[5]

It doesn't stop there. The aristocrat won't be satisfied when his children do well only in absolute terms. He'll also care how they fare relative to other people's children, and that will make him willing to impoverish future societies so long as his children end up on top. He'll want the abysmal public schools, the open borders, the regulatory barriers, all the things that place a stumbling block in the path of the Ragged Dicks who seek to rise. Instead of a meritocratic society, he'll want something like seventeenth-century France.

While we began as a meritocratic society, the meritocrats have manipulated the rules to pass on their advantages to their children, and a corrupt meritocracy has turned into an aristocracy. They've jiggered the legal and regulatory regime to burden those beneath them, while praising themselves for their intellectual, cultural, and moral superiority over the deplorables and publicans at the back of the Temple.

That is a betrayal of the American Dream, the idea that, whoever you were, wherever you came from, you can flourish and your children will have it better than you did. That's always been at the core of the American idea of liberalism. We can tolerate inequalities if we think that our children can get ahead. What we can't abide is an aristocracy, where children are locked into the same economic and social class as their parents. That, we had thought, was what we left behind in the countries from which so many of our ancestors came. It wasn't supposed to happen here.

We owe the idea of the American Dream to Abraham Lincoln, who gave a new meaning to the Declaration of Independence. He revered the Founders, especially Jefferson, and understood that Jefferson's egalitarianism was incompatible with the institution of slavery. However, he thought that equality was also a guarantee of social mobility.

> This progress by which the poor, honest, industrious, and res-
> olute man raises himself, that he may work on his own account
> ... is that progress that human nature is entitled to, is that im-
> provement in condition that is intended to be secured by those
> institutions under which we live, is the great principle for which
> this government was really formed.[6]

Lincoln didn't just believe this. He lived it, and from his personal rise he took an understanding of society that in time led to the Emancipation Proclamation and the Thirteenth Amendment's abolition of slavery. That was how, he told Congress on July 4, 1861, the fight to preserve the Union should be seen. It was about a principle more encompassing than slavery.

> This is essentially a people's contest. On the side of the Union
> it is a struggle for maintaining in the world that form and sub-
> stance of government whose leading object is to elevate the
> condition of men; to lift artificial weights from all shoulders; to
> clear the paths of laudable pursuit for all; to afford all an unfet-
> tered start and a fair chance in the race of life.

Lincoln hated the idea that social classes are fixed, that a superior culture-bearing and leisured aristocracy would be served by a permanent underclass. Before the Civil War, Southerners called this the mudsill theory, a metaphor for the way in which gorgeous antebellum mansions rested upon the bare earth, the slaveholder upon the slaves.[7] Sadly, however, the mudsill lives on in America among those who think that the deplorables are doomed to permanent inferiority by their broken homes and drug dependencies, like the family members J. D. Vance ratted out in *Hillbilly Elegy*. An older left had allied itself to America's underclass, to the coal miners of Harlan County and the Joads of *The Grapes of Wrath*, but the modern Democratic Party abandoned them in favor of policies that serve their elites.

So just how much mobility is there in America? Historically, a lot. In Jefferson's day, Virginia's Tidewater planters lived in the strongest aristocracy that America has ever known, Gordon Wood tells us.[8] In the nineteenth century, however, the Declaration's affirmation that all men are created equal became a self-fulfilling prophecy. When jobs were lacking, a person could strike out for Frederick Jackson Turner's frontier, until that closed in 1890. In the 1950s and 1960s, more people than ever before went to college, and on graduation they found good jobs waiting for them and better homes than the ones they grew up in. Women and minorities still faced discriminatory barriers, but these had receded with feminism and the civil-rights movement. We sensed correctly that things were getting better for everyone, and that America was the land of opportunity. More recently, however, income mobility has slowed, and today there is much less chance for a family to move up the ranks.[9]

What is embarrassing is that the American Dream really isn't dead. It's just moved offshore, to more mobile countries. The Pew Economic Mobility Project ranks countries on an immobility scale, where a higher score means less mobility (a closer correlation between the incomes of fathers and sons). At zero there is no correlation and the society is perfectly mobile. Denmark has a ranking of 0.15 and is relatively mobile, while a relatively immobile Britain has a ranking of 0.50. Remarkably, the U.S. is one of the least mobile societies in the First World. Our score of 0.47, high as it is, might even be too low. Bhashkar Mazumder would put it at 0.60.[10]

Liberalism is sometimes confused with a radical egalitarianism that seeks to equalize all of us, in our wealth, status, and education. That's an impossible goal, and an undesirable one as well. We sort ourselves out by our character and preferences, and they will resist the radical egalitarian's procrustean bed. We trade off labor and leisure, human capital investments and consumption, and always in a different manner. Some of us are frugal ants, others *plus cigale que fourmi*. If somehow we were all made equal, we'd immediately sort ourselves out again and become unequal. As Robert Nozick noted, the professional egalitarian would have a full-time job correcting departures from his naïve ideal.

That's not what the true liberal would want. What he will seek to do, however, is eliminate the unjust barriers through which an aristocracy cements its privileges and prevents a lower class from rising. The country to emulate, on that score, is Denmark. In part, that means adopting a right-wing agenda: tighter immigration restrictions, better K–12 schools, lower regulatory barriers, and a stronger rule of law. In addition, we might emulate some of the more left-wing things Denmark does to promote intergenerational mobility. Make college affordable by capping tuition and provide relief from catastrophic medical conditions with a decent health-care system. Leaving right- and left-wing labels aside, that's a liberal agenda.

7.

RELIGION

Derek Parfit offered the following summary of the history of ethics:

1. Forbidden by God.
2. Forbidden by God, therefore wrong.
3. Wrong, therefore forbidden by God.
4. Wrong.[1]

The first of these is a theory of religion, not ethics. In theory God might command things that are wrong, and in practice this included the human sacrifices of pagan religions. The second is a Divine Command theory which was affirmed by Jewish scriptures and defended by Aquinas. God's commands cannot be second-guessed, and Jews and Christians still believe this. If autonomy were all that mattered, Adam would have been right to eat of the Tree of Knowledge and God would have been wrong to punish him. As an example of the third theory, Kant thought that moral laws were prior to religious beliefs. In the *Groundwork of the Metaphysics of Morals* (1785), he wrote that "even the Holy One of the Gospel must first be compared with our idea of moral perfection before he is recognized as one."[2] Parfit subscribed to the fourth option, which is what one must do if, like him, one is a moral philosopher and an atheist.

Religious believers will take issue with Parfit. Dostoevsky thought that, on any theory of morals, it was impossible to take God out of the picture. Either Christ rose from the dead, or everything is permitted. That's an argument for religious belief that assumes a prior need for moral requirements and would seem to subordinate God to ethics. If we start with the need for a moral code, why not stop there without bringing God into it? Dostoevsky's answer is that religion adds something to the mix, an idea of the holy and a deeply internalized sense of personal responsibility and guilt. Before ascending to moral knowledge, the sinner must abandon himself to God and accept suffering as the path to moral purification and salvation. Absent the transformative power of religious belief, we too easily might become a self-excusing Raskolnikov capable of the vilest acts.

The Founders also believed that morality required a firm grounding in religious belief. In his *Farewell Address*, Washington warned his countrymen not to "indulge the supposition that morality can be maintained without religion." At the time most Americans would have agreed with him. The 1787 Northwest Ordinance authorized federal funding for religious schools, and this was renewed by the Congress that drafted the First Amendment. The most frequently cited book in the political literature of the time wasn't Locke or Montesquieu. It was the Bible.[3]

Today, however, nearly everyone accepts that unbelievers may act morally. What's more in question is whether the same might be said of believers. For "New Atheists" such as Richard Dawkins and Christopher Hitchens, religions are nothing more than superstitions that do no one any good, and which historically have done much harm. They point to 9/11 and blame Christians for what they regard as retrograde beliefs about same-sex marriage.

Religious beliefs are not illiberal, however, so long as they permit people freely to choose or exit their religion and do not impose a crushing illiberalism. Nor do they, anywhere in the West. If that hasn't always been the case, it is nevertheless now true in countries with a Christian heritage, where liberalism first arose and flourished.

That points to another way in which liberalism is associated with religious belief. From its sense of progression, Parfit's typology suggests that the origins of our commonsense morality, and the intuitions behind his thought experiments, lie in an inherited religious tradition. They came first, and we live in their shadow. The Enlightenment thinkers, including the Moral Sense philosophers we saw in Chapter Three, had themselves plagiarized from writers who lived hundreds of years earlier. Parfit's fourth category of abstract morality might thus appear to be parasitic upon the religious beliefs that preceded it.

If we live in a liberal state, our Judeo-Christian heritage can take much of the credit. In the West, religion has favored liberalism in four ways. It privileges the individual over his family; it provides what would otherwise be lacking, an argument for treating people equally; it defends the autonomy of free choices; and it's the source of our sense of the limits of political authority.

INDIVIDUALISM

One of the core ideas of liberalism is the central importance of individuals. They are the repository of rights that cannot be infringed and form a border that bars the state from intruding on a plea of advancing social justice or the common good. That is why forms of communism, which think that only the collectivity matters, regard individualism as an unjust bourgeois morality.

But where did the concern for individuals come from? It wasn't to be found in ancient Greece and Rome, whose religion was that of the selfish gene. What mattered then was the family through all its generations, and not any individual.

In *The Ancient City* (1864), Fustel de Coulanges described the premodern religious practices that regarded the family as a single entity, whether deceased, alive today, or yet to be born. Ancestors were honored as titular deities who, if worshiped, would protect their descendants and who, if neglected, would become malign spirits. They were the *lars* and *penates*, the family gods of Roman households, and were represented in the sacred fire that burned in every house. They required descendants who would honor them, and every man had a sacred obligation to marry and beget sons to continue the line.

Each household had its separate religion, and the marriage ceremony was one in which the bride renounced her old religion and took on that of her husband. It was performed not in a temple but at the new family's hearth, and this was the source of the notion that marriage was a gift exchange in which fathers gave away brides. She was a member of her family's religion by virtue of her descent from her father, and only he could detach her from it. This was also the idea behind the custom of the groom carrying the bride over the doorstep and into membership in his religion.

What brought an end to the religion of the selfish gene was Christianity. "Whosoever shall do the will of my Father, that is in heaven," said Christ, "he is my brother, and sister, and mother."[4] In a universal religion, distinctions between stranger and brother, non-family and family, were swept away. What Christianity had done, said Larry Siedentop, was invent the individual, and the conservative who faults our culture for its individualism must ask himself if he is also objecting to our religious heritage.

People joined the new religion through baptism and not through birth into a family or marriage. Henceforth, they would be judged as individuals for their own actions. Salvation did not depend on having someone perform the funeral rites, as Priam wished to do for Hector and as Antigone did for Polynices. If the dead body was covered with earth, the shades of the deceased could cross the river to the Elysian Fields and join those who had gone before them. Otherwise, said Virgil, they would remain stranded in limbo for as long as a hundred years, "holding out their hands in longing for the farther shore."[5] But in Christianity, salvation was an individual matter. "We shall die alone," said Pascal.[6]

It was no longer possible to regard women as chattels to be given away in marriage. The marriage ceremony was a sacrament performed in church and would not be valid without the bride's consent. Christianity also put an end to female infanticide, which was not uncommon in the ancient world. In Christianity's early years, many of the saints were women and women were more likely than men to become Christians. When the pagan writer Celsus (*ca.* 175 A.D.) wanted to mock the early Christians, he called them "slaves, women, and children." In the Middle Ages, the Cult of the Virgin gave women a prominence that they had never enjoyed during the classical period.

Christianity also served to promote a property-rights economy. In earliest Greece and Rome, property rights inhered in the family and were not alienable. On death, property passed automatically to the eldest son. These rules were liberalized over time, and the Church's canon lawyers hastened the move to make questions of property and succession turn on consent and free will. Aquinas taught that private ownership contributed to the common good, making the economist's point that it would remedy the incentive problem of the tragedy of the commons. "Everyone takes more care of things for which he is privately responsible than of things held in common, the responsibility for which is left to the next man."[7]

Siedentop insisted that the West's culture could be traced back to the earliest years of Christianity and argued that the importance of the Renaissance had been grossly inflated.[8] Renaissance humanists gave us a new emphasis on cultivating the self, which Siedentop called a cult of individuality, but this was overlaid upon a religion that had invented the individual. The people we associate with the new learning—Nicholas of Cusa in Germany, Thomas More and John Colet in England, Petrarch, Pico della Mirandola, and Torquato Tasso in Italy—were pious believers. In France, Joachim du Bellay had been a canon of Notre-Dame in Paris and Pierre de Ronsard met his end at a priory. In Italy the arts flourished under the patronage of humanist popes such as Sixtus IV and Leo X. Botticelli is said to have burned some of his paintings in Savonarola's Bonfire of the Vanities. The rediscovery of the classics of Greece and Rome gave rise to a new humanism, but one that retained its Catholic roots.

EQUALITY

The Declaration of Independence asserts that it is a self-evident truth that all men are created equal. Calling it self-evident nicely finesses the question of how its truth might be verified, for it doesn't look like an empirical proposition. Looking about, one sees similarities among people, but also differences. We're composed of the long and the short and the tall, the clever and the slow. If one had to pick a single attribute to define what makes us equal, such as intelligence, we'd observe differences and not commonality. Rationality is not uniformly distributed among us, and if that is what mattered we'd have returned to the highly stratified world of ancient Greece and Rome, with the difference that the world would now be divided between Big and Little Brains.

Suppose instead that what matters is the ability to feel pain. Whether felt by a human being or a mouse, pain is bad, and it's cruel to torture animals. That doesn't mean that we must treat them as humans, but if the feeling of pain were the criterion of humanity, we'd commit the modern sin of speciesism if we gave priority to humans. At the farther edges of precious leftism, there are even people who think that plants feel pain. In *The Life of Plants* (2018), philosopher Emanuele Coccia puts plants at the top of the moral hierarchy and humans down at the bottom. If that's not how we think, Coccia blames religion for getting it wrong.

None of this explains the radical idea of human equality. If intelligence were the criterion, we'd find it difficult to ascribe full humanity to the severely retarded or the newly born child. Philosopher Peter Singer argues that it is not wrong per se to kill a newborn baby. It would be wrong, to the extent that it pains the child's parents, but as to the child himself it would be permissible.

Philosophical accounts of equality are often of this form: assuming equality is a good, what does this entail? What must a just state do to ensure that people are treated equally? What is left unanswered, however, is why equality is a good. Even Ronald Dworkin, who thinks that a government that doesn't show an equal concern for each of its citizens is illegitimate, and who describes equality as the state's "Sovereign Virtue," has little to say about why equality matters in the first place.[9] The thesis is simply asserted, and those who dissent from it (aristocrats, racists, alt-right Nietzscheans) are unworthy of attention. Not that I disagree with this. I'd just like to know where it came from.

The United Nations' Universal Declaration of Human Rights is a model statement of what every person is owed and was a consensus document produced by people with very different ideas about good government. Catholic philosopher Jacques Maritain was one of the draftsmen and noted how surprised everyone was that people could be brought to agree on how to define those rights. "Yes, they replied, we agree on those rights, *providing we are not asked why*."[10]

Historically, the assumption of equality was religious in origin and a product of our Judeo-Christian heritage. Without it, commonly accepted moral theories would not get off the ground. Utilitarianism commends itself to many moral philosophers, but it rests on Bentham's belief that everyone counts as one and no one counts as more than one. Without equality, the Kantian would lack a basis for the idea that people should be treated as ends and not used as means. What lay at the root of these intuitions was a religious tradition.

Rawls's *Theory of Justice* is a resolutely secular book, and Rawls expressly denied that his ideas depended on our moral or religious intuitions. He never published anything about his own religious beliefs, but two posthumous essays reveal that he had been deeply religious as a younger man, and it's been suggested that some of his ideas about faith survived in the latter work. Joshua Cohen and Thomas Nagel wrote that "those who have studied Rawls's work, and even more, those who knew him personally, are aware of a deeply religious temperament that informed his life and writings, whatever may have been his beliefs."[11]

If egalitarianism was religious in origin, Christians didn't always live up to its requirements. They've been faulted them for failing to condemn slavery, and priests and even a pope were slaveholders. Shamefully, Georgetown University owes its existence to the sale by the Jesuits of 272 slaves. But it mattered that the Church had set its face against slavery, as Paul III did in 1537. His prohibition of slavery was repeated by Pope Gregory XIV in *Cum sicuti* in 1591 and reaffirmed by Urban VIII in *Commissum nobis* in 1639. The Church stood out for its disapproval of slavery at a time when it was accepted everywhere else and existed in the New World only because the state condoned it in the face of the Church's opposition. And while we're asked to believe that emancipation was a product of the Enlightenment, Locke, Voltaire, and Hume were prepared to tolerate slavery.

In England, the anti-slavery movement was led by the Clapham sect in the Church of England and by religious dissenters such as Josiah Wedgwood. Thomas Clarkson, the founder of the Society for the Abolition of the Slave Trade, began his career as an Anglican deacon. His friend William Wilberforce experienced a religious conversion and was converted to the anti-slavery cause by John Newton, the composer of "Amazing Grace."

It's no answer to say that basing the idea of equality on some passages in the Bible arbitrarily privileges the Judeo-Christian tradition. In that tradition, nothing is arbitrary, and its beliefs anchor a demand for equality because they are Judeo-Christian beliefs. That was how the dissenting judge in the *Dred Scot* case arrived at his rejection of slavery. "A slave is not a mere chattel. He bears the impress of his Maker, and is amenable to the laws of God and man; and he is destined to an endless existence."[12]

Within the Christian tradition, the message is passed on in various ways. When I was a child in the second grade, the teachers introduced an imbecilic, hydrocephalic boy to the class. He could not talk, but from the way he smiled he seemed very happy to join us. I imagine his parents felt the experience would be good for him, and that our teachers—the Sisters of Charity—thought the experience would be good for us. We learned that he was one of us.

Biblical narratives have always shaped our culture and the ideal of equality. The anti-slavery cause and the 1960s civil-rights movement situated themselves in the struggle of the Jewish people in the Book of Exodus. Cain's plea "Am I my brother's keeper?" and the parable of the Good Samaritan express the liberal requirements of solidarity and charity. Even purely secular ideas such as the Marxist notion of a common humanity have their roots in a religious tradition.

Among wiser socialists, that's led to a new respect for religion, as a foundation for their deepest beliefs. The German philosopher Jürgen Habermas was one of them. Without abandoning his atheism, he was willing to debate then-Cardinal Joseph Ratzinger and announce his openness to learning from the egalitarian content of religious traditions.[13]

Autonomy

Liberalism has meant several different things, but it has always excluded forced conversions. It demands that the state not take sides in debates about religion and remain neutral in its ideas about ultimate human ends.

For all the pride the English might take in their freedoms, that didn't include religious liberty until relatively recently. We remember Elizabeth I as a more tolerant monarch than Bloody Mary, but Elizabeth's Parliament made it a capital crime to be a Catholic priest in England, and 183 Catholics were executed during her reign. In the seventeenth century, many of the classic defenses of liberty in the English language, such as Milton's *Areopagitica* (1644) and Locke's *Letter Concerning Toleration* (1689), proposed that Protestant dissent be tolerated while simultaneously defending the suppression of powerless Catholic families, who might reasonably have felt that they were being asked to pay for the sins of their Spanish coreligionists.

Today, no one in the West would defend religious persecutions. The liberal may have his own beliefs about ultimate ends, but he won't want the state to enforce them. Nor does the Church. Echoing Milton, Pope Pius XII stated in his 1943 encyclical *Mystici Corporis Christi* that "it is absolutely necessary that conversion should come about through free choice, since no man can believe unless he is willing." The principle of free choice was reaffirmed in Vatican II's Declaration of Religious Freedom, *Dignitatis Humanae*.

Liberalism is now better defended within than without the West's religious traditions. Many schools teach a set of beliefs on sexual matters that are opposed by religious parents. The classes are given to children as young as eight or nine, and the schools have denied the right of parents to take their children out of them. They've hidden from parents what they're teaching and have even encouraged gender transitioning without consulting parents. For the left, a substantive sexual-justice agenda trumps the rights of parents.

Whatever one might think of this, it's wholly inconsistent with liberalism and was explicitly condemned in *Dignitatis Humanae*.

> Parents ... have the right to determine, in accordance with their own religious beliefs, the kind of religious education that their children are to receive. Government, in consequence, must acknowledge the right of parents to make a genuinely free choice of schools and of other means of education, and the use of this freedom of choice is not to be made a reason for imposing unjust burdens on parents, whether directly or indirectly. Besides, the right of parents are violated, if their children are forced to attend lessons or instructions which are not in agreement with their religious beliefs.

Vatican II recognized that that Church had not always adhered to these principles. Nevertheless, the tolerant liberal of today is more likely to be a Christian parent than a fashionable leftist.

LIBERALISM

Integralists regret the wall of separation between church and state, but this was one of liberalism's greatest accomplishments, one which legal historian Harold Berman said we owed to the eleventh-century investiture crisis when pope and emperor fought over who could appoint bishops.[14] Holy Roman Emperor Henry IV had claimed that he had the right to do so, and for this he was excommunicated by Pope Gregory VII (1073–85). The emperor conceded the point, begging absolution, and Berman said that this was the origin of separationism, when the sacred was divorced from the secular and liberalism was born.

Without a wall of separation, an Erastian state might legislate over religious matters, as Parliament has done and may do for Anglicans in England, and as states would do in America were they not restrained by First Amendment free-exercise protections. The Integralist who imagines that, were the wall removed, he'd find himself back in Pio Nono's papal states, has forgotten how in 1922 an anti-Catholic Oregon banned parochial schools until the Supreme Court ruled that "the child is not the mere creature of the State," and that parents had the right to give their children a religious education.[15]

Separationism meant the "freedom of the church" and released a burst of ecclesiastical energy and creativity. Churchmen worked out the details of canon law, and the first universities were created as religious institutions. Separate from the state, the Church was also an institution within the state and had to work out its relation to the secular power.

Two possibilities presented themselves. One was a blanket abstention from participating in the affairs of government, like that practiced by the ultra-orthodox in Israel.[16] On the other hand, the Church could and did assert the right to pass judgment on the actions of rulers, and in extreme cases to free the faithful from the allegiance to them. In *On Kingship* (1265–66), Aquinas wrote that, "if to provide itself with a king belongs to the right of a given multitude, it is not unjust that the king be deposed or have his power restricted by that same multitude if, becoming a tyrant, he abuses the royal power."[17]

John Locke's right of revolution against unjust kings had merely restated what Catholic theologians had said four hundred years earlier, and which had been repeated by people such as Francisco Suárez (1548–1617). Locke and the Founders had not invented the idea that political legitimacy depended on the consent of the governed, for Aquinas and Saint Robert Bellarmine (1542–1621) had said the same thing. What separationism provided were the grounds to resist the totalitarian instincts of a state that asserts the power to command allegiance over matters of faith and morals, and to override the rights of individuals to obey their conscience. That is why the true totalitarian, whether in China or here, understands that the Church is his enemy.

The Church has its own rules, of course, and the left might not like them. But it has no right to demand that it be liked or its beliefs respected, and the only danger to liberty arises when it prosecutes religious beliefs as hate crimes. However exacting their moral code might be, churches offer the exit rights that illiberal states refuse to their subjects.

Religious belief offered one thing more for liberals: the sense of foundational constraints that saved them from extreme and illiberal policies right and left. The right-wing ideologue might think that fidelity to free bargaining is all that matters, but the believer knows that it's more complicated than that. He is also wiser than the leftist who imagines he can create a Heavenly City peopled by New Soviet Men; and, conscious of his own sins, he is less ready to indulge in the everyday hatreds of the *Washington Post*.

Do you want to know why university presidents struggle to condemn genocide, why woke Zoomers excuse Hamas, and why alt-right crazies hate democracy? I suspect it's because they're atheists who have lost their religion. They might be fabulous people but might lack a still, small voice to tell them that they're not nearly as wonderful as they think they are.

In our politics and moral beliefs, religion divides Americans. Those who admire a nun's humility, who believe that Isaac Jogues was a martyr and not a colonialist oppressor, and who think it nobler to suffer rather than to make others suffer, were raised in a Judeo-Christian religious tradition. They aren't pantheists who worship nature or Randians who make a virtue of selfishness. They part company with people who take their rage to the streets. They are liberals.

8.

THE COMMON LAW

The common lawyer will think it odd that, in a book about liberalism, I have given him only one chapter. I deserve the whole book, he'll insist. The same kind of complaint might also be made by people who think I've given short shrift to religion, *doux commerce*, and other things I've covered. In my defense, I've wanted to write about the many different origins of liberalism, and not to highlight one only of them. Like victory, liberalism has more than a single father. I also have a special reason to limit the contribution of common lawyers to a single chapter.

THE SELF-INTERESTED LIBERAL

Without denying that lawyers plying their trade have promoted liberalism, I want to distinguish between their disinterested and self-interested motives for doing so. This is a book about liberal virtues, and there's nothing virtuous about the person who, for personal profit, inserts himself in the interstices between which power and money pass.

What lawyers add to the mechanics of governance is a concern for procedural justice, and it's the procedure that keeps them employed. The non-lawyer might desire a particular end, but he'll not get there unless he first overcomes the procedural hurdles. If it's liberty that's desired, the libertarian must turn to the lawyer for help, and in that sense the lawyer sometimes seems more like liberty's camp follower than its general.

An English king needs his lawyers, Sir Edward Coke told a skeptical James I. The king wasn't buying it. The law was founded on reason, said James, and he was as smart as any lawyer. Indeed, Your Majesty has excellent science and great endowments of nature, said the obsequious lawyer, but you're going to need me because legal questions "are not to be decided by natural reason, but by the artificial reason and judgment of law, which law is an act which requires long study and experience before that a man can attain to the cognisance of it."[1] Don't try to practice law without a license.

Thrusting lawyers put the grit in the machinery, and when the threat to liberalism came from an all-powerful king exercising the royal prerogative, lawyers were on the side of liberty. Coke wrote that the king could not direct a judge how to rule (*Jentleman's Case*) or excuse a person from complying with criminal laws (*Penal Statutes*). His prosecutors couldn't recharge a person who has been found innocent (*Vaux's Case*), and he couldn't sell monopoly privileges (*the Case of Monopolies*). Any offices he created should be for the public benefit (*Walter Chute's Case*). In all these ways the lawyers clipped the king's wings.

Parliamentary sovereignty was a lawyer's invention that blocked attempts by English monarchs to rule without the consent of the House of Commons. John Fortescue (*ca.* 1394–1479) reminded English kings that the country had a mixed form of government, and that laws could be enacted only with the consent of Commons, Lords, and King.[2] This was a cardinal component of English constitutional law, which Charles I raised as a defense when tried by a court appointed by the House of Commons. It was also the principle that informed the Declaration of Breda (1660) by which Charles II returned to the throne, and the 1688 Bill of Rights by which another

Stuart monarch was deposed. Parliamentary sovereignty became identified as the cornerstone of English liberties and was the rallying cry of eighteenth-century Whigs.

All this changed with the rise of an all-powerful House of Commons in the nineteenth century. Now the threat to liberty came from a supreme and effectively unicameral Parliament. Jean-Louis de Lolme (1740–1806) wrote that Parliament could do everything except make a woman a man and a man a woman—and of course now it can do that, too.

The rise of an all-powerful Parliament, and the expansion of the state, erased the nexus between the lawyer's artificial reason and liberty. For every defense lawyer seeking to free his client, there'll be a prosecutor trying to convict him. He might be someone like Coke, whom G. M. Trevelyan called "one of the most disagreeable figures in our history" for his vituperative prosecutions of the Earl of Essex and Sir Walter Raleigh.[3] And for every new liberticide regulation, there will be lawyers on each side. If the choice were between Leviathan on the one hand and the rule of law on the other, then we could thank lawyers for our liberty. But that's not really the choice today, so expansive has the law become, and so easily can we find ourselves caught in its maw.

No one knows just how many federal criminal offenses there are. One commentator described federal criminal law as "an incomprehensible, random and incoherent, duplicative, incomplete, and organizationally nonsensical mass of federal legislation."[4] What makes it worse is that the crimes often dispense with the requirement of a criminal intention or guilty mind (the lawyer's mens rea). That's a throwback to Anglo-Saxon law, where the act alone was enough to convict. The mens rea requirement, imported by the canonists, served liberty by excusing innocent actions. For public-welfare crimes, however, lawyers have brought us back to the Anglo-Saxon period by dispensing with the accused's defense that he didn't intend any harm. Because of this, and the threat advantages of partisan and publicity-seeking prosecutors, American criminal law poses a serious threat to liberty.[5] When intention is irrelevant and the criminal offenses are technical and numberless, we all commit three felonies a day, according to defense counsel Harvey Silverglate. Worse still, when politically-minded prosecutors turn misdemeanors into felonies to criminalize political differences and take down presidential candidates, lawfare can make us look like a Third World country.

Lawyers have given us more law, but can anyone say this has made us freer? Law professor Grant Gilmore thought not. "The worse the society, the more law there will be," he wrote. "In Hell there will be nothing but law, and due process will be meticulously observed."[6]

SOMERSET'S CASE

There have nevertheless been moments when lawyers crucially defended liberty, more so in England than in America when it came to slavery. In 1772, a slave from Virginia named James Somerset had been brought to London and kept there against his will. He sought out Granville Sharp, a prominent abolitionist, and Sharp retained a lawyer to seek a writ of habeas corpus to free Somerset. The question came before Lord Mansfield, who tried as best he could to dodge it. He knew that if he held slavery illegal this would impose a severe financial burden on the slaveowners. Perhaps this was a matter for the legislator, he suggested, and not the courts. He delayed rendering a decision, hoping the parties might settle out of court. But when he was finally pressed for a decision, he gave one of the noblest judgements ever delivered in a British court.

> The state of slavery is of such a nature, that it is incapable of being introduced on any reasons, moral or political; but only positive law, which preserves its force long after the reasons, occasion, and time itself from whence it was created is erased from memory: it's so odious, that nothing can be suffered to support it, but positive law. Whatever inconveniences, therefore, may follow from a decision, I cannot say this case is allowed or approved by the law of England; and therefore the black must be discharged.[7]

ENFORCING PATRIOTISM

Have I been unfair to the legal profession? The question won't keep me up at night, but I must acknowledge that American courts have often defended liberty, and in ringing language too. In *Brown v. Board of Education* (1954), the Supreme Court struck down the "separate but equal" argument for racial segregation.[8] Of course, it had been another set of judges that had justified segregation and Jim Crow in the first place.[9]

If you ask a lawyer for a case in which his profession has unselfishly defended freedom, he might point you to *West Virginia State Board of Education v. Barnette* (1943).[10] The West Virginia legislature had required the state's schools to teach the ideals, principles, and spirit of Americanism, and the Board of Education had ordered its students to salute the flag. The plaintiff, a Jehovah's Witness, refused to comply, saying that the flag was a "graven image" and that saluting it was contrary to his religion. Children of that religion were expelled from school, and their parents were threatened with prosecution for contributing to the delinquency of a minor.

The Supreme Court held that a state was permitted to see that its students were taught American history and the principles of our government. What it could not do, however, was compel a student to declare his belief in an ideology, even that of American liberalism. Barnette was a Jehovah's Witness, but the issue at hand was broader than religious liberty. Whether the refusal to salute the flag was prompted by religious beliefs or by some other motive did not matter. Public education should be politically neutral and not the enemy of any party or faction.

The case came to the Court in the middle of the Second World War, when the need for patriotism and national unity was all too clear. But a higher patriotism is faithful to the liberal principles of the Founders in crafting the Bill of Rights. In a unanimous judgment written by Justice Jackson, the Court held that:

> If there is any fixed star in our constitutional constellation, it
> is that no official, high or petty, can prescribe what shall be
> orthodox in politics, nationalism, religion, or other matters

of opinion, or force citizens to confess by word or act their faith therein.[11]

The same issue arose in *Texas v. Johnson* (1989),[12] in which a Texas statute had criminalized flag burning. The flag is a symbol of America, and the prohibition was meant to promote patriotism, like the flag salute in *Barnette*. But as in the earlier case, the Court ruled that the Bill of Rights was a more fundamental icon of what it means to be an American than a physical symbol such as the flag. The words of the Declaration of Independence and the freedoms protected by the Bill of Rights are what define us as Americans, and anything that trenches on them to promote patriotism is self-defeating and diminishes the country more than the desecration of the flag.

There is, besides, one more thing to be said on behalf of lawyers. When the Intergralist pushes his illiberal policies, the lawyer will nod his head and ask how he proposes to get there. Would he prefer a parliamentary form of government, without a separation of powers? Restrictions on campaign spending? A Congress of a thousand representatives (which Cardinal de Retz said would be no better than a mob)? Within the strictures of our constitution, radical change comes slowly. That's what the Framers intended, and this can't be bypassed without a revolution.

9.

THE AGE OF CHIVALRY

The nuns in my little Leoville knew that their pupils hungered after adventure stories and they regaled us with tales of the heroes of New France. They told us how Dollard des Ormeau and his companions had sacrificed themselves to save Montreal, and of how the fourteen-year-old Madeleine de Vershères took command of a fort to stave off an attack. We heard of voyageurs who thought nothing of stepping onto a canoe in Quebec and stepping off in Louisville, St. Louis, or Louisiana. But we always returned to the Conquest, to James Wolfe and the Marquis de Montcalm, and the fall of Quebec in the 1759 Battle of the Plains of Abraham. From those stories we learned that the age of chivalry still lived and that it imposed a code of courage against an enemy, benevolence for the defenseless, and magnanimity for a defeated foe.

Advienne que pourra

The capital of New France had the strongest natural defenses of any city in North America, and a three-month siege had failed to dislodge Montcalm. With winter approaching, it seemed as though the British would be forced to retire before the St. Lawrence froze over and that Quebec would remain French. Rather than admit defeat, however, Wolfe made a last, desperate gamble, *advienne que pourra*—whatever might happen. He had his army rowed in absolute silence across the St. Lawrence to a point a half mile downstream from the city. The army then pulled itself up a 175-foot cliff, and in the morning stood before the city ramparts arrayed for battle.

Quebec is a walled city, and the French might have stayed in their fort and waited out the attacker. Like Hector, however, they came out to meet the enemy. They fired first but in a desultory manner, and the British continued their advance. Finally, when the two sides were forty paces apart, Wolfe gave the command to fire. His troops were loaded with double shot, and the volley cut down the French line. In the melee Wolfe received a third wound and was carried to the rear. Asked whether he needed a surgeon, he answered, "there is no need. It is all over with me." As he lay, a soldier brought him news of the battle. "They run, see how they run," he said. "Who runs?" asked Wolfe. The French, he was told. "I die content," he said, and immediately expired.

Mounted on his horse, Montcalm was an easy target for the British. Moments after Wolfe fell, he also was shot and was led on his horse into the walled city. How many hours do I have to live, he asked his surgeon? Not much past three in the morning was the answer. "So much the better," he answered. "I will not see the English in Quebec."

The battle was a word-historical event. It invited Britons to imagine an empire on which the sun would never set. For Americans, it meant a future from which both the threat of French invasion and the need for British protection were removed and made possible the Declaration of Independence seventeen years later. For Canadians, the battle became the founding event in the country's history. For three leading liberal democracies, it was a decisive turning point.

The battle became the stuff of myths and a symbol of how lives may be lived according to the highest precepts of knightly virtue. In Francis Parkman's account of the battle,[1] Wolfe recited Thomas Gray's *Elegy Written in a Country Graveyard* as he was carried across the river. He paused on the line that "The paths of glory lead but to the grave," and having done so added that he would rather have written that poem than take Quebec. In his last letter to his mother, Wolfe denied this had happened, but perhaps he had really said it, then or on an earlier occasion. While Parkman's story might lack what in Texas is called the added advantage of truthfulness, Simon Schama writes that "the sources are strong enough to resist the automatic modern assumption of apocrypha."[2]

In any event, the tale had gotten out. Wolfe's fiancée had given him a copy of Gray's poem, and he had underscored the line. Whether he really recited the poem, the story took the battle from the pages of history to the highest plane of romance. And then there was Wolfe's desperate gamble, in a battle that decided the fate of empires, one in which both generals would fall. If all that weren't enough to capture one's imagination, *The Death of General Wolfe* (1770), by the Anglo-American Benjamin West, became one of the most famous paintings of its time. In the center lies Wolfe at the moment of death. An American ranger breaks through a crowd of British officers to bring news of the battle, while a native in a classical pose stoically looks on. West's painting became one of the most frequently reproduced images in the eighteenth century and took its place in our collective memory as an icon of the British Empire and of the heroic deaths of two knights.

A KNIGHT-ERRANT FOR OUR TIME

"The Age of Chivalry is gone," mourned Edmund Burke. The knight-errant who rode out in search of honorable advancement had been replaced by lawyers, economists, and utilitarians. A mercantile class had prospered and come to power, and as that happened Burke lamented that we had lost our antique sense of virtue. But we're never without the need for chivalry or for knights such as Lt. General Roméo Dallaire.

In 1993 Dallaire's career in the Canadian Army was on pause when he took a call that changed his life. Is there any reason why you couldn't accept an overseas posting on a peacekeeping mission, he was asked? None whatsoever, said Dallaire. It's in Rwanda, he was told. "Rwanda, that's somewhere in Africa?" asked Dallaire.[3]

Rwanda had been riven by a civil war between the Hutu-dominated Rwandan government and the Tutsi Rwandan Patriotic Front. Then in August 1993 the two sides signed a peace accord in Arusha, Tanzania, which established an interim unity government with Rwandan President Habyarimana to remain as president. To make it work, the accord would be supervised by the United Nations Assistance Mission in Rwanda (UNAMIR).

The Hutus were French-speaking and the Tutsis English-speaking, so the UN thought it natural to ask a bilingual French-Canadian general like Dallaire to oversee the military mission. Besides, unlike France, Belgium, and Britain, Canada didn't have a problematical history as a colonial power, and Canadians had founded the National University of Rwanda. Many of the country's leaders had studied in Quebec. As for Dallaire, the posting appealed because, growing up in a Catholic milieu, he had been captivated by stories about missionaries in Africa. He would also be reporting to an old Canadian Army friend at the UN, General Maurice Baril.

Dallaire arrived in Kigali, Rwanda's capital, in August 1993 to head up UNAMIR's military operations. To patrol the eighty-mile-long demilitarized zone he thought he'd need five thousand soldiers. He was offered only 2,500, however, and of these the thousand Bangladeshis hid at the first sign of trouble. When things got rough, Dallaire sent them all packing. The major powers—Britain, France, and the United States—were unwilling to provide men and materiel to a mission they thought doomed from the start. Rwanda was regarded as a sideshow and, after the debacle of Somalia, peacekeeping fatigue had set in.

Dallaire quickly realized he couldn't rely on Jacques-Roger Booh-Booh, his immediate superior in Rwanda. Booh-Booh was a friend of UN Secretary-General Boutros Boutros-Ghali and a former Cameroonian foreign minister. He couldn't speak English and brought nothing to the table. He rarely arrived at the office before ten in the morning, took two-hour lunches, and left before five. Booh-Booh favored the francophone Hutus, and one of his staff members appears to have served as a spy for a Hutu official who was subsequently sentenced to life imprisonment for genocide.

Dallaire found that the Arusha Accords had failed to stop the violence. In a country that was 85 percent illiterate, people got their news from the radio, and *Radio Mille Collines*, the Hutu radio station, called the Tutsis cockroaches and urged its listeners to kill them. Dallaire asked his superiors in New York, who included future UN secretary-general Kofi Annan, for permission to shut down the station but was told this would exceed his mandate. And so the killings continued, and individual Tutsis and moderate Hutus were murdered.

The bloodiest Hutu group was the Interahamwe, which was closely connected to the Hutu government. On January 10, 1994, a whistleblower from the group told Dallaire that the Hutus had drawn up lists of prominent Tutsis to be rounded up and killed. They also planned to kill Belgian peacekeepers. They thought that the Belgians had no stomach for casualties, and that if any of their troops were killed, their government would withdraw them from Dallaire's command.

When he heard this, Dallaire sprang into action. "I had to catch these guys off guard, send them a signal that I knew who they were and what they were up to, and that I fully intended to shut them down."[4] He told Maurice Baril what he planned to do in what came to be known as the "genocide fax." It said that the whistleblower had been ordered to register all the local Tutsis with an eye to their extermination. "Example he gave was that in 20 minutes his personnel could kill up to 1,000 Tutsis." The fax was in English, but the final paragraph was in French. "Peux ce que veut. Allons-y," it read. "If you want, you can do it. Let's go." Those were the mottos of his high school and regiment back in Canada, and Dallaire believed that Baril would recognize the appeal to knightly virtue.

It wasn't to be. Years later Dallaire realized that, ensconced in the United Nations, Baril had gone native. The next morning Dallaire received a fax from Kofi Annan that ordered him to suspend the search for the arms and to share his information with the Rwandan government. The request that the whistleblower be given asylum was denied, and sharing his information appears to have gotten him killed.

Thereafter things got worse. Dallaire kept pressing for more troops on the ground, without any luck. Then on April 6 a plane carrying President Habyarimana was shot down, killing all aboard. It was never proven who was responsible, but within an hour Interahamwe had swung into action and the mass killings began. Government killers went from house to house with a list of names, just as the whistleblower had predicted. By noon the next day, all the moderate Rwandan leaders had been killed or were in hiding, and the Arusha Accords were dead. With this, the big powers—the Americans, French, and British—finally reacted. They sent in planes and soldiers, but only to evacuate their nationals. They left the Rwandans behind.

Dallaire thought that, with Habyarimana's death, the country's prime minister, Agathe Uwilingiyimana, should become the head of government. He sent out ten Belgian peacekeepers to protect her, but they were killed along with her. At this, the Belgian government withdrew all its forces from UNAMIR, just as the Interahamwe had anticipated.

That's when the real genocide began. It lasted a hundred days, and when it was over 800,000 Rwandans, mostly Tutsis, had been slaughtered. One used to think that genocide required the murderous technologies employed during the Holocaust, the rail cars and the gas chambers. What the Hutus had was machetes, but still they killed at a quicker rate than the Nazis. Even so, that was hard work. One's arms got tired. But it was made easier when the Hutus discovered that they could immobilize their victims by severing their Achilles tendons. The murderers could then go off for lunch and come back later to finish the job.

In Hollywood's fictionalized version of the genocide, *Hotel Rwanda* (2004), Dallaire was played by Nick Nolte and made to seem in a constant state of panic. That's not how it was. Dallaire was in command throughout, even after the genocide began. His original mission was over, but he thought it would be immoral to cut and run in the midst of the killings.

He told the UN that he could stop the genocide with as few as five thousand troops. When it was all over, everyone thought he had been right, but the UN turned him down. Instead of sending in more peacekeepers, it reduced their number from 2,500 to 250. Rwanda was a far-off country, and news about the genocide was pushed aside by the latest stories about Tonya Harding and O. J. Simpson. Boutros Boutros-Ghali called Dallaire on April 29 to order him to leave Rwanda. No, said Dallaire. I'm staying. An angered Secretary-General repeated the order. Dallaire said no again, and Boutros-Ghali hung up. For first time Dallaire had disobeyed a direct order. He stayed put in Kigali, along with the Ghanaians who also refused to leave, and together they saved the lives of thirty thousand Rwandans.

By August the Tutsi forces had won the war and ended the genocide, and Dallaire finally left Rwanda. He was not the same person who had arrived in Kigali a year before. His failure to prevent the genocide had scarred him emotionally, and he now had a death wish. He recognized that he was cracking up and asked to be relieved.

Dallaire exemplified the best of liberalism, in risking his life for marginalized people at a time when liberalism's high officials—the UN secretary-general, the U.S. president, the president of the French Republic—were doing their best to ignore them. Dallaire is especially scathing in his comments about President Clinton, who had told his staff not to tell him what was going on. In 1998, Clinton paid a three-hour visit to Kigali to issue a non-apology apology. "The international community, together with nations in Africa, must bear its share of responsibility for this tragedy," he said. "We did not act quickly enough." And then he went back to his plane. He had never left the airfield, and his plane had kept its engines running the whole time he was there.

Unlike Clinton, Dallaire wasn't a politician and self-proclaimed liberal. He was a soldier and acted as he understood soldiers were supposed to act. That meant something more than ordering people about and taking orders from one's superiors. There was a content to what he understood as his duty that was derived from a tradition that could be traced all the way back to the days of knighthood.

I asked Dallaire how he came to act as he did, and he returned to his decision to disobey the order to leave Rwanda. "I had no tactical or strategic reason to stay," he told me. "I refused a lawful command and became a rogue commander. I didn't know if I could save anyone, and the enormity of what I did went beyond all my training." So why did he do it? "There was a romantic dimension to it," he said, from instincts formed from boyhood stories about Bayard, the chevalier *sans peur et sans reproche*. The image of Saint Michael the Archangel stuck with him, as did the "peux ce que veut" motto from his Catholic School. "It never left me." He'd also absorbed the traditions of his regiment, which incorporated a code of knighthood derived from soldiers who had served centuries before. Edmund Burke had been wrong. The age of chivalry still lived.

LIBERALISM AS VITA ACTIVA

In every tale of chivalry, a knight like Sir Launfal goes forth on a quest. That's what brought Dallaire to Rwanda. Imagine you're a fireman, he asked. During your entire career you've never seen a fire. That might look like success, but it's not enough. Dallaire's father had served in the Canadian army and helped liberate Holland, but what followed for Canadians was years of peace, and Dallaire had not seen combat himself. And then he was given the chance to go to Rwanda. "It was like God had given me finally a real challenge for my skills. I just lapped it up. I couldn't get enough of it."[5]

In the urban dictionary, there's an acronym for this: FOMO. The fear of missing out. It's the anxiety we feel when we think that other people are living better lives than we are. That's what brought Oliver Wendell Holmes Jr. (1841–1935) into battle. As a judge he sat for fifty years on the bench, but before this he had been a soldier. When he was twenty, he left Harvard College without taking his degree to fight for the North in the Civil War, where he was shot three times and left for dead at Antietam. He hated slavery and wanted the Union preserved, but it wasn't the grand political issues that made him enlist. On both sides of the contest, "hearts were touched by fire," and no one wanted to miss out. "As life is action and passion," he concluded, and "it is required of a man that he should share in the action and passion of his time at peril of being judged not to have lived."[6]

What Dallaire and Holmes understood was the imperative of leading an active life, a *vita activa* as opposed to a *vita contemplativa*. As between the two, many have argued for the superiority of the contemplative life. Aristotle preferred the philosopher's *bios theōrētikos* to the active life, and in the Catholic tradition there's a special cachet for the religious contemplatives who spend their days adoring God. In the New Testament, Mary was a contemplative, unlike Martha who fussed around with the chores of caring for Christ and His disciples. Martha complained that she wasn't getting any help, but Christ told her that Mary had chosen the better part.

The academic leftist is a contemplative. He has rules about things not to do rather than about things we ought to do, apart from voting for a woke candidate. He never has to make the hard choices to which Dallaire was put in Rwanda. If it's just a matter of respecting the rights of others, he can be a perfect liberal saint, wrapped up in his bed at night. He offends no one under the covers, or at his workshop. But then his is a cheap and lifeless liberalism, and he can't teach us much about what is due other people and the affirmative actions we're required to take to help them.

When it's a matter of taking a stand, John Milton had little use for the academic's lifeless liberalism. "I cannot praise a fugitive and cloistered virtue, unexercised and unbreathed, that never sallies out and sees her adversary, but slinks out of the race where that immortal garland is to be run for, not without dust and heat."[7] Instead, the moral lessons come from our instinctive admiration for people like Dallaire and Holmes, or perhaps James Lawrence, USN.

In the War of 1812 Lawrence commanded the USS *Chesapeake* in Boston's harbor. Off the Boston Light lay the Royal Navy's HMS *Shannon*, patrolling the waters to keep the *Chesapeake* bottled up. In their guns and numbers of men the two ships were almost identical. What happened next will be familiar to readers of Patrick O'Brian's Aubrey-Maturin novel *The Fortunes of War* (1979). The *Shannon's* captain, Philip Broke, was eager to engage the *Chesapeake* and sent Lawrence a letter that was a model of chivalry. "As the *Chesapeake* appears now ready for sea," he wrote, "I request you will do me the favor to meet the *Shannon* with her, ship to ship, to try the fortune of our respective flags." Broke then described the *Shannon's* arms and men, to persuade Lawrence that it would be a fair fight. He also said he'd send away other Royal Navy ships, to make it *mano a mano*. "Choose your terms, but let us meet."

The letter might have been drafted by Sir Walter Scott in a novel about medieval knights. Lawrence never received Broke's letter, but the presence of the *Shannon* off Boston harbor was enough to bring the *Chesapeake* out. It steered a course to close with the *Shannon* and fired a gun to ask the *Shannon* to wait for her. As the two ships approached, the *Chesapeake* had the weather gage and could have passed by the *Shannon's* stern and raked her. Instead, the *Chesapeake* altered course to come abreast the British ship. For its part, the *Shannon* might have maneuvered into a better position but declined to do so. Both sides agreed to have at it, as quickly as possible. "It could have been a medieval jousting match," wrote a naval historian.[8]

The superior gunnery of the *Shannon* quickly decided the contest. Within two minutes, a hundred out of 150 men on the *Chesapeake's* upper deck were killed or wounded. Lawrence himself was mortally wounded and carried below. Realizing that his ship was lost, he gave a command that lives on in the American Navy as a proud symbol of defiance in the face of hopeless odds: "Don't give up the ship." But the *Chesapeake's* losses were so great that it struck a few minutes later. It was the bloodiest naval action of the war, with 228 men dead or wounded. Broke himself scarcely survived the battle, but with Lawrence he provided the world an example of how the spirit of chivalry still lived among those who lead a *vita activa*.

The great theorist of the *vita activa* was Hannah Arendt (1906–75), a refugee from Hitler's Germany who escaped from a French internment camp and made her way to the United States. In *The Human Condition* (1958) she wrote that it's the actions we perform, particularly in the public sphere, that give meaning to our lives. "A life without speech and without action . . . is literally dead to the world; it has ceased to be human life because it is no longer lived among men."[9] But through an active life we might attain a heroic immortality.

That's what kept Dallaire at his post and brought knights out on their quests. What they sought was the chivalrous advancement that comes from a *vita activa*, and in doing so they followed a code that was one of the sources of liberalism.

THE CODE OF CHIVALRY

Chivalry was a code of conduct for French *chevaliers* and (after the Norman Invasion) English knights. If that was a time of strong class distinctions, the Code of Chivalry incorporated a sense of benevolence and proto-liberal virtues such as magnanimity, liberality, and the duty to protect the vulnerable. Knights were also expected to adhere to their religion and, with allowances made for departures from perfect chastity, to follow its commandments. Finally, chivalry elevated the position of women through the invention of courtly love.

After a victory, the liberal virtue of magnanimity was famously displayed at the Battle of Poitiers. In 1356, Edward III's son, the Black Prince, had led an Anglo-Gascon army in France. He intended to move fast, never letting the much larger French army trap him, but at Poitiers the French King cut across the English line of march. While the French outnumbered the English by at least three to one, the English archers decided the contest. Not merely were the French defeated, but the King of France was taken prisoner along with the cream of the country's nobility. That night, wrote Froissart, the Black Prince waited upon them, as a servant would do. He knelt before the French King and addressed him:

> Beloved sire . . . you have good cause to be cheerful, although the battle did not go in your favor, for today you have won the highest renown as a warrior, excelling the best of your knights. I do not say this to flatter you, for everyone on our side, having seen how each man fought, unanimously agrees with this and awards you the palm and the crown, if you will consent to wear them.[10]

It wasn't always so noble-minded and magnanimous. The Battle of Eversham (1265) was a massacre. Simon de Montfort was killed and his body mutilated. Further, chivalry did not exclude the possibility of cruelty against those who had held out in a siege, like the people of Limoges whom the Black Prince put to the sword. Froissart put the number of people who were killed at three thousand, but the correct number seems to have been about one-tenth of that.[11]

Knights were also expected to liberal, in the older sense of that word, and free with their money. Not that they weren't motivated by wealth. It was the opportunities for plunder and ransom that brought English knights to France in their *chevauchées*. Arthur Conan Doyle's White Company was little more than a gang of mercenaries who roamed France and Italy in search of loot. Once he became wealthy, however, a knight was asked to show a complete disregard for how he spent his money. Liberality also meant that a knight should be charitable to the poor, like Saint Louis (1214–70), who in Joinville's telling fed twenty-six poor people daily at his house, waiting upon them himself. When he traveled, he always enquired about widows and poor young women in need of a dowry.

It was chivalrous to protect the weak, and "just as judges profess the office of judging," wrote Ramon Llull (*ca.* 1232–1316), "so knights profess the office of upholding justice."[12] In Leon Gautier's commandments of chivalry, the last was "thou shall be everywhere and always the champion of the right and the Good against injustice and evil." That explains the Dudley-Do-Right quality to knighthood. In the tales of chivalry, the knight was always the Randolph Scott or Jack Reacher character who wandered into town and took up the cause of an unjustly persecuted stranger.

Christianity radically changed what was asked of the warrior. The pre-Christian hero was a person who, as José Ortega y Gasset observed, simply wanted to be himself, *contra mundum*.[13] The Sophoclean hero was even an outcast from the gods. Rejected by Athena, Ajax says "I am hateful to the gods." Antigone also thinks she's been forsaken by them. What makes such people heroic is their refusal to compromise, when all their friends ask them to give up and the gods have abandoned them.

With chivalry, by contrast, knighthood was a Christian vocation, and the Code of Chivalry was much more than a warrior ethic. The knight was a devout son of the church, and knighthood was a divinely ordered estate. In the nineteenth century, Gautier wrote that chivalry and Christianity so complemented each other that "chivalry is the Christian form of the military profession: the knight is the Christian soldier."[14] In his *The Book of the Order of Chivalry*, Llull wrote that knighthood was a kind of secular priesthood, and "just as our Lord God has chosen the clergy to uphold the holy faith . . . so the God of glory has chosen the knight to conquer and overcome by force of arms the Infidels who contrive every day to destroy the holy Church."[15]

The ceremony of knighthood was almost sacramental. In his rules for knighthood, Llull described how the candidate would keep a vigil the evening before he was dubbed, and after confessing his sins would assist at Mass in the morning. There he'd hear a sermon that recounted the articles of Faith and receive communion. He'd then be clothed with his armor and told of the virtues that each piece represented. When given his sword, he'd be told it resembled a cross and should be used to defeat the Church's enemies.

The unity of chivalry and Christianity was symbolized in the legend of the Holy Grail, the chalice in which Christ performed the miracle of transubstantiation during the Last Supper. The Fourth Lateran Council in 1215 proclaimed as dogma the real presence of Christ in the Eucharist. The host was really Christ's body and the wine was really His blood. The Grail was thus the most precious of relics, and one which the legend said had been brought to England by Joseph of Arimathea. The Grail romances told its readers that miracles were still possible, that the sacred could be grasped in your hand, and that holiness might lie at the end of the lane.

We first see the Grail in Chrétien de Troyes' *Perceval* (*ca.* 1182–90), at the home of the Fisher King, a descendant of Joseph whose father refrains from eating anything except a host brought to him from the Grail. In Malory's *Morte d'Arthur* (1485), the Grail is more clearly identified as the chalice from the Last Supper, and the Knights of the Round Table are summoned on a quest for it. As a punishment for his adulterous affair with Guinevere, Lancelot is not permitted to see the Grail, but his son Galahad, the perfect and sinless knight, will find it, and when he does his soul is transported to Heaven by a company of angels.

We'll not understand the period unless we realize how deeply pious it was. Monastic orders of knighthood arose to defend the Holy Land and the pilgrims. The Knights Hospitaliers of St. John was created in 1113, and the Knights Templars in 1120. The greatest of knights, William Marshal (1147–1219), joined the Templars before he died, and King John of England was buried as a Benedictine monk. We recall Henry V as Shakespeare's heroic warrior, but he was also the king who established monastic communities with the idea that their prayers would assist his armies in battle. Louis IX of France, canonized as Saint Louis, led the Seventh and Eighth Crusades, and Joinville tells us that he heard the Hours sung and a Requiem Mass each day and the vespers and compline before bed. It was all for the greater glory of God, which became the motto for the Jesuits.

The ideals of chivalry remain with us. You'll find them in Hollywood Westerns, Star Wars fantasies, and the Boy Scout Handbook. Onscreen, superheroes fight for truth and justice, aided by miraculous powers. Magnanimity and liberality still are virtues, and the duty to protect the weak calls forth rescuers when people are attacked on a subway. Policemen still choose to serve and protect, and soldiers volunteer to defend their country. Tear back the cynicism of an elite culture and you might even find knights in shining armor.

COURTLY LOVE

Chivalry elevated the position of women and invested them with new powers. The courtly literature of the troubadours told of how a knight would venerate his lady as the sovereign of all his thoughts, feelings, and actions, and how to honor her he would seek out yet more glorious passages of arms. Before Percival sets forth as a knight, his mother instructs him that, "should you encounter, near or far, a lady in need of aid, or a maiden in distress, make yourself ready to assist them if they ask for your help, for it is the most honorable thing to do. He who fails to honor ladies will find his own honor dead inside him."[16]

The very purpose of a knight was to do battle on behalf of a lady. Why, asked La Belle Iseult, are you a knight and not a lover? "Ye may not be called a good knight [but] if ye make a quarrel for a lady."[17] No period in Western literature was so concerned with love and lovers as the medieval, with a conception of love that differed radically from every other type of sexual love known, celebrated, or taught before then.

Women were there to be worshipped by men, and, in the nineteenth century, Gaston Paris identified courtly love as a distinctive genre in Western literature.[18] It had been there all the time, in Malory and the troubadours, but Paris defined what he said were its essential elements. Courtly love, like that of Lancelot and Guinevere, is illicit and adulterous and therefore furtive. The knight is inferior and continually begs the favor of an elevated and even disdainful lady and must earn her affection by undergoing many tests of his valor and devotion, as in the *Lancelot* of Chrétien de Troyes.

One of the greatest medieval works of literature was the *Roman de la Rose*, a long allegorical poem by Guillaume de Lorris (*ca.* 1200–40) and Jean de Meun (*ca.* 1240–1305). The poem begins with the Lover asleep in a garden next to a Rose, which symbolizes his love. He becomes a vassal of Cupid, who tells him what he must do to become acceptable to his lady. The sense of physical desire was clearly present, and as in Dante the theme of earthy love mingles with the sacred.

Courtly love was a science and also subject to its own strict rules. In *The Art of Courtly Love*, a Latin treatise of the late twelfth or early thirteenth century, Andreas Capellanus told how every one of a lover's actions should end in the thought of his beloved. He should never take her for granted and should express his feelings in delicate sighs and moans. He should turn pale in the presence of his beloved and be quick to jealousy. Love was naturally adulterous, since in the arranged marriages of the time there could be no love between a husband and wife. But then marriage should not prevent anyone from taking a lover.

There was even a Court of Love, whose judgments were recorded and whose judges were the leading noblewomen of the day. In one case, the court ruled that a lady was obliged to accept a young man as her lover. She had told him she could not do so because she already had a lover, but that he'd be next in line. Then she married the first man, and the court ruled she was bound to accept the second as her lover. Since love was incompatible with marriage, she could not love her husband.

Courtly love was associated with the cult of the Virgin, which arose at the same time. The Gothic cathedrals at Chartres, Paris, Amiens, Rouen, Bayeux, and Coutances were the palaces of the Queen of Heaven and of the World. She was, said Saint Bernard, the Star of the Sea, the source of light, and the sun of justice. On Earth, her place was taken by the extraordinarily powerful women of the period, notably Eleanor of Aquitaine (*ca.* 1124–1204). Eleanor was for fifteen years Queen of France, and after divorcing the king was for fifty more the Queen of England as the wife of Henry II and the mother of Richard the Lionheart. As a model of female empowerment, she has no equal. She was said to have had many lovers, including Saladin while she was on a crusade.

Does anything remain of the code of courtly love? Some customs, such as holding a door open for women, might seem presumptuous and sexist in a modern office. Other customs remain, however, especially in restaurants. A man need not hold a chair for a woman, but he should let her sit first, and shouldn't order before any of the women at table. At an elevator, women enter and leave first. Many women still expect that these differences will be observed. One lady came in for some ribbing when she complained that she wanted to find a man who would pay on the first date and open the door for her—but that the only men who did so today were conservatives.

On a subway a man might refuse to help a man but must help a woman when she is being attacked. One psychological study found that men are more likely to be altruistic and incur costs when they're asked to protect a woman.[19] The instinct of chivalry can also be seen at sentencing in criminal trials, with female offenders receiving more lenient treatment than male offenders who have committed the same crime.[20]

In one respect, however, the code of knighthood differed greatly from modern liberalism. As a code of honor, chivalry condemned privately immoral behavior. That didn't exclude the adulterous romances of courtly love. In matters of religion, the knight was pious, but in his amours he wasn't prim. Still, those affairs were conducted according to the rigid rules that required knights to show themselves worthy of love and to shun everything ignoble. It's difficult to imagine anything as removed from today's hookup culture as the code of courtly love. Where it does survive—in its condemnation of sexual relations tainted by force, fraud, or undue influence—is in the Me Too movement. If that came as a surprise to men raised on the Playboy Philosophy, it's a sign of how far we've come from the ideals of chivalry.

10.

THE BOOK OF THE GENTLEMAN

With the rise of commerce in the fifteenth century, a new class of landed gentry, wealthy merchants, and lawyers emerged. They were called gentlemen and were the recognized leaders in every community. While they weren't knights, the Code of Chivalry had taught them what it meant to be a gentleman, and this included a sense of benevolence and the virtues of liberalism.

For those who wanted lessons on the subject, there were classic texts. Aristotle's great-souled man, in Book IV of the *Nicomachean Ethics*, was the very model of a gentleman. He'd confer benefits on others but would be ashamed to receive them. As he was contemptuous of the opinion of the crowd, he wouldn't hide his opinions. Conscious of his own merit, he'd never bootlick or cringe before someone more powerful. One might also turn to Cicero's *On Duties* for lessons on magnanimity, or to his *Tusculum Disputations* for its stoicism.

In the modern era, the Code of the Gentleman incorporated the virtues of knighthood. In the nineteenth century, the dashing youths of England tried to relive the twelfth century, and in 1839 they organized the Woodstock of the day, the Eglington Tournament, a mock-medieval pageant of chivalric splendor.[1] Readers poured over the novels of Sir Walter Scott and studied Kenelm Henry Digby's tales about knighthood. Digby's book was *The Broad-Stone of Honour* (1822), and its subtitle was "Rules for the Gentlemen of England."

AT WAR AND ON THE PLAYING FIELD

Digby's readers learned that a gentleman should never boast of his deeds and when praised should be embarrassed.[2] Without having to be told, he should know that he shouldn't crow over a defeated enemy. In 1941 the German battleship *Bismarck* managed to elude the Royal Navy and reach the North Atlantic, where it threatened to cut off the supplies Britain desperately needed. The *Bismarck* had sunk *HMS Hood* and forced *HMS Prince of Wales* to retire but was itself damaged and made for safety at a French port. Before reaching it, the German ship was sunk by the Royal Navy and the RAF. The British Ministry of Information was charged with wartime propaganda, and its parliamentary secretary, Harold Nicolson, asked the Admiralty for a photo of the ship as it went down. No such picture had been taken, however. No Englishman would have felt right taking snapshots of a fine ship sinking, Nicolson was told. Afterwards, he reported that he felt ashamed for having asked.[3]

That's also part of the tradition of baseball. When a team is up 10–0, it's supposed to ease off. Its players won't try to steal bases, and it'll send in its B team. It won't try to embarrass the losing team. That's called unsportsmanlike conduct, and there are no rules about it. People just know. Same thing with schoolyard fights. You don't kick a kid when he's down. Instead, you offer a hand to help him up. From far off, the players had somehow learned to emulate the Black Prince at Poitiers.

People who ignored these rules weren't gentlemen. They might be "bounders," a word that has almost disappeared from our language, along with "cad" and "rogue." That's a pity, because it described a kind of person all too present today, the person who oversteps his natural place and demands more than his due. He is the vain, strutting person who always brings the conversation back to himself, and who is guilty of the vice the Greeks called *pleonexia*. General Montgomery, who courted popularity with his troops and blotted his copybook in the failed Market Garden operation, was a bounder. Viscount Alexander, who quietly got the job done in the invasion of Italy, was every inch a gentleman.

George S. Patton, who loved swordplay and horseback riding, was another gentleman. He knew that chivalry meant that officers must be courteous and should protect the weak and oppressed. In an address to fellow officers, he said:

> In the days of chivalry—the golden age of our profession—knights (officers) were noted as well for courtesy and gentleness of behavior, as for death-defying courage. . . . From their acts of courtesy and benevolence was derived the word, now pronounced as one, Gentle Man. . . . Let us be GENTLE. That is courteous and considerate for the rights of others. Let us be MEN. That is fearless and untiring in doing our duty as we see it.[4]

That didn't stop a gentleman from being a fighter, as Patton showed. The Code of Chivalry not only sent knights out to battle but also constrained how they were to conduct themselves in a fight. A warrior-gentleman would treat others with respect, and perhaps even with the exquisite courtesy shown at the battle of Fontenay in 1745. In Voltaire's account, an English officer named Charles Hay waited till the French army was only twenty or thirty paces away and then cried out, "Gentlemen of the French Guard, fire!" To which a French officer replied, "Gentlemen, we never fire first. Fire yourself."[5] If that sounds a little precious, it's also how they arrange these affairs in Hollywood Westerns.

The same sense of restraint can make gentlemen out of hockey players, even with all the fights in the game. When skaters armed with sticks cross-check each other at twenty miles an hour, or slam another player into the boards, they get their blood up. It's a game that elicits violence, unlike football, where the violence is momentary and ends immediately when the play is over. In hockey, by contrast, the players crash into each other and go on playing. What brings an element of nobility to the contest is the way in which, without formal rules, the violence has been ritualized.

In hockey, some things are just not done, or call for retribution if they are done. A goalie is too well padded to fight, and if he is attacked everyone on his team will jump the player who did it. You also pick on your own size. The heavyweights don't attack the middleweights. Some exceptionally skilled players such as Wayne Gretzky and Sidney Crosby are too valuable to risk an injury, and they are permitted to resist a challenge. Instead, they'd be protected by their team's "enforcer." Without Dave Semenko to serve as his bodyguard, Gretzky would likely have had a much shorter NHL career. As it was, Crosby lost a season and a half in the NHL due to concussions and needed a set of enforcers.

Before a fight begins, there will often be an express challenge. "You wanna go?" they'll ask. The two players will then drop their gloves at the same time, since the "instigators" who start a fight are penalized with an extra penalty. They'll also drop their helmets, to protect the other player from a hand injury that could prevent him from playing. When one of the fighters drops to his knees, the round ends and they'll permit the referees to separate them.

Off the ice, no one was more of a gentleman than Mr. Hockey, Gordie Howe, who played in the NHL from 1946 to 1980, and who on the ice had the sharpest elbows in the league. He pioneered what came to be called the Gordie Howe hat trick: One goal, one assist, and one fight.

Sportsmanship teaches us to transcend the Schmittian categories of friends and enemies. The members of the team on the other side are opponents, not enemies. If they're to be treated with dignity, it's because of both what we owe them and what we owe ourselves as gentlemen. When a hockey series is over, the players will line up and shake each other's hand, a North American sports tradition seen only in that game.

Since the gentleman refuses to play dirty, he might be seen as weak, at least as compared to someone less scrupulous. George H. W. Bush tried without success to shed the image of a gentleman. And in truth he seemed to lack resolve. He might have let Saddam Hussein keep Kuwait if Margaret Thatcher hadn't told him that this was no time to go wobbly, and in 1992 he was turfed out in favor of the ungentlemanly Bill Clinton. In 2016 we wanted a fighter, but from Trump we learned that there is something to be said for gentlemanly behavior. Better than all of them was a Franklin Roosevelt, who combined the qualities of a quintessential gentleman with a hockey player's willingness to mix it up against the boards.

LARGE AND LIBERAL LEARNING

Gentlemen were expected to possess a fund of liberal learning, which they'd recognize as civilizing and worthy of pursuit for its own sake. Matthew Arnold thought this would dissipate provincialism, cure intolerance, and purge away pettiness: all sins of a philistine middle class.[6] It would free one from the tyranny of *idées reçues* and the narrowness of unquestioned lies and half-truths, which is why it was called "*large* and liberal learning." By its turn to simple-minded politics, American higher education has abandoned this goal and created a dead zone in which nothing in the humanities written over the last fifty years is thought worthy of study.

A person with large and liberal views could not be a xenophobe or bigot. If he was English, he might have taken the Grand Tour and learned that the culture of France and the religion of Rome were not to be scorned. Charles Kingsley, who mocked the vows of chastity taken by Catholic priests and nuns and who wrote the racist *Water-Babies*, was a vulgar illiberal and a perfect foil for Cardinal Newman. George Washington, who attended a Catholic Mass in Philadelphia while at the 1787 Constitutional Convention, and who sent his good wishes to the Jewish Congregation of Newport, Rhode Island, was the First Gentleman of America as well as the person George III called the greatest man in the world.

Gentlemen would recognize that racial prejudice was shameful, and its victims would see them as allies. "There are two classes of people in the North," said Booker T. Washington. "One that is just as narrow and unreasonable toward the white man at the South as any Southern white man can be toward the Negro or a Northern white man. I have always chosen to deal with the other white man at the North—the man with large and liberal views."[7]

One could even find a degree of liberalism in the postbellum South. In South Carolina, a conservative, white patrician class led by Wade Hampton rose to power after Reconstruction. Hampton had been a large slaveowner and a general in the Confederate Army, and after the war supported anti-black intimidation. By today's standards, he was a racist—as were most Americans of his day. By the standards of his society, however, he was a courtly gentleman and a liberal who ran for governor in 1876 as a racial moderate. He sought the votes of blacks, and the Jim Crow laws that made them second-class citizens were enacted only after he left office and the viciously racist "Pitchfork Ben" Tillman was elected in his place. Before then, there had been no laws about blacks sitting at the back of the bus or eating in separate restaurants.

Tillman was a populist, and what he disliked about Hampton was that he was a gentleman. As between the Reconstruction Republicans on the one hand and Hampton and Tillman on the other, it was the former who had the right of it. But as between the latter two, the gentlemanly Hampton was the liberal. As Edmund Burke put it, vice lost half its evil by losing all its grossness.

Large and liberal views imposed the requirement that, even in a racist society, a gentleman would not mistreat inferiors. As Cardinal Newman said, "it is almost a definition of a gentleman to say he is one who never inflicts pain."

> He has his eyes on all his company; he is tender towards the bashful, gentle towards the distant, and merciful towards the absurd; he can recollect to whom he is speaking; he guards against unseasonable allusions, or topics which may irritate; he is seldom prominent in conversation, and never wearisome. He makes light of favours while he does them, and seems to be receiving when he is conferring.[8]

Newman provided one of the classic statements of a liberal education when in the early 1850s he was asked to serve as the rector for a new Irish university. While the new university would serve Catholic students excluded from Oxford and Cambridge, it would not be a religious institution. Instead, it would seek to train students in the qualities of a gentleman. To explain what that meant he delivered a series of lectures, which became *The Idea of a University* (1852).

> Liberal Education makes not the Christian, not the Catholic,
> but the gentleman. It is well to be a gentlemen, it is well to have
> a cultivated intellect, a delicate taste, a candid, equitable, dis-
> passionate mind, a noble and courteous bearing in the conduct
> of life;—these are the connatural qualities of a large knowledge;
> they are the objects of a University.[9]

A liberal education, he said, should inculcate in students a sense of freedom, equitability, calmness, and moderation, and these were valuable in themselves, quite apart from their utility in equipping a person for a profession.

The same ideas informed an 1828 Yale report on university education. It had been suggested that Latin and Greek be dropped from the curriculum and replaced by courses better suited to the "business character of the nation." The report wanted none of that, and instead upheld the ideal of a liberal education, one designed "both to strengthen and enlarge the faculties of the mind, and to familiarize it with the leading principles of the great objects of human investigation and knowledge." The college's mission was to educate students to perform their duties to their fellow students and their country, and to do so its graduates should have "large and liberal views."

Higher education had a special purpose in a republic, said the report. The graduate should be able to take his place in the deliberative assemblies of Hannah Arendt's *vita activa*. America was newly democratic in 1828, and so, far from threatening the university, this gave it a mission which had hitherto been lacking, the education of students in civic virtue.

In time, America's public-school system would be infused with the same liberal spirit. Along with providing a basic education, reformers such as Horace Mann said that our K–12 schools would

Americanize their students by teaching them the liberal ideals of the Founders. This was so successful, before those ideals were trashed by a woke professoriate, that Adlai Stevenson said that the public-school system was the most American thing about America.

The Code of the Gentleman was anything but egalitarian, but in the nineteenth and twentieth centuries it promoted democratic liberalism when chivalric ideals became a model for instructing the youth of every class. The public schools taught the virtues of the country's republican heroes, and the Boy Scout Handbook insisted that a good scout must be chivalrous. Gentlemanly conduct also protects liberalism against its excesses by decrying brutish, self-seeking behavior. If progressives make an idol of the uninhibited cultivation of individuality, if they require the state to be neutral between different conceptions of the good, if they support soulless university presidents whose institutions train students to be loutish barbarians, the fault lies in the abandonment of the Code of the Gentleman.

A Man of Parts

Henry Dwight Sedgwick, the grandfather of the 1960s actress Edie Sedgwick, said that a gentleman must be what used to be called a man of parts. What this would require is both athletic prowess and a knowledge of how "all human intercourse may be embellished, how conduct may become a fine art, how animal mating may be idealized by courtly love, how speech may be more than purely utilitarian."[10] The gentleman would recognize his duty to contribute to the happiness of those around him through a lighthearted cheerfulness.

As a model for what was asked of him, he might consult Baldassare Castiglione's *The Book of the Courtier* (1528), a treatise on the special qualities sought in a *cortegiano*. The courtier should be cultivated and a generalist of wide learning, amorous but not gross, conscious of his honor, and intrepid in defense of his lord. While well educated, he should avoid the charge of pedantry and instead should adopt a pose of *sprezzatura* which masks his wit under a cover of nonchalance and spontaneity.

A gentleman will be tolerant of ordinary human failings but will quietly unfriend the boor or blowhard. He'll know that the mark of elegance is simplicity, while that of vulgarity is loudness. He might not be a believer, but he'll have no truck with the village atheist who scorns religion and mocks the sense of the sacred. From the code of courtly love, the gentleman will have inherited the duty to treat women of every condition with utmost courtesy, and if he fails to do so will be told "You're no gentleman!"

Before the Revolution, the sixteen-year-old George Washington had learned the courtly ideals of a gentleman. He copied out 110 *Rules of Civility & Decent Behavior in Company and Conversation* to remind him of his duties.

1. Every Action done in Company, ought to be with Some Sign of Respect, to those that are Present.

19. Let your Countenance be pleasant but in Serious Matters Somewhat grave.

25. Superfluous Complements and all Affectation of Ceremony are to be avoided, yet where due they are not to be Neglected.

26. In Pulling off your Hat to Persons of Distinction, as Noblemen, Justices, Churchmen &c make a Reverence, bowing more or less according to the Custom of the Better Bred, and Quality of the Person.

29. When you meet with one of Greater Quality than yourself, Stop, and retire especially if it be at a Door or any Straight place to give way for him to Pass.

36. Artificers & Persons of low Degree ought not to use many ceremonies to Lords, or Others of high Degree but Respect and highly Honor them, and those of high Degree ought to treat them with affability & Courtesy, without Arrogance.[11]

Movies used to supply us with models of courtly behavior in people like Cary Grant. When dispatching his villains, Sean Connery's James Bond displayed an elegant sprezzatura. In *The Philadelphia Story* (1940), Jimmy Stewart didn't take advantage of an inebriated Katherine Hepburn, because there were rules about that sort of thing. Even the film noir heroes had a quiet nobility, a code of honor they'd not traduce. Sam Spade will send his lover to the clink because, when a man's partner is killed, he's supposed to do something about it. *Casablanca*'s Rick Blaine poses as a cynic but is really a sentimentalist and a patriot. Slobs and louts who dress in hoodies and shorts and mock anything that suggests courtliness and nobility will sneer at this, but they can't help but recognize their inferiority to such people.

* * *

The legends of chivalry told of a world that had never really existed, to which was contrasted a sadly mediocre present. Writing in 1935, Sedgwick lamented that "now even the ideal is gone, like an old fashion of dress, not spoken of but to be laughed at."[12] Even Malory, writing in the late fifteenth century, complained that lovers were no longer as faithful as they had been in olden times.[13]

The legends had a measure of authenticity, however, even in Sedgwick's day. Not so long ago, a gentleman didn't have be told to check his privilege. He recognized that his advantages were unearned and that he had an obligation to give back to society. In wartime, he'd be the first to volunteer and like the knights of old would seek the honorable advancement that comes from a passage of arms. At Harvard, Memorial Hall stands as an enduring symbol of what people such as Oliver Wendell Holmes Jr. understood as their duty.

Since then, the Code of the Gentleman has been radically weakened. The sense of *noblesse oblige*, of duties to serve and protect other Americans, was abandoned, and the Ivy League graduate who was first to volunteer to defend his country in previous wars found excuses from enlisting after the Vietnam War. He let the deplorables fight on his behalf.

And yet the Code of the Gentleman still survives, in the shame we feel when it is traduced. If we're fascinated by the Page Six freaks and knaves, it's because of the *nostalgie de la boue*, the perverse attraction of the scabrous. But that's not to say we'd like to emulate any of them. Instead, the secret message is: Don't go there. As the *New York*

Post reminds readers, if you don't want to see yourself in Page Six, don't do it. The world presents us with a photographic negative of virtue, and our minds reverse the image to recall the glory of knighthood and the desire to be chivalrous. Those stories of loyal lovers, of knights who battle against fantastic giants and furious beasts, conveyed a sense of grandeur and left readers with an image of what a life would resemble if lived according to the highest dictates of honor and glory.

11.

THE CHIVALROUS LAWS OF WAR

The U.S. armed services inherited their traditions from those of the British army, which held officers to the elevated moral standards of a gentleman. What was tolerated in common soldiers was not permitted a gentleman-officer, and in *Henry V* that was a badge of honor. At night before battle the king walks about his camp, and Pistol fails to recognize him.

> PISTOL: Discuss unto me; art thou officer?
>
>   Or art thou base, common and popular?
>
> KING HENRY V: I am a gentleman of a company.[1]

Asked who he is, Pistol answers "As good a gentleman as the emperor." Then you are better than the king, answers Henry.

The army asks its officer corps to be the bearer of the noblest traditions in the service. The enlisted man's loyalty is primarily to the comrade next to him. It's different with officers, General Dallaire told me. When you're put in charge of the lives of other people, they're always in your thoughts and there's never a time when you're not a commander. For that reason, officers are held to the most sensitive standards of honor and can be cashiered for conduct unbecoming an officer and gentleman.

An Officer and a Gentleman

The reference to gentlemanly behavior was dropped in the 1956 Code of Military Justice, which substituted "conduct unbecoming an officer,"[2] but military courts continue to punish male officers whose conduct has been less than gentlemanly, and this was upheld by the Supreme Court in *Parker v. Levy* (1974).[3] In the middle of the Vietnam War, Captain Levy had urged African-American soldiers to disobey orders, and the Court convicted him of conduct unbecoming "an officer and a gentleman" and sentenced him to three years in prison. That standard would have been held to be unconstitutionally vague had it trenched on the free-speech rights of civilians, but the Court ruled that a higher standard was imposed on officers, given the need for discipline in the services. In addition, the longstanding customs of the military had given content to what it means to be a gentleman.

Faults and omissions that are encountered every day in civilian life might get an officer punished. In *U.S. v. Voorhees* (2019),[4] the accused had made suggestive comments to other service members and gave one of them a back massage, and this was held to be conduct unbecoming an officer. Then, in *U.S. v. Conliffe* (2009),[5] a West Point cadet had secretly filmed female cadets in the shower room, and his creepiness was found to be inconsistent with the duties of an officer and a gentleman. Lying, cheating at cards, treating women with disrespect, public drunkenness, and even adultery aren't crimes, but are still offenses under the Code of Military Justice.[6] Failing to pay a due debt happens often enough outside the military but was enough to get an officer court-martialed in *Fletcher v. United States.*[7]

The content of an officer's duties can be traced back to the code of knighthood, described in detail by Christine de Pisan (1364–1430) in her *Book of Deeds of Arms and of Chivalry (ca.* 1410). There was even a specialized Court of Chivalry to resolve disputed questions over such matters as how to deal with prisoners. Those duties became the Code of the Gentleman, and from them, incorporated into the collective memory of his corps, an officer would learn what was due to his enemy.

One of the most striking examples of the power of chivalry to shape military decisions came at the end of the First Gulf War in 1992. The coalition forces, with those of the United States in the lead, had crushed Saddam Hussein's army, whose path of retreat had become a killing zone. The carnage stretched for miles, with hundreds of army vehicles strewn along what came to be called the Highway of Death. The Iraqis had lost the ability to put up a fight, and the way to Bagdad lay open when the Americans decided to stop the fighting. Joint Chief of Staff General Colin Powell told the White House that the Iraqi Army was so thoroughly dismembered that allied intelligence "can't find divisions, can't find brigades, can't find battalions. It's all just shattered." To continue the killing would have been "un-American and unchivalrous."[8]

THE GENEVA CONVENTION'S CODE OF CHIVALRY

The Code of Chivalry amounted to what historian Nigel Saul calls a proto-version of the Geneva Convention.[9] Under Article Three of the Third Geneva Convention, prisoners of war are to be treated humanely without being discriminated against based on their race, sex, or religion, and outrages to their personal dignity are banned. Article Fifteen requires signatories to provide free medical care for prisoners, and suitable clothing must be given them under Article Twenty-seven. They are also to be provided with baths, soap, and laundry facilities under Article Twenty-nine. The treaty formally obligates only countries that have signed the treaty, but as 186 have done so, it is considered to be part of the customary law of war and binding on all nations.

Violations of the treaty by citizens of a signatory might be prosecuted by the courts of that country. In addition, any state may assert jurisdiction over international crimes such as genocide, wherever the crime occurred. States that (unlike the United States) are parties to the 2002 Rome Statute that created the International Court of Justice might also refer one of their nationals to the ICJ for prosecution, and even without a referral the ICJ is empowered to try people who have committed crimes against humanity. Further, the UN Security Council has established special courts to try those guilty of such crimes, as it did in establishing the International Criminal Tribunal for Rwanda. That Court sentenced the people behind *Radio Mille Collines*, which was an ex post recognition of the wisdom of General Dallaire's request to shut down the station before the killings began.

All of that seems very noble, but another self-interested story may be told about all this. Without denying that there was an element of chivalry in Colin Powell's thinking, the decision to abandon the fight in 1991 was also a prudent one. Powell was the person who said, "if you break it, you own it." He knew that pursuing the enemy and deposing Saddam Hussein would result in the United States taking ownership of the Iraqi government, and the Second Iraq War showed just how disastrous this might be.

The Geneva Convention and the Code of Chivalry can also be seen as self-interested insurance contracts. The protections they offer to prisoners of war benefit all combatants, when they aren't sure whether they'll win or lose. If defeated, the knight might have to pay a ransom, but that was better than being slaughtered. Similarly, the rules of the Geneva Convention benefited signatories such as the Germans and Western Allies in the Second World War. On both sides the prisoners were as well-treated as conditions permitted. In the United States and Canada, the POWs formed symphonic orchestras and played baseball and hockey, with instruments and gear supplied by the host country. The neutral Red Cross came to film the prisoners playing gymnastics or visiting the camp doctor to show the Germans how well their troops were treated in captivity, in the hope that they'd reciprocate in how they treated prisoners of the Western Allies. And so they did, as compared to how they treated their Russian POWs. Russia had not signed the Geneva Convention, and three million of its prisoners died in German captivity. The

Russians took three million Germans prisoner, a third of whom died in captivity.

The same idea of reciprocity explains diplomatic immunity in international law. Under the 1961 Vienna Convention on Diplomatic Relations, the premises of a foreign mission are inviolable, and diplomatic agents cannot be arrested by the host country unless this is waived by the sending state. The idea of legal immunity, which long predates the Convention, rankles the locals in New York City as they observe the double-parked cars with diplomatic plates, but it's meant to protect our diplomats abroad. If we won't prosecute their diplomats, it's in the expectation that they won't prosecute ours on what might be trumped-up charges. That explains why Iran's seizure of American diplomats in 1979 was so deeply shocking. We had thought that countries didn't behave like that.

The Geneva Convention offers a bargaining solution to a prisoner's dilemma game. When countries face each other in wartime, they can be seen as opponents in a prisoner's dilemma game in which they are put to an election between cooperating and defecting. Cooperating means signing on to the Geneva Convention to ensure that their troops will be well treated if taken prisoner, and adhering to its rules. Defecting means failing to care of prisoners of war. Joint cooperation is win-win, and defection is a distinctly inferior strategy. The problem is that, while it is collectively rational to cooperate, it is individually rational to defect and treat a cooperating party as a patsy. Knowing this, both parties will defect and lose the gains from cooperating.

This turns out to be a trust problem. The other side may tell you he'll cooperate, but how can you believe him? In private-law contracting, the trust problem can be solved by making promises legally enforceable, so that the party in breach must pay damages. The problem is that there's nothing like this in international law. Even if the states have bound themselves by signing the Geneva Convention, there are no enforcement mechanisms for breaches of the treaty.

In practice, treaties do get honored, however, even by rogue states, when the parties deal with each other on a repeat basis. As we saw in Chapter Four, PD games change in character when they are iterated or repeated, and each party is able to react to how the other has behaved and respond tit for tat. There was an example of TFT in action in the Second World War, when German and Canadian forces handcuffed each other's POWs. After the disastrous 1942 Dieppe raid, the Germans found Canadian documents that asked their troops to bind the hands of the Germans they captured, since the Canadians weren't planning to hang around and take prisoners. The Germans were outraged at this and announced that they'd handcuff their Canadian prisoners. The Canadians responded in turn, until finally both sides relented and released the handcuffs. The law of war in customary international law and the Geneva Convention can thus be seen as the product of an implicit bargain to cooperate.[10]

While TFT protects the soldiers of both sides, it's still a limited moral code. The Third Geneva Convention binds signatories and probably non-signatory states as well, but it might seem to exclude stateless groups that can't be expected to reciprocate and cooperate. In the Second Iraq War, the George W. Bush administration used this as a justification for refusing to extend Geneva Convention protections to the irregular soldiers it had captured.

After a few years, however, the toughness didn't sit well with American voters. In 2004, they were shocked by the revelation of human-rights abuses in the Abu Ghraib prison in Iraq, which included photos of prisoners being physically and sexually abused and of Army interrogators gleefully looking on. Humanitarian organizations such as Amnesty International and Human Rights Watch reported that these were not isolated incidents but part of a broader pattern of torture in other U.S. prisons, including Guantanamo Bay. Then, in the 2006 congressional election, voters repudiated the way in which the Bush administration had prosecuted the War on Terror, and Democrats won control of both houses. In addition, U.S. federal courts, which had stood down in the early years of the War on Terror, became more assertive in defending Guantanamo prisoners under American constitutional and statutory law, and in doing so upheld the Code of Chivalry.

THE SUPREME COURT WEIGHS IN

The Supreme Court, which refrained from ruling on the status of the Guantanamo prisoners in the early years of the War on Terror, soon began to rein in the Bush administration. This began in 2004 with *Rasul v. Bush*, when the Court granted irregular Taliban and al-Qaeda prisoners a right to have their cases removed from military tribunals and adjudicated in federal courts through a habeas corpus petition.[11] On a decision released the same day as *Rasul*, the Court in *Hamdi v. Rumsfeld* rejected the argument that the government was entitled to hold an American member of the Taliban indefinitely, without access to counsel and without formal charges.[12] The Court conceded that the military could detain a prisoner during the hostilities, and that captivity was merely a temporary detention and not a punishment, but as Hamdi had been captured three years before, this would not justify his perpetual detention. At a minimum, therefore, Hamdi had to be accorded some opportunity to make his case, and federal courts had to have some ability to review the matter.

In response to these cases, Congress in 2005 passed the Detainee Treatment Act (DTA), which eliminated statutory habeas jurisdiction in favor of a more limited form of judicial review. The Defense Department had established Combatant Status Review Tribunals to decide whether the prisoners were in fact enemy combatants, and the DTA limited their appeal rights to a review of the tribunal's decisions by the D.C. Court of Appeals.

The next year, however, the Court took up the case of an al-Qaeda member in *Hamdan v. Rumsfeld*,[13] and rejected the government's argument that the prisoner's rights were limited by the DTA. Stateless prisoners such as Hamdan could still rely on the protections provided by other parts of the Geneva Convention, in particular Article Three, which bans cruel, humiliating, and degrading treatment. It also requires that prisoners be offered the judicial procedures recognized as indispensable by civilized peoples, which the Court thought meant something more than a Combatant Status Review Tribunal. This was a rejection of a TFT understanding of the law of war, since al-Qaeda was in no position to reciprocate, and as a terrorist organization wouldn't have done so even if they could have. No matter. The less virtue in them, the more in us.

In response to these cases, Congress in 2006 passed the Military Commissions Act (MCA) which included a lengthy code of criminal justice, with extensive procedural protections for the prisoners. The MCA stated that these were deemed to codify Article Three protections and barred any separate invocation of the Convention in habeas proceedings. In short order, however, the Supreme Court held the MCA unconstitutional in *Boumediene v. Bush* (2008), insofar as it purported to restrict habeas rights under Art. I, § 9 of the Constitution.[14] The government had argued that the Guantanamo prisoners had no constitutional rights, but the Court disagreed. The right to habeas relief was a core principle of liberty and a defense against arbitrary assertions of executive power by kings or presidents. In doing so, the Court repudiated the TFT view of international law and vindicated of the Code of Chivalry. Somehow, we've retained the memory of and admiration for the Black Prince.

If Schmitt's categories of friends and enemies ever commended itself, it would be in wartime, but even here it has been rejected in customary international law and in American legislation and Supreme Court jurisprudence. In the end, however, it's more than a matter of statutes and judges, and comes down to people like Generals Dallaire and Powell and an officer corps that has incorporated a code of conduct that excludes barbarous and unchivalrous behavior. As military historian Sir John Keegan (1934–2012) observed, "there is no substitute for honor as a medium of enforcing decency on the battlefield; never has been and never will be."[15]

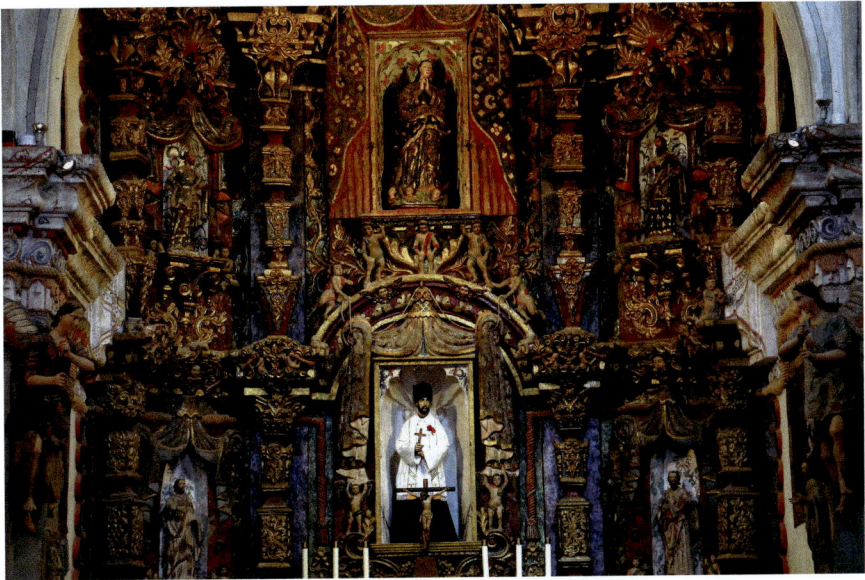

St. Xavier del Bac Mission, Arizona

Source: Wikimedia Commons, Philcomanforterie

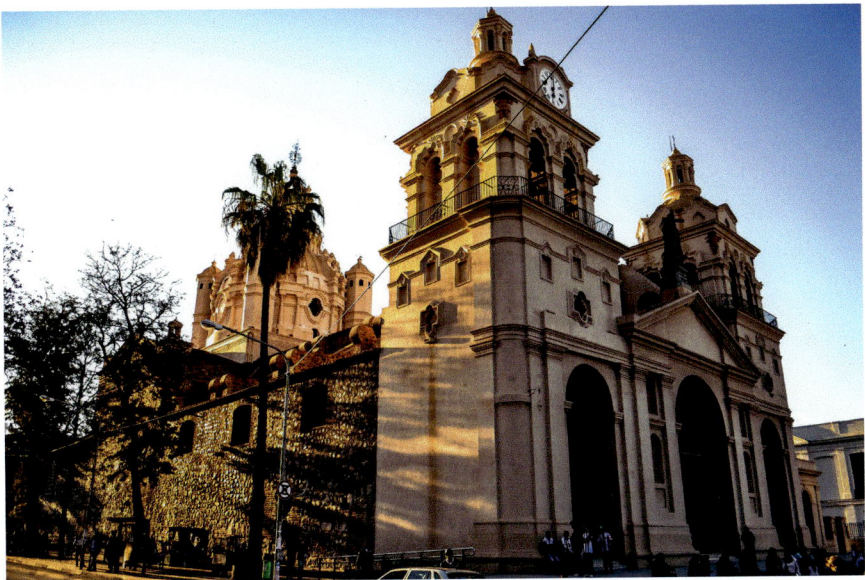

Cathedral of Cordoba, Argentina

Source: Wikimedia Commons, Nicolás Riofrio

The Holy Grail appears to the Knights of the Round Table,
Everard d'Espinques

Source: Gallica Digital Library

The Death of General Wolfe, **Benjamin West**
"I die content."

Roméo Dallaire in 2017
St. Joseph Health Care Foundation, London Ontario

Source: Wikimedia Commons, Michelle Campbell

The Allegory of Good and Bad Government,
Ambrogio Lorenzetti
"See how much good comes from her and how sweet life is and full of peace in the city."
Source: Bridgeman Images

***Oliver Twist*, George Cruikshank**

Source: *Oliver Twist*, Richard Bentley, New Burlington Street edition

Cleveland Monsters Hockey

"You wanna go?"

Source: Wikimedia Commons, Erik Drost

Pericles's Funeral Oration, **Philipp Foltz**

"There is no exclusiveness in our public life, and in our private business we are not suspicious of one another, nor angry with our neighbor if he does what he likes."

Source: Rijksmuseum Houses

Wanderer above the Sea of Fog, **Caspar David Friedrich**

Source: Wikimedia Commons, Cybershot800i

12.

CIVIC VIRTUE

Liberalism rests on a foundation of civic virtue and the desire of citizens or public officials to promote the common good. The antonym of civic virtue is public corruption. It's not corrupt to favor a subset of society where it is just to do so, for example to alleviate poverty or to correct an historical wrong. But that apart, the voter or official who unjustifiably favors a part only of society is corrupt and reveals himself to be illiberal. He in the public realm is like the faithless employee in the private realm who steals from his employer.

To promote the common good, it doesn't suffice to uphold a thick set of individual rights, since these might be asserted in an illiberal manner. Without virtues such as moderation, a selfish person might demand his rights be respected when the benefits to him are greatly exceeded by the costs he'd impose on everyone else. And without a sense of benevolence, a person wouldn't care if his rights trenched on the common good. A liberal society will defend individual rights, but rights shorn of virtuous rights-bearers can be a menace.

The sense of civic virtue might arise in two ways. First, it might result from a bottom-up sense of solidarity and loyalty that citizens feel for each other. Employing a distinction made by Aristotle, this is the virtue of the many, who recognize their duties to each other and who are thereby made capable of self-government. Second, the virtue of the few assumes that individuals are by nature corrupt and that a regime of virtue should be imposed upon them from above, by virtuous officials.

Many Americans subscribe to the virtue of the many, the idea that the voters are pure and that only the government is corrupt, and that our political ills arise because political leaders fail to represent the interests of their constituents. A self-interested elite, sure of itself and contemptuous of outsiders in flyover country, constitutes a new aristocracy and rings down the curtain on the American Dream of a mobile country where everyone is empowered to get ahead. These are the complaints of a Country Party, and they have been a constant in our politics from the time of the Patriots at the American Revolution onward.

Many on the left subscribe to the idea of the virtue of the few, the thought that many, perhaps most, Americans are deplorable racists and semi-fascists, and that good government depends on guidance from scientific experts and an elite class that rises above the mob's mistaken and vicious beliefs. If Country Party members remain skeptical about climate change or how COVID arose, that just shows how irredeemable they are. These are the beliefs of a Court Party and are seen today in the attempt to use court proceedings to suppress a Country Party candidate for the presidency.

Country and Court Parties quarrel over the meaning of virtue, but right-wing Constitutional Conservatives would have us do without civic virtue altogether. They call themselves Never-Trumpers and scorn the Country Party's charges that we've turned into an aristocracy. They're ideologically opposed to the left-wing Court Party, but culturally have more in common with it than they do with the Country Party and can be seen as aristocrats themselves. They're to be found in high Republican Party circles, the Federalist Society, and national think tanks, and they try to pass themselves off as the official voice of conservatism.

Constitutional Conservatives agree with Madison in *Federalist* 10 that everyone is naturally self-interested, and that it's too much to expect virtue from anyone. The desire for virtuous government is even dangerous, because it threatens liberty. We can do without civic virtue, however, if we get the institutions of government right. Corrupt groups will arise, but they'll be rendered harmless by the Constitution's separation of powers. Their self-interested desires will be checked in their competition with each other, and only the common good will emerge.

Constitutional Conservatives revere Madison and tell us we live under a Madisonian constitution. In doing so, however, they betray their ignorance about how the Framers crafted the Constitution. They also fail to recognize how the separation of powers has failed to cabin corruption, and how parliamentary countries that lack a separation of powers rank higher than we do on measures of both civic virtue and freedom.

The Virtue of the Many

The Age of Chivalry ended in Italy before anywhere else. During the Late Middle Ages (1150–1300), it became the wealthiest and most highly urbanized region in Europe. Money came to replace property as the most basic form of wealth, and new cities arose. What they offered were markets where goods could be bought and sold and where people could make themselves wealthy. The feudal lords found they could not keep up and sought the friendship and protection of urban life. As this happened, a more democratic form of government arose, one in which guild merchants were permitted to participate. The city republics gave birth to a secular culture that differed from both the chivalry of the aristocracy and the scholasticism of the clerics.

With the revival of urbanism and commerce came a different kind of morality, one suited to people who rubbed shoulders in the piazza and traded in their stalls. What emerged from their shared experiences were the bourgeois virtues of Montesquieu's *doux commerce*, the merchant's industry, prudence, and temperance, where what mattered was the here and now, the temporal as opposed to the eternal. The city dwellers weren't Augustinians who believed that our real home is the City of God. Instead, their world was the City of Man, and their concern was for peace, prosperity, and civility, and these are not to be scorned. The new ethos also included the civic virtues that asked the citizen to support his city, participate in its government, and fight in its wars.

In Siena, a hill town thirty miles south of Florence, the revolution in commerce and government began in the early twelfth century. The city's government was called a commune, and was led by a *Podestà*, a salaried city manager appointed for a limited term. He in turn was supervised by an assembly of twenty-four representatives—the *Ventiquattro*—in the city's council. In time, the Twenty-four gave way to the Nine—the *Nove*. Both assemblies were chosen by the people, and Siena was one of the earliest democracies. While it owed formal allegiance to the Holy Roman Emperor, it was effectively a self-governing republic.

Siena had become a rich and bourgeois city, and more democratic than America was at its founding. In 1451 a visitor complained that it was ruled by "grocers, tanners, shoemakers and rustics."[1] The Sienese traded in cloth and spices, but its banks were what made the city rich. They were the principal lenders to the Church, whose patronage helped make the city one of the leading financial centers of medieval Europe.

In the early fourteenth century, its city fathers took stock. They had founded the eighth-oldest university in 1240 and defeated the Florentines in the Battle of Montaperti (1260). The city was at peace, prosperous, and happy, and its council commissioned an artist to tell its story in the Palazzo Pubblico, the city's council hall. The result was a series of frescoes called *The Allegory of Good and Bad Government* (1338–39), and the artist was Ambrogio Lorenzetti.

In one panel, set in a city that is recognizably Siena, craftsmen ply their trades, and gorgeously attired maidens dance hand in hand. A wedding party brings a bride to her new home, while behind them men play at a board game. In another panel, set in the country, farmers work the soil, from tilling and planting to harvesting and threshing, and shepherds bring their wool to market. The allegorical figure of Security hovers above, holding a scroll on which is written, "Without fear every man may travel freely, and each may till and sow, so long as this commune shall maintain this lady [Justice] sovereign, for she has stripped the wicked of all power."

A third panel, in the center of the room, shows how all this had come about, through civic virtues represented by six female figures: Fortitude, Prudence, Temperance, Justice, Magnanimity, and a reclining figure of Peace. The first four of these are the Cardinal Virtues of the Church, and to them Lorenzetti added the chivalric virtue of magnanimity, shown as a lady dispensing coins from a bowl. Above them hover the Church's theological virtues of Faith, Hope, and Charity. Peace is what will follow from the practice of these virtues. She is not crowned, as the virtues are, but bears a laurel wreath to symbolize victory.

In the turbulent politics of early Renaissance Italy, peace was recognized as good government's sine qua non. Dante (1265–1321) and Marsilius of Padua (1270–1342) both praised its tranquility.[2] Without peace, everything is at risk, and Montesquieu described political liberty as the "tranquility of mind arising from the opinion each person has of his safety."[3] If we had forgotten this, the left reminded us of it when it allied itself to criminals and tolerated lawlessness.

Justice is enthroned on the fresco's left, above a door through which the Nine would enter when they met. The inscription below spells out what they were to do to ensure that Siena was well governed:

> Turn your eyes, you who rule, to look carefully at Justice, who, for her glory, is presented and crowned here. She always gives each man his rightful due. See how much good comes from her and how sweet life is and full of peace in the city where this virtue is to be seen, which is more resplendent than any other.

For inspiration, Justice looks reverently upwards to the figure of Divine Wisdom, and on either side holds a balance from which angels dispense distributive and corrective justice (the latter with a sword). Below them, a cord descends to the figure of Concord, which binds the Sienese together as common citizens. Concord bears a heavy carpenter's plane, symbolizing equality, and levels society so that no one person stands above everyone else.

The cord then passes to a group of twenty-four citizens who symbolize the *Ventiquattri*, all of whom look equal. Each one hands it to the person in front of him. Crucially, they hold it and aren't held by it, since everyone is asked to take an active role in maintaining justice. From the *Ventiquattri*, the cord passes upwards to a scepter borne by a regal figure who is surrounded by the virtues. He bears a shield with the image of the Virgin, to whom the city was dedicated, and around his head are the four letters CSCV, for *Commune Saenorum, Civitatis Virginis*: the Commune of Siena, the City of the Virgin. The godlike figure personifies the common good, and the fresco shows how this is brought about through a virtuous citizenry that takes part in the city's government.[4]

The frescos were painted in 1338–39, and there had not been anything quite like this in Western art. Lorenzetti was a near-contemporary of Giotto, and like him he portrayed identifiable faces in his fresco, likely of known Sienese citizens. His figures of Peace in the center panel and of the dancing maidens in the side panel have a sweetness that will not be seen for another hundred years in Italian art. And while religious ideas and imagery are present, the theme is wholly secular. There are no popes, bishops, or priests to be found. Instead of sermons, a lay scholar lectures a group of attentive students, likely on Roman law.

Lorenzetti's allegory conveys the idea that wisdom leads to virtue, but what is equally important is how this comes about. The cord runs from Justice through the *popolo*, who've been made equal by Concord, and from them to the city government or Commune. The direction is bottom-up, and not top-down from the Commune to the people. The common good emerges from the citizens and their representatives, informed by a sense of justice. When republics fall, it is from their selfishness and vices, as portrayed in a companion Lorenzetti fresco, *The City State under Tyranny*, where "no one is ever in accord with the Common Good."

The frescoes introduced the idea of civic virtue, the idea that goodness could be defined by something other than the relationship between man and God. Virtue had become political, and the citizens of Siena were asked to have a sense of civic consciousness, and to see themselves as charged with duties to support their neighbors and promote the common good. Along with the impulse to make a gift, the call to chivalry, and the Code of the Gentleman, this is one of the sources of liberalism.

THE VIRTUE OF THE FEW

The fresco stood in the city's council chamber, and Machiavelli must have seen it when he was sent by Florence on a mission to Siena. The two towns were the principal city-republics in Renaissance Tuscany, and Machiavelli agreed with Lorenzetti on the need for civic virtue, the virtue shown by citizens who are willing to defend their country and to share in the responsibilities of government. For Renaissance Italian writers this became a major theme in what historian Hans Baron labeled *Bürgerhumanismus*, or civic humanism.

Civic humanism was an ideology about what it meant to be a *civis*, or citizen. The merchants and shoemakers were asked to see themselves as members of a *città* and to share in their duties to advance the common good. In this, the civic humanists took their inspiration not from Aristotle or Aquinas so much as from classical Roman authors such as Seneca and Cicero, and especially the latter's description of the common good.[5] The common good is the good of all citizens and is opposed to self-interested factions that prefer the good of their guild or neighborhood to that of the whole.

Civic humanists nevertheless disagreed on the form of government that virtue politics would entail. What Cicero had in mind was the virtue of the many, in a non-monarchical republican government. As we saw, Lorenzetti agreed with him, as did Marsilius of Padua.[6] So did Leonardo Bruni (1370–1444), whom Hans Baron credited with a Copernican Revolution in historiography by attributing the fall of Rome to the decline in republican virtue.[7] In the latter part of the fourteenth century, however, the forms of communal government found in Lorenzetti's Siena and other cities in Northern

Italy had given way to principalities ruled by *signori* such as the Medici in Florence, and many of the civic humanists abandoned the virtue of the many to embrace the virtue of the few.

Machiavelli was one of them in *The Prince*, which described the qualities required for a ruler who wants to preserve his power. Machiavelli's *virtù* was the *vir virtutis*, the spirited manliness that wins honor and glory, and which is prepared to use cruelty and deceit to stay on top. The *virtuoso* prince will not be bound by conventional morality and will know when to depart from it. "If everything is considered carefully, it will be found that something which looks like virtue, if followed, would be his ruin; whilst something else, which looks like vice, yet followed brings him security and prosperity."[8] To keep himself in power, he should even be prepared to employ beastly methods.[9] That's virtue of a kind, but it made Machiavelli seem like the person Leo Strauss called "a teacher of evil."[10]

Virtue meant something very different for Machiavelli than it had for Lorenzetti. The Sienese painter was an orthodox Christian who thought that what mattered was the Church's cardinal and theological virtues. However, Machiavelli thought that Christianity was the religion of a monkish *vita contemplativa* that denigrated the honor of the world, against which he preferred the religion of the ancients and their *vita activa*.

> Our religion has glorified humble and contemplative more than active men. It has then placed the highest good in humility, abjectness, and contempt of things human; the other placed it in greatness of spirit, strength of body, and all other things capable of making men strong. And if our religion asks that you have strength in yourself, it wishes you to be capable more of suffering than of doing something strong. This mode of life seems to have rendered the world weak and given it in prey to criminal men, who can manage it securely, seeing that the collectivity of men, so as to go to paradise, think more of enduring the beatings than of avenging them.[11]

Though he described himself as a Christian, Machiavelli did not bother to hide his scorn for the religion's "effeminate" spirit, and he nowhere expressed any interest in its truth or the salvation of his soul.[12]

In addition to *The Prince*, Machiavelli wrote *The Discourses on Livy* to encourage the rebirth of the ancient Roman Republic. It is the common good that makes cities great, he said, and added that this will only be found in republics. The two books were written alongside each other, but some have argued that the *Discourses* was the author's mature reflection on political theory, and that the earlier work was an isolated composition. That might make Machiavelli appear a champion of the virtue of the many, and so he was taken by "Cambridge School" historians such as Quentin Skinner.[13]

There are no sharp differences between the two works, however.[14] In the *Discourses*, Machiavelli spoke of the need for virtue amongst the common people.[15] On the other hand, he also wrote that they are easily corrupted and that one shouldn't expect to find disinterested virtue from *il vulgo*.[16] A well-ordered society rests "not so much from the goodness of the peoples, which is in good part lacking, as from having one king that maintains them united not only through his virtue but through the order of those kingdoms."[17] As such, both books may be taken to represent the Court Party's top-down virtue and rule by the few.

THE VIRTUE OF THE FOUNDERS

If ever any event was overdetermined, it was the American Revolution, so many were the reasons for Independence. They included the Quebec Act's barrier to westward land-development schemes and religious paranoia over the toleration of Catholicism in that province. More than anything was the sense that, after the Conquest of New France, America no longer required Britain's protection, that it had no need for imperial popinjays, and that it was ready for self-government.

Nevertheless, it was remarkable that the Thirteen Colonies united to oppose Great Britain, when only Massachusetts was directly attacked. What that took, said a New Hampshire divine, was the willingness of a united citizenry "to sacrifice their private interests to the public good, and unite like a band of brothers, to make the cause of one state, and even of one town, a common cause; and that they should continue firm and united amidst the greatest discouragements and the most trying reverses of fortune." Rev. Samuel Mc-Clintock was speaking to the delegates to the New Hampshire constitutional convention and warned them that what would be needed was the virtue of the many.[18]

These were commonplace observations during the Revolution and immediately afterwards. John Adams wrote that "public virtue cannot exist in a Nation without private Virtue, and public Virtue is the only Foundation of Republics."[19] Washington warned that "Human rights can only be assured among a virtuous people,"[20] and in his Farewell Address decried the baneful influence of factions and party politics, which at the time were buzzwords for public corruption.

The Revolution itself was a reaction to corruption in the mother country, as described by Country Party writers in Britain such as John Trenchard and Thomas Gordon. Between 1720 and 1724, the two co-authored *Cato's Letters*, a series of attacks on the South Sea Scandal and Robert Walpole's government, and these were widely read in America. John Adams studied them and concluded that the electors and elected in Britain were "one mass of corruption."[21] American visitors to Britain brought back their personal reports of the mother country's appalling level of public vice. John Dickinson was the strongest Anglophile at the Revolution, and yet the young visitor from America was shocked by how the British conducted their elections. "It is astonishing to think what impudence & villainy are practizd on this occasion. If a man cannot be brought to vote as he is desird, he is made dead drunk & kept in that state, never heard of by his family or friends till all is over & he can do no harm."[22]

In eighteenth-century British politics, all sides thought it legitimate to offer plums to political friends and to feast on whatever was put their way. The parties weren't divided by ideology or even dynastic allegiances, wrote Sir Lewis Namier, but only by partisan friendships and the spoils that might come their way. "Men . . . no more dreamt of a seat in the House in order to benefit humanity," he observed, "than a child dreams of a birthday cake that others may eat it."[23]

The Patriots thought they could do better, and in the language of republican virtue found a justification for the break from a corrupt and monarchical Britain. Kings would breed a Court Party that would milk the public purse. To answer this, said the Patriots, we'd need a republic, one from which selfish dealings and corrupt bargains would be banished, a government founded on republican virtue, the virtue of the many shown by citizens who champion the general welfare in a personally disinterested manner.

Historian J. G. A. Pocock described the revival of virtue politics in Britain and America as a "Machiavellian Moment." The Revolution had been seen as embodying Lockean principles, but Pocock took issue with this, building on the work of two historians who had located the Patriot cause in the tradition of republican virtue. The first of these in 1967 was Bernard Bailyn with his *The Ideological Origins of the American Revolution*, a study of the political pamphlets written to oppose the Stamp Act. Two years later, in *The Creation of the American Republic*, Gordon Wood argued that the Revolution was motivated by the Patriots' disinterested desire to defend their local communities against what was seen as a foreign invader. While Pocock labeled this as Machiavellian virtue, it was really a Lorenzetti moment that rested on the virtue of the many.

The true Machiavellian, the advocate of the virtue of the few, was James Madison. In an essay entitled the "Vices of the Political System of the United States," written a month before the 1787 Constitutional Convention began,[24] he disparaged the many, whom he said would not choose wisely in a democracy. "How easily are base and selfish measures, masked by pretexts of public good and apparent expediency?" The people themselves are divided into different factions and cannot be expected to support the common good. Sadly, the voices of the few, those virtuous "individuals of extended views and of national pride" (ahem!), were silenced by the demagogues.

For an answer, Madison borrowed an idea from David Hume, whom he had studied at Princeton. In a 1754 essay on the "Idea of a Perfect Commonwealth," Hume had proposed a highly artificial scheme of government that began with a division of Great Britain and Ireland into a hundred counties, each with a hundred parishes, and built up from there with parish meetings, county-town assemblies, county magistrates, and senators.[25] This was a theory of refinement or *filtration* of representatives, in which ordinary voters would elect local representatives, who would then elect higher and more virtuous representatives, and so on up the ladder. Cream would rise to the top.

Madison adopted the filtration theory in his "Vices" essay, which envisaged "a process of elections" designed to ensure that the most senior places in government would be occupied by "the purest and noblest characters" in society. Such a system would "extract from the mass of the Society" those who "feel most strongly the proper motives to pursue the end of their appointment, and be most capable to devise the proper means of attaining it." In the Constitutional Convention, he described this as a "policy of refining the popular appointments by successive filtrations."[26]

The Virginia Plan, which he drafted and which the Virginia delegates presented at the Convention, incorporated Madison's filtration principle. While providing for a formal separation of powers between the branches, only the members of the House of Representatives would be popularly elected. The Senators would be selected by the Representatives from a list of nominees provided by the state legislatures, and together the two branches would elect the president. In this way, he thought, civic virtue would emerge from on high.

Between 1776 and the 1787 Convention, the many had begun to seem less virtuous. The mobs that had played so important a role in the Revolution were less welcome when they threatened the new American governments.[27] After Shays' Rebellion in western Massachusetts, this was particularly true of delegates from that state, such as Elbridge Gerry. As Alexander Hamilton observed, "the members most tenacious of republicanism . . . were as loud as any in declaiming against the vices of democracy."[28]

Filtration survives as the principle behind parliamentary government. Without a separation of powers, only individual Members of Parliament are elected directly by the people. A majority of MPs then choose the Prime Minister, who in turn appoints members to a nearly powerless upper house (the House of Lords in Britain, the

Senate in Canada). While political campaigns ask voters to support one party over another, there is still an element of refinement in the way votes are filtered by the way in which a Prime Minister might be turfed out when he loses the confidence of his MPs—as Margaret Thatcher, Theresa May, and Boris Johnson discovered, to their cost.

America's Constitutional Secret

Madison quickly abandoned the idea of filtration. On July 16, 1787, the small-state delegates united around the Connecticut Compromise to reject the Virginia Plan. Now the members of the Senate would be chosen by a method devised by the state legislatures, with equal representation for the states in the Senate. With the House, they would then elect a president. There would be filtration, but the states would be doing the filtering, and as a strong nationalist who wanted to draw power away from the states Madison hated this.

Madison met with other nationalist delegates the next morning to decide what to do. Virtually all his ideas had been rejected, and he must have wondered whether anything could be rescued of the Convention. The person who is popularly taken to be the father of the Constitution seems to have wanted to stage a walkout that would have ended the Convention and possibly split up the country. He wrote that the Connecticut Compromise caused "serious anxiety" that the Convention would prove a failure.[29] In the end, however, nothing was decided. "The time was wasted in vague conversation."[30] When the Convention was about to adjourn, Madison wrote to Jefferson to confess that he had lost.[31]

Happily, Gouverneur Morris arrived at a way to rescue the Convention. Later that same morning he proposed that the president be popularly elected. This was an explicit rejection of the filtration principle, which up to then he had supported, but he would have realized that an elected president would draw power to the national government as the only person elected by the entire country. Forced to choose between his nationalism and filtration, Morris opted for nationalism, and two days later brought Madison along with him.

A difficulty remained, however. How could the country get corruption-free government without filtration and the virtue of the few? For most of the delegates that wouldn't be a problem. They were suspicious of democracy and the virtue of the many but hadn't given up on the virtue of the few. They thought that filtration would survive, since they believed that (after Washington) presidential elections would most often be decided in the House of Representatives because no candidate would get the needed majority of votes in the Electoral College.[32] In that case, the choice of president would be thrown to the House, voting by state, as prescribed by Art. II, § 1, cl. 3. The virtue of the few would thus be preserved. However, the last time that a presidential election was decided by the House was in 1824. Technological changes since the Framers' day have made it easier for national candidates to emerge and win a majority of Electoral votes, and that has spelled the end of filtration by the House.

Corruption was a problem for Madison, however. He had rejected the virtue of the many and had given up on filtration. That would have excluded any possibility of civic virtue, thought Machiavelli. If the people and the officials are corrupt, the best institutions wouldn't give us good government, he thought. And if they are virtuous, the institutions wouldn't matter.[33] But Madison disagreed and thought that a country could do without virtuous voters or officials if it got its institutions right. In place of virtue politics, he placed his faith in the structure of the constitution and its separation of powers.

Madison naively thought that, with the separation of powers, ambition would check ambition, and that politicians would not find a way around this. But politicians are savvy enough to bargain with each other, and we've elected a Congress of mutual backscratchers in which wheels are greased through corrupt legislative deals. Congressman A trades off a steel tariff about which he doesn't care in favor of milk subsidies that do matter to his voters, with a Congressman B who has opposite preferences. The first public official achieves more of his principal objective while surrendering something about which he cares less, but about which the second politician cares more strongly.

Machiavelli was right. We're not going to be saved by our institutions or by the separation of powers. Parliamentary countries with an all-powerful House of Commons that lack a separation of powers are less corrupt than presidential ones that do have a separation of powers.[34] Separationism encourages corruption by giving individual congressmen the incentive to favor their own districts, as opposed to the country as a whole. The competition between the branches also encourages Congress to trench on presidential powers by micromanaging the executive through overlong legislation. That's given us thousand-page bills in which corrupt interest-group bargains may easily be hidden.[35] The division of powers also means that it's hard to say who is responsible for corruption. Instead, it leads to a lot of finger-pointing and things that don't get fixed.[36] Finally, the separation of powers makes it hard to reverse legislation that, with the benefit of hindsight, is found to be wasteful.[37] If the "Madisonian Constitution" was meant to promote civic virtue and cure the problem of corruption through the machinery of government, it's been a conspicuous failure.

What about political freedom? When I compared the fifty-odd parliamentary regimes to the ninety-odd presidential ones in a regression analysis, I found that the former were significantly freer.[38] Prime ministers aren't heads of state. They have to expose themselves to the daily slanging matches during Question Period. They aren't insulated from accountability by the separation of powers. All of this has helped keep parliamentary countries free.

But what about us? We're free, even if our Constitution did not export well. In other presidential governments, power cycled between presidents-for-life and military juntas. If that didn't happen here, what's the secret to American Exceptionalism? While we remained free, this was evidently in spite of and not because of the Constitution. Something else made the difference, and this could only have been a sense of things that citizens owe to each other, of limits that should not be transgressed, and of the requirements of liberalism. But why here and not in Russia or Venezuela? What made the difference was something you'll find in Lorenzetti's fresco. What made the difference was civic virtue, something we'll need as much today as ever we did.

13.

LIBERTY, EQUALITY, FRATERNITY, NATIONALISM

Machiavelli advised the Prince to employ immoral means to remain in power. But that fact doesn't entirely summarize the man, for he was also a Florentine and Italian patriot. Near the end of his life he wrote, "I love my native city more than my own soul,"[1] and he ended *The Prince* with an exhortation for a new ruler who would free Italy from "the cruel and arrogant domination of their foreigners."[2] The immoral means should be employed for that moral end, aided by what Petrarch called that "antique valor which is not yet dead in Italian hearts."[3] If Lorenzetti's virtue arose from a sense of civic neighborliness, Machiavelli's *virtù* was a product of his nationalism, and it is nationalism that accounts for American liberty, equality, and fraternity.

Why Nationalism Matters

In this, as in other things, Machiavelli was ahead of his time. Most of his contemporaries felt the tug of loyalty to their cities, not to their nation, and in later centuries people identified themselves by their religion. Machiavelli's nationalism was more of a nineteenth- and twentieth-century phenomenon, for that was when three changes gave rise to a sense of membership in a national community.

The first was the realization that the universal values of the eighteenth-century Enlightenment project had dissolved local ties but failed to produce a just society. If Wordsworth thought it bliss to be alive when the French Revolution began, the sense of elation quickly dissipated when it began to massacre its victims.

Second, the ruthless way in which invading French armies exported liberal universalism provoked a reaction from the conquered peoples of Germany, Russia, and Spain. There was a romantic rebellion against the Enlightenment's universal principles in Germany, where Johann Gottfried von Herder (1744–1803) argued that a country's national spirit must be understood in terms of its literature and folkloric traditions. Similarly, in his *Address to the German Nation* (1808), Johann Gottlieb Fichte wrote that political principles could not be applied across national and linguistic borders in the same way to all people. The German language created a national identity that was distinct from the ideals held by the French troops who were occupying Berlin. During the Nazi era, those ideas became highly unfashionable, but the notion that our language cabins in our thoughts is not so wild an idea and was endorsed by Charles Taylor in *The Language Animal* (2016).

Third, nationalism was a response to the wound of modernity. The new technologies of the Industrial Revolution, aided by contract law's laissez-faire principles, ushered in extraordinary wealth gains, but the "almost miraculous improvement in the tools of production . . . was accompanied by a catastrophic dislocation of the lives of the common people," wrote Karl Polyani.[4] Before then, market economies had been subordinated to political, religious, and social

150

ends. This was reversed in the nineteenth century, however, when advanced thinkers proposed that society be ruled by the economy, a misstep that persisted until it was corrected by the welfare state and a newer kind of liberalism.

The Industrial Revolution had also brought people from their villages to the cities and weakened their sense of connection with each other. The sense of social solidarity (which Ferdinand Tönnies called *Gemeinschaft*) had formerly come from one's local community, while membership in a state (Tönnies's *Gesellschaft*) was a bloodless and purely legal relationship. But nationalism changed this, argued philosopher Ernest Gellner. If the deserted village had been abandoned, its place was taken by the nation, and "a mobile anonymous society simulated a closed cosy community" with "Gesellschaft using the idiom of Gemeinschaft."[5] As Charles Taylor put it, people entered in as peasants and emerged as Frenchmen.

Nationalism is what Benedict Anderson calls an imagined community. That makes it seem unreal, its bonds mystic and chimerical. It also doesn't tell us why the sense of attachment to the nation has any moral significance. Immanuel Kant said that rules aren't moral unless they can be applied universally, and, in *The Language of Morals* (1961), R. M. Hare argued that moral language is universally prescriptive. To count as a moral judgment, any prescription or command would have to apply in the same way to any person in the same circumstances, whatever his nationality. That is why Robert Goodin and Philip Pettit excluded nationalism from the topics to be covered in their collection of essays on political philosophy. "Nationalism ... does not figure, on the grounds that it hardly counts as a principled way of thinking about things."[6]

William Godwin (1756–1836) expressed the same idea in a book he wrote to counter Edmund Burke's *Reflections on the Revolution in France*.[7] In a thought experiment, Godwin asked the reader to imagine two people in a burning house where only one can be saved. The first is a great benefactor of humanity (Godwin had Fénelon in mind), and the second is a common chambermaid. Godwin was a utilitarian who thought that people should act in such a way as to maximize human happiness and concluded that they should save the benefactor. Moreover, he added, one should do so even if the chambermaid is one's mother. To count as a moral imperative, duties must be universalizable, he said, and this implies an objective perspective which ignores personal ties.

If this seems repellent, it's because love of family and friends constitutes the sense of solidarity or community that is one of the most basic of human goods. Ignoring such bonds drains life and ideals of the content that alone gives them meaning, and an atomistic society without them would be deeply lonely.[8] If the utilitarian asked us to sacrifice our mother, utilitarianism would make us all unhappy and would be self-defeating. But it's not. We'd be happier in a world where particularistic family duties are permitted to overrule universal ones, and where I owe special duties to my mother. And that is consistent with utilitarianism.

The same is true for the weaker requirements of nationhood. Like our families, nationalism is one of the particularistic emotions that binds us to others. The nation is one's home, the place where, as Robert Frost said, "when you have to go there, they have to take you in."[9] I found the sense of belonging to my country very comforting when, during a disastrous trip abroad, I thought I had lost my passport. I hadn't, as it turned out, but I briefly felt like Philip Nolan, the banished conspirator in Edward Everett Hale's *The Man Without a Country* (1863). I phoned up my embassy and asked whether I could return home without a password. Don't worry, I was told. We have to take you in.

Matthew Arnold said that there are things we do not understand unless we understand that they are beautiful. So too, there are things we do not understand unless we understand that they are loved.

The sense of comfort in belonging to a nation doesn't exclude the possibility that nationalism might be troubling, however. Revolutionary France sought to unify France by eliminating all traces of local differences, and this policy was continued with the nineteenth-century educational reforms of François Guizot, where a dominant, centralizing state imposed its language on weaker, regional cultures. In particular, nationalism was dismissed as morally tainted after the example of Nazi Germany's ethnic nationalism. In *The Open Society and its Enemies*, written in 1945, Sir Karl Popper called nationalism "the most reactionary and servile political philosophy that had ever been imposed upon meek and long-suffering mankind," one that "appeals to our tribal instincts, to passion and to prejudice, and to our desire to be relieved from the strain of individual responsibility."[10]

In addition to excusing illiberalism, nationalism has been charged with provoking wars. Max Weber argued that Germany should win the First World War because it defended *Kultur*, while Emile Durkheim supported France in the name of its *mission civilisatrice*. How much better it might have been if each side had more fully appreciated the other's culture, and a destructive war averted.

After the savage wars of the twentieth century, it was therefore unsurprising that nationalism was in disfavor, and that Popper's jeremiad caught on. But then nationalism had also rallied the Western Allies in combating Nazi Germany. What had kept a beleaguered Britain on its feet in 1941, said George Orwell, was

> chiefly the atavistic emotion of patriotism, the ingrained feeling of English-speaking peoples that they are superior to foreigners. For the last twenty years the main object of English left-wing intellectuals has been to break this feeling down, and if they had succeeded, we might be watching SS men patrolling the London streets at this moment.[11]

Crucially, English nationalism was liberal nationalism and rooted in the way in which in England had historically been identified with the cause of liberty. So too, the genius of American nationalism is liberal nationalism. One can thus be an English or an American nationalist and a liberal at the same time. There might be perverse forms of illiberal nationalism in other countries, but as an American nationalist I needn't take any interest in them.

THE NECESSITY OF LIBERAL NATIONALISM

In recent years, a group called National Conservatives (or NatCons) has proposed to do a leveraged buy-out of the right by conjoining the ideas of nationalism and conservatism. They're conservatives who reject liberalism, and make nice to illiberal nationalists such as Hungary's Viktor Orbán. They're welcome to him, but in America nationalism is necessarily liberal and National Conservatism is self-defeating.

The NatCons reject the liberal principles that are constitutive of our identities as Americans. They call this "credal nationalism," and say that we're more than a creed. We're also a people, with a culture that includes figures such as George Washington and Abraham Lincoln. But if we're not credal nationalists, there is not much left of a common American culture, and the NatCon is or ought to be a secessionist. A secessionist cannot be a nationalist, however, and that is a second way in which National Conservatism is self-defeating. Third, National Conservatism is a right-wing movement most of whose members oppose the welfare state and refuses to recognize nationalism's leftward gravitational force. The true nationalist knows that the bond of fraternity he feels with his fellow citizens imposes a duty to care for the least well-off, and National Conservatism is self-defeating if it fails to understand this.

I. LIBERTY AND EQUALITY

The American nationalist must be a liberal because what makes one American is an American creed of fidelity to the liberal principles of the Founders and the idea that America has a special mission to promote liberty and equality, as promised by the Declaration of Independence and guaranteed by the Bill of Rights. Other countries had their common cultures or religions. What America had was an idea. Robert Penn Warren wrote, "to be an American is not . . . a matter of blood; it is a matter of an idea—and [American] history is the image of that idea."[12]

That was what the Supreme Court held in *West Virginia Board of Education v. Barnette* and *Texas v. Johnson*, and it was also Lincoln's idea of American nationalism. In a speech on July 10, 1858, he asked what it was which made someone an American. Some in his audience were descendants of the Founders, some not. It didn't matter, said Lincoln. They were all entitled to call themselves Americans, for what made them so was something other than ties of blood.

> When they look through that old Declaration of Independence they find that those old men say that "We hold these truths to be self-evident, that all men are created equal," and then they feel that that moral sentiment taught in that day evidences their relation to those men, that it is the father of all moral principle in them, and that they have a right to claim it as though they were blood of the blood, and flesh of the flesh, of the men who wrote that Declaration, and so they are. That is the electric cord in that Declaration that links the hearts of Patriotic and liberty-loving men together, that will link those patriotic hearts as long as the love of freedom exists in the minds of men throughout the world.[13]

That sounds like a paradox. If every liberty-loving person supports the principles of the Declaration, what makes this a badge of American nationhood? John Quincy Adams explained why in an 1821 Independence Day Address. You might be a lover of liberty in Albania, but the respect for liberal principles is strengthened when they become a national symbol. "The tie which binds us to our country is not more holy in the sight of God, but it is more deeply seated in our nature, more tender and endearing, than that common link which merely connects us with our fellow-mortal, man." We value constitutionally protected liberties not merely because they are admirable in themselves, but because they are *American* liberties.

Unlike the Know Nothing movement, whose xenophobia he thought should be excised from the new Republican Party, Lincoln welcomed the new arrivals who had immigrated to America. But the NatCons who reject Lincoln's liberalism oppose immigration and renounce the "electric cord" that Lincoln said links the hearts of patriotic and liberty-loving Americans. The incongruity recalls an anti-Gaullist slogan that Pétainists adopted during the German Occupation. On a poster bearing the image of Marshal Pétain, they wrote *Êtes-vous plus Français que lui?* Are you more French than the Marshal? The same question might be asked of the American NatCon who doesn't care for the electric cord of credal nationalism. Are you more American than Lincoln?

II. SECESSIONISM

Some illiberal NatCons will nevertheless tell me I've missed something. I've defined American nationalism in terms of the beliefs of the Founders. They tell me that we're more than a creed. We're a people. As indeed we are, and easily recognizable as Americans when we travel elsewhere. However, credal nationalism doesn't exclude a sense of membership in a nation and a feeling of kinship with fellow Americans. We're not Hungarians, who are rescued from the dislocations of modernity by a nationalism based on religion and a common language. But if we don't have that, we do have a history in which our legal and constitutional liberties were defended and enlarged, from Bunker Hill to Selma, Alabama. We are People of the Book, and the sense of community and of Tönnies's *Gemeinschaft* is no less strong for that.

That's why the true American nationalist doesn't think he's been replaced in America, in the way that Éric Zemmour complains he's being replaced in France. It takes a generation to make someone a Frenchman. In America it takes only fifteen minutes. Like Lincoln, we know that we've always been replaced, and that we're none the worse for it. We don't feel that, without leaving America, America has left us. Instead, we live in a country that remained America when it welcomed new arrivals who were faithful to the American creed.

The NatCon who denies that credal nationalism supplies our sense of solidarity as Americans, who insists on the need for something more, is obliged to tell us what this may be. And the problem is that, like Gertrude Stein's Oakland, there's no there there.

In an 1882 essay entitled "What is a Nation," Ernest Renan defined France's non-credal nationalism as a collective memory of his country's glorious moments as well as an amnesia about the inglorious ones. "Forgetfulness, and even historical error, are essential factors in the creation of a nation."[14] Similarly, Fustel de Coulanges said that "true patriotism is not the love of the soil, it is the love of the past, it is the respect for the generations that have preceded us."[15]

But if that's right, is America still a nation? The only memories about our country we'll find in our popular media are ones about how shameful America is, and the only amnesia is about anything great in our history. As taught in our schools, American history is a list of events which should never have happened. Thus, if Renan was right about what makes for nationalism, the NatCon must ask himself whether he is or ought to be a secessionist. If he is, he's not a nationalist. If he's not, if we are a nation, he must recognize that it's only credal nationalism that unites us. That is a second way in which, for Americans, National Conservatism is self-defeating.

III. FRATERNITY

There is another sense in which the nationalist must be a liberal, and to see this one must recognize that nationalism can take two different forms. *Vertical* nationalism desires its country's glory, its preeminence over other countries. That's the nationalism of the right-wing Trump supporter who wants to Make America Great Again.

There's another kind of nationalism, however, called *horizontal* nationalism, which the NatCon fails to recognize. It rests on a sense of fraternity with fellow citizens and implies a generous social safety net for those who need help. Shortly before his death, Bobby Kennedy said that "when one part of the United States does badly, it also has an effect on the rest of the United States." If you can't feel this, you're not much of a nationalist.

Those who take a dim view of nationalism fault it for stirring up prejudice against foreigners. What they miss, however, is the heightened sense of solidarity that nationalists feel for fellow citizens. The charge of prejudice assumes that remote and universal ties always outweigh local ones and that loyalty to one's country always comes at the cost of loyalty to more encompassing groups, such as humanity in general. One kind of solidarity waxes, the other wanes. But our sympathies are naturally constrained, and the alternative to national or local bonds is often not universal bonds but no bonds at all.

The moral health of a society depends importantly upon an expanded sense of solidarity with people who don't belong to the same club, religion, or race. In a diverse society such as the United States, nothing promotes solidarity of this kind so much as nationalism. Think of people who've been left behind in our society. "Do we say that these people must be helped because they are our fellow human beings?" asks Richard Rorty. "We may, but it is much more persuasive, morally as well as politically, to describe them as our fellow *Americans*—to insist that it is outrageous that an *American* should live without hope."[16]

We naturally feel a kinship to fellow Americans. Moreover, we ought to feel a special attachment to them. Morality is positional. We are more than mere individuals, and radically independent of anyone else. Rather, we're members of a family, of a religion, and of a country. We occupy different stations, and duties are attached to these stations, wrote F. H. Bradley. We should promote the common good, but the common good of fellow citizens takes priority.

Nationalism implies fraternity. American nationalists take the side of their fellow Americans, even as they prefer their friends over people they don't know. The norm of nationality and friendship is partiality. You're not a true friend if you're indifferent between your supposed friend and a stranger. So too, you're not a nationalist if you don't care for your countrymen any more than you do for those from other countries. But as the nationalist does care for his countrymen, he'll want his country to provide for those in need. If the NatCon claims that he's a nationalist but as a right-winger opposes a decent health-care system for all Americans, he's sailing under a false flag. Once again, National Conservatism is self-defeating.

14.

INDIVIDUALISM

The American nationalist must be tolerant, as he's asked to share a bond of common citizenship with people who, apart from their allegiance to a common creed, might be very different from him. Their cultural ties, their religion, their color, even their language might not be the same as his. That is why credal nationalists can't be accused of racial or ethnic prejudice. Their creed imposes a requirement of tolerance.

Tolerance implies a willingness to accept lifestyle differences that don't pick your pocket or break your leg. The American who dislikes patriotic Muslims, socialists, or gays cannot call himself a nationalist if they're Americans who subscribe to Lincoln's principles. One is not required to share all their tastes, any more than one is required to enjoy every cuisine or musical genre that's out there, but at a minimum nationalism implies the same fraternity Lincoln felt with the newly naturalized Irish or German immigrant.

HARMLESS ECCENTRICITY

One of the classic statements of liberalism was given in 430 B.C. in honor of the Athenian war dead. In his Funeral Oration, Pericles extolled Athens's superiority over its illiberal enemy, Sparta. Athens was a democracy, with equal justice for all, and its offices were open to everyone however poor they might be. As a seaport, it enjoyed the fruits of the whole earth and met foreigners in a free and fearless spirit. It punished the transgressor's crimes but befriended eccentrics who did not injure anyone.

> There is no exclusiveness in our public life, and in our private business we are not suspicious of one another, nor angry with our neighbor if he does what he likes; we do not put on sour looks at him which, though harmless, are not pleasant.

The crucial distinction is between harmless eccentricity and harmful deviance. The latter might be prosecuted as crimes or punished by the social sanctions Pericles called the "unwritten laws which bring upon the transgressor of them the reprobation of the general sentiment." These might be "sour looks" or, more seriously, the merchant might find himself ostracized. But then there are the harmless eccentrics who dance to a different drummer but don't set a bad example.

John Stuart Mill's *On Liberty* (1859) is the classic modern statement of Periclean liberalism, and in it Mill made the same distinctions. Harms come in two kinds, he said. Some people harm others directly, and this might merit a legal response. Other harms injure by the bad example they set, and while this doesn't justify a legal penalty they do merit a social stigma, Pericles' "sour looks." The way in which we frown on the drunkard discourages others from emulating him and permits society to promote its vision of good behavior without heavy-handed penal prosecutions.

What drew Mill's ire were sanctions, whether legal or social, directed against people who live their lives against the grain but who don't harm anyone else, either by direct action or by their example. Even if they're not prosecuted as criminals, they might be chilled by oppressive social norms. "Our merely social intolerance kills no one, roots out no opinions, but induces men to disguise them, or to abstain from any active effort for their diffusion."[1] The most active and inquiring minds will be silenced and only the conformist will be heard, sacrificing a society's moral courage and its awareness of hidden evils.

That leaves four possible responses to abnormal behavior. Liberals will accept harmless eccentricities, while prudes will condemn them. The progressive is willing to tolerate truly harmful behavior and might excuse real crimes by refusing to see them policed or prosecuted. For example, San Francisco declined to go after shoplifters even after downtown stores were pillaged by professional thieves. The progressive will also refuse to condemn behavior that doesn't rise to the level of criminality, but which is nevertheless socially harmful and deserving of reputational sanctions. We know enough about the costs of fatherless households to realize that out-of-wedlock birth rates are not to be celebrated.

Table B   *The Condone and Blame Game*

	HARMLESS ECCENTRICITY	HARMFUL DEVIANCE
Condone	Liberals	Progressives
Blame	Prudes	Conservatives, Liberals

Harmful deviance will be properly condemned by both conservatives and liberals, and if libertarians like Mill are sometimes mocked it's because they fail to do so. Mill asked his readers to tolerate what he called "experiments in living," at least until experience has shown them to be harmful. But now the evidence is in, and we've found that some of those experiments were mistakes indeed. In *Jules et Jim*, Henri-Pierre Roché's 1953 novel about a fatal love triangle, Jim concludes that it's fine to want to rediscover the laws of human life, but it's more practical to conform to the existing ones. We played with the sources of human life. We met them in armed combat, lost, and now roll in their waves.[2] The state recognizes this by refusing to sanction "throuple" marriages, and most of us would agree with this. But not Mill, perhaps. With his concern for slippery slopes, he might argue that they should be legitimized. If so, that shows the problematical overreach of such arguments.

Mill is popular with the progressive left because of his anti-clericalism. His moral heroes were the heretics who broke things, who abandoned established religions and beliefs, and he claimed that "every single improvement which has taken place either in the human mind or in institutions, may be traced distinctly" to periods when "the yoke of authority was broken."[3] That foolishly overstates things, as it ignores improvements made by people who worked within the bounds of established institutions and beliefs: the Dantes, Bachs, and Burkes. Mill was on firmer ground, however, when he defended individualism and the idea "that in things which do not primarily concern others, individuality should assert itself."[4] In departing from conventional morality such people might merit social sanctions, but then they might be harmless eccentrics who by their example do no injury to anyone except possibly themselves.

The Good of Individualism

Individualism was more than a psychological datum for Mill, observed Isaiah Berlin. Rather, it was an ideal,[5] something people should cultivate for its own sake. Its heroes would include the splendid eccentrics you'll find in Edith Sitwell's *English Eccentrics* (1933). So long as they are harmless, they're to be celebrated for the way in which they entertain us.

Eccentrics are people who have decided to depart from customary behavior. That assumes a conscious decision on their part and excludes people who are simply mad. Prince Philip's mother, Princess Alice, believed she enjoyed carnal relations with Christ. At Queen Elizabeth's Coronation she could be seen wearing a nun's habit, but she really wasn't a member of any religious order. She wasn't an eccentric, just off her rocker. The profanity-spewing homeless person who suffers from Tourette's Syndrome isn't an eccentric either. He's just someone who was mistakenly released from a mental institution.

The eccentric often lives a life of conventional morality, one eccentricity apart. He doesn't harm anyone by setting a bad example because no one will wish to emulate him. He might be kind, generous, and forgiving, and possess all the virtues except those of prudence and moderation, the virtues of chartered accountants. And while the eccentric is immoderate, not everyone who is immoderate is an eccentric. Stoners and drunks are immoderate but lack what makes the eccentric of interest. They're simply crashing bores.

Moderation or prudence may indeed be praiseworthy, and for Aristotle they were the touchstone of the virtues, establishing a mean between blameworthy extremes at each end. The brave man is neither cowardly nor foolhardy; the generous man is neither miserly nor wasteful with his money. Aquinas also made prudence a virtue,[6] although what he had in mind was not overindulging in physical appetites.

Those who pursue sanctity aren't moderates, however. Judged by the goods of the world, nothing was more imprudent than Isaac Jogues' desire for martyrdom. The Church of Laodicea was neither hot nor cold, but that wasn't high praise. Some saints, such as Saint Benedict, were paragons of moderation, but we're more likely to remember the eccentrics, such as Saint Francis.

Harmless rule-breaking is thus to be encouraged, and England is famous for its eccentrics. Mad Jack Mytton (1796–1834) risked life and limb for the sheer sport of it. He hunted in the coldest weather, wearing the thinnest of clothes, and once was found stark naked pursuing some ducks on an iced-over pond. He kept a bear as a pet and alarmed his dinner guests by riding it into the dining room. The animal bit his leg clean through, but Mytton didn't let that get in the way of his dinner. It was a wonder, concluded Sitwell, that he reached the age of thirty-eight before he died.

Eccentrics court attention. The dandy stands out from the rest of us by his extreme attention to style and manners. He was Gérard de Nerval, taking his pet lobster out for a walk in a leash; or Anthony Blanche, reciting *The Waste Land* through a megaphone to an Oxford quad in Evelyn Waugh's *Brideshead Revisited*. Earlier still, the dandies were Beau Brummell and his circle, leaning out from the bay window of White's to mock the neckcloths of passersby.

Dandyism espoused frivolity to show its rejection of everything normal, sensible, and efficient in modernity. The eighteenth-century cult of the love of nature and melancholia was replaced by a hard-edged ennui about the goods of the world. In "Le Peintre de la vie modern" (1859–60), Baudelaire said that the dandy takes a proud satisfaction in being blasé. That's how to show your superiority, as a friend tells Julien Sorel in Stendhal's *The Red and the Black* (1830). It's not *bon ton* to seem sad. It shows that you've failed at something, that you're inferior. Instead, you must seem bored. That way you show that you're better than the people who try to please you.[7]

Some nineteenth-century writers complained that, with its thick set of social norms, prudish Americans frowned on eccentrics. Stendhal thought that America's small-town social sanctions amounted to a tyranny, and Alexis de Tocqueville said that "I know no country where, in general, less independence of mind and genuine freedom of discussion reign than in America."[8] (Why conservatives think Tocqueville liked America is a mystery to me.) George Santayana felt the same way: "Even what is best about America is compulsory, the idealism, the zeal, the beautiful happy unison of its great moments."[9]

However, a country that invented so many odd religions wouldn't seem very repressive, and part of baseball's charm is its welcome mat for eccentrics. Bill "Spaceman" Lee showed up for a game in a space-man costume, and since he had been accused of throwing spitballs once carried a bucket of water to the mound. Casey Stengel gave the bird to the umpires by lifting his cap and letting a bird fly out. Dizzy Dean became an American folk hero, and the sayings of Yogi Berra ("It ain't over till it's over" and "The future ain't what it used to be") are part of the American lexicon.

We're really not all that far behind Europe when it comes to eccentrics. They had Chinese Gordon; we had George Patton. They had Baudelaire; we had Edgar Allen Poe. They had Beau Brummell; we had Tom Wolfe. To say nothing of John Randolph of Roanoke, the communards of Brook Farm, Allen Ginsberg, and the Beats.

That was then, however. From many of the Zoomers, all I see is the dull conformism of a Lost Generation. The kind of tolerance we used to display for eccentrics is threatened by Internet mobs that descend on anyone who voices a conservative opinion on social media. We've become a nation of prudes, like the ones of whom Tocqueville complained, and the penalties imposed by the wokerati are far greater than sour looks. In the case of Brendan Eich, it cost him his job as the Mozilla CEO. He had contributed to an anti-same-sex marriage proposition and was outed by the *Los Angeles Times*. What followed was a blacklist and his forced resignation.[10]

Conservatives should welcome individuality since they are today's eccentrics. When they ask themselves how higher education might be turned around, the best they can realistically imagine is the 1950s academy, when nearly every professor was a liberal but where conservatives were tolerated as the department's Mad Jack Mytton. For conservatives it wouldn't get better than this. But that would be a vast improvement.

In higher education, conservatives have learned to keep their heads down until they receive tenure, and even that no longer protects them on campus. Joshua T. Katz, a tenured Princeton academic who was fired after he wrote articles criticizing the university's progressive agenda, described what it's like when the woke mobs turn against one.

> Colleagues who used to laugh with me every day no longer acknowledged my existence. Students who had previously asked for my attention around the clock removed me from the acknowledgments of their work. Professors across the country issued calls for right-minded people to stop citing my publications and for academic journals and presses to refuse to publish anything I might write, effectively obliterating my career. Is it a surprise that I had trouble sleeping when the husband of a psychologist I had been encouraged to see took to social media to denounce me?[11]

Purges like that have a multiplier effect. For every Katz, there are hundreds of other academics who see what's happened and, burrowing down, choose to remain silent. When inoffensive statements are made into firing offenses, the message is that no one is safe if he publicly dissents from woke pieties.

In sum, conservatives have paid a heavy price for the dull conformism enforced by the prudes on the left, and what is needed today is a revival of Periclean liberalism and a willingness to accept those with whom one disagrees.

15.

PRIVACY

Jeremy Bentham didn't think much of privacy, or at least didn't think that prisoners in jail deserved any. He designed a "panopticon," a prison built in a circle with each cell facing a guard at the center. At a glance, the guard could see into each cell, and the absence of privacy would keep the prisoners in line.

The same idea would work elsewhere, Bentham thought. If applied to asylums and hospitals, doctors could monitor their patients more easily. Further, since people were breaking rules all over the place, panopticons might be built for schools and the new factories spawned by the Industrial Revolution, with an all-seeing principal or office manager at the center.

The panopticon became famous as a metaphor for the loss of privacy in modern society. In *Discipline and Punish*, Michel Foucault (1926–84) argued that, like Bentham's prison, modern society creates a docile citizenry through its schools, factories, and the military. It wasn't that we were being spied on by a prison guard. Rather, society and all its repressive institutions had cabined us in by making it impossible to imagine an alternative world. Foucault was a man of the left, but today conservatives might feel that they're the ones being silenced by a dominant left-wing establishment.

Liberals will share the desire for privacy, from wherever it comes, and will instinctively dislike the meddlesome person who sticks his nose where it's not meant to be. "The most hateful of all names in an English ear is Nosey Parker," wrote George Orwell.[1] We recognize that what's behind the inquisitiveness is an *animus dominandi*, an illiberal desire for power over others. You'll instinctively recognize this when you avert your eyes before a person's unblinking gaze, like that of the cop who has stopped you for speeding.

There's a greater loss of privacy today than in Foucault's time, as a result of technological change. Social media and its online bullies silence conservatives, obscuring their ideas like a fog that blankets a valley. The Biden White House pressured the social-media giants to suppress content with which it disagreed, and when a judge ruled this illegal it was the illiberal left that objected and wanted the censorship to continue.[2] In addition, the way in which closed-circuit television cameras spy on us begins to resemble the panopticon. The tyranny of *idées reçues* has never been more oppressive.

The Role of Technology

At one time we thought that new technologies would be on the side of privacy. No longer. Modern technology facilitates forms of social control that Foucault could not have imagined. We live an important part of our lives online, where we can be canceled by the cyberbullies of social media. Logging off, and taking a solitary stroll down the street, we might also be observed by a closed-circuit TV camera.

America is reportedly the second most spied-on country in the world, based on the number of CCTV cameras per citizen and the number of attempts by governments to gain our personal data from social media. Atlanta has 25,000 CCTV cameras, or forty-nine per one thousand people. Washington, DC has 11,000 of them. The police use them to see who's been at a crime scene, and during a demonstration the DC police monitors protestors from a Joint Operations Command Center, relaying information back to police on the ground. That doesn't count the security cameras at the 7-Eleven or at one's front door. When asked, people usually share the film with the police.

Many of us will take comfort in this, given the spike in violent-crime rates. If, unprovoked, someone has been pushed onto the subway tracks or sucker punched, there's probably a video of it somewhere. It's getting dangerous out there, and the cameras help the police catch the bad guys. On the other hand, camera surveillance has been abused. The American Civil Liberties Union reports that rogue cops have used the cameras to stalk women and track estranged spouses. But it's really in China where the curiosity of the police and public officials tramples most on personal and political liberty.

There are 540 million CCTV cameras in China, almost one camera for every two citizens. They'll watch you as you shop and dine, and they can record audio conversations from three hundred feet away. The cameras might even be installed in your house without your consent. In schools, cameras record the facial expressions of the students and report whether they look happy, upset, angry, fearful, or disgusted. With the assistance of the country's sophisticated facial-recognition software, China expects to be able to identify everyone, everywhere within three seconds of anything happening. The degree of control over people's lives exceeds that of any country at any time, more than the panopticon, more even than George Orwell imagined in his dystopian *Nineteen Eighty-Four*.

China uses the information to produce a *bien rangé* populace. Its "social credit system" identifies people who've been caught speeding or jaywalking, playing music too loud on the train or putting their trash into the wrong bin. They can also be punished for spreading "misinformation" about the Communist Party. There are sanctions for that. People with low social credit have their Internet speeds reduced and are banned from air or train travel. Their children are kept out of prestigious schools, and their dogs can be taken from them.

We're not there yet, but our government's snooping powers increased with the Foreign Intelligence Surveillance Act. Under section 702 of the Act, the National Security Agency is permitted to intercept the communications of foreigners without a warrant. While the Act prohibits targeting aliens who are within the United States or Americans located in or outside the United States, section 702 powers have been used to search through the private data of Americans in this country. Before he defected to Russia, Edward Snowden revealed that the National Security Agency was intercepting phone calls and harvesting millions of our emails and instant messages.

The NSA obtains full copies of everything that is carried along major domestic fiber-optic cable networks and obtains communications directly from U.S. tech and social-media companies like Facebook, Google, and Apple. The information is passed on to the FBI, which can conduct "backdoor searches" of Americans provided they are suspected to be involved with foreign terrorists, spies, cybercriminals, and so forth. However, the Bureau has conducted millions of searches on Americans in cases that have nothing to do with national security, and they've done this without going to the trouble of obtaining a search warrant. One such search was for information about a Republican congressman, Darin LaHood (R-IL).[3] That's a violation of the Fourth Amendment guarantee against unlawful searches and seizures.

In recent years, the discovery that highly partisan FBI agents launched the Russia-collusion hoax without any evidence has made Republicans worried about the surveillance state. More recently, it was reported that the Bureau was investigating parents who objected to the transgender agenda being pushed at their public schools. A parent who complained that a school had covered up his daughter's rape by a transgender student was arrested at the direction of the school board. National School Board leaders complained to President Biden that they were the true victims and asked the White House to treat disruptive parents as domestic terrorists.[4]

President Biden has come close to describing millions of Americans as domestic terrorists. "Donald Trump and the MAGA Republicans represent an extremism that threatens the very foundations of our republic," he said.[5] He left open who the MAGA Republicans are, but he subsequently said it included those who challenge the 2020 election results and support election reforms, and that's at least half the Republican Party. He also conveniently ignored the prominent election deniers in his own party, such as Stacy Adams, Jimmy Carter, and Al Gore.

There are real domestic terrorists out there, but Biden's charges used to be called McCarthyism. The problem is that, because we're so polarized, Biden can get more mileage from his inflammatory language than a president could in the 1950s, and that should alarm liberals. The tools that the government can use to snoop on ordinary Americans, on the pretext that they are domestic terrorists, represent an extraordinary threat to our privacy.

Rights to Privacy

The common law has long protected our privacy, and blackmail has always been a criminal offense. In blackmail, two rights paradoxically make a wrong. The blackmailer has a right to reveal the information if it's true, and he also has the right to ask the victim for money. But put the two together, and you have a crime, and the criminalization is justified by the threat to privacy were blackmail made legal. Blackmailers would incur costs to seek out information about their victims, who in turn would either change their behavior or invest in efforts to keep it confidential. If the victim's behavior really was terrible, this might be thought to serve a social purpose, but there are also things, not discreditable in themselves, that we'd not want to see spread over the Internet. We simply don't want to be observed by a twenty-four-hour spy cam.

In a famous law-review article, Samuel Warren and Louis Brandeis described the ban on blackmail as an element of a more-encompassing right to be left alone.[6] More recently, the Supreme Court in *Griswold v. Connecticut* (1965) and *Lawrence v. Texas* (2003) held that privacy rights prevent the government from banning contraceptives and sodomy.[7] Privacy rights also served to ground a right to abortion in *Roe v. Wade* (1973), before this was reversed in *Dobbs v. Jackson Women's Health Organization* (2022).

Liberals are permitted to disagree about abortion, but they'll nevertheless think that the government should stay out of our bedrooms and will not want to see *Griswold* and *Lawrence* reversed. And while conservatives might disagree about some of those rulings, they should realize that they'd be the beneficiaries were privacy better respected. We had thought that we had put the Inquisition long behind us, but the right to conservative beliefs is threatened when "the personal is political" and people can be bullied for wrongthink.

Trump's press secretary, Sarah Huckabee Sanders, was refused service at a Lexington, VA, restaurant when the staff complained. After that happened, Congresswoman Maxine Waters (D-CA) told people at a rally "if you see anybody from [Trump's] cabinet in a restaurant, in a department store, at a gasoline station, you get out and you create a crowd" and then "push back on them."[8] That's what happened to Senate Majority Leader Mitch McConnell (R-KY) as he left a restaurant, and to Senator Rand Paul (R-KY) at a Republican event. Trump's homeland security secretary was driven out of a restaurant by protestors from the Democratic Socialists of America, who said she should never be allowed to eat and drink in public again as punishment for Trump's border policies.

The protests are especially troubling when they come for you at your home. The word home means something more than our residence or the house in which we live. It's our refuge and rookery. Sir Edward Coke said it was our castle and fortress.[9] It's where Robert Frost's hired man came to die.

That's why the protests outside the homes of Chief Justice Roberts, Justice Kavanaugh, and Justice Alito were so shocking. They came after a draft of Justice Alito's opinion in *Dobbs* was leaked. Since the Supreme Court had not officially reached a decision, and since a switch by Kavanaugh or Alito would have changed the result, this was an attempt to intimidate the members of the Court. The group outside Justice Alito's house chanted "Alito is a coward." A sarcastic sign read, "Oh sorry, does this feel INTRUSIVE?"

It's a crime to parade or picket outside the home of a judge with the intent of influencing his opinions, but Biden's Justice Department declined to prosecute the demonstrators, and Biden's press secretary said that the administration encouraged the protests so long as they were peaceful. They weren't entirely so. One protestor was charged with attempting to murder Justice Kavanaugh. Doing so would have preserved abortion rights, which was the point of it all.

Our homes are threatened when we're doxed and our addresses are revealed. That's what happened to Brendan Eich, when his views on same-sex marriage were revealed by the *Los Angeles Times*. We might also lose our online privacy when we've written under a pseudonym and our identity is revealed. A columnist for the *Washington Post*, Taylor Lorenz, wrote an article in the *Post* outing Chaya Raichik as the right-winger who had written anonymously as "libsoftiktok." "Meet the woman behind Libs of TikTok, secretly fueling the right's outrage machine," sneered the headline.[10] The article mentioned that Raichik was an orthodox Jew, and an online version of the article initially included a link to her real-estate license. When Lorenz was criticized for this, she played the victim card and complained that she suffered from severe post-traumatic stress disorder from online harassment.

Technological changes have shrunk our private spaces, and we need better legal protection for our privacy. Publishing private information about public officials, such as their home addresses, can get you arrested, but there are few consequences for revealing the address of an ordinary citizen. That needs to change, and if it does the principal beneficiaries will be conservatives.

16.

THE LIBERAL IMAGINATION

In *The Liberal Imagination* (1950), Lionel Trilling tried to explain the nexus between literature and politics. Unlike the then-fashionable New Critics, Trilling thought that content mattered and that literature should reveal the writer's politics.[1] The Stalinists would have agreed with this, but Trilling didn't have much use for them either. Tendentious propaganda hampers a writer's moral imagination and diminishes the literary value of a work. A liberal imagination wouldn't suffer from this, however. Instead, it would reveal the complexity of moral choices, including the contentious ways in which we're asked to form a good society. In America these are ideas about liberal democracy, which means that our literature—Mark Twain, Walt Whitman, and Trilling's *The Middle of the Journey* (1947)—is liberal.

THE INVENTION OF KINDNESS

The nineteenth-century novel was also liberal. Charles Dickens and George Eliot wrote against the backdrop of their time, and the Industrial Revolution had proven a mixed blessing. It produced an enormous increase in wealth but had also created a new class of urban poor. This resulted in what Polyani called a double movement, in which capitalist production was both promoted and challenged by a new concern for those left behind.[2] The dialectic confounded placid Enlightenment beliefs about progress and led to the invention of kindness and the birth of modern liberalism.

In his landmark television series *Civilisation* (1969), Kenneth Clark noted how a cult of kindness had arisen at that time.[3] Before the nineteenth century, if you had asked people what was most important to them, they wouldn't have said kindness. The Black Prince might have mentioned magnanimity. The Princesse de Clèves thought that nothing mattered more than honor. Friedrich Schiller would have said beauty. But that changed, with the wretched new urban conditions described by Friedrich Engels in *The Condition of the Working Class in England* in 1845, and in the same year by Disraeli in *Sybil*. Dickens almost created the genre, from *Oliver Twist* in 1837 to *Hard Times* in 1854. In America, Harriet Beecher Stowe's *Uncle Tom's Cabin*, published in 1852, showed how powerfully the literature of kindness might inspire a demand for reform.

Kind people are benevolent. But the difference between benevolence and kindness is the difference between the eighteenth and nineteenth centuries. Before 1800, the benevolent approached the world with a smiling imperturbability. They were David Hume—*le bon David*—in a Parisian salon. When presented with a moral challenge, they would do the right thing, but they shunned enthusiasm as vulgar. What was missing was the kind of indignation Tolstoy felt a century later when he saw people arrested for begging:

> I understood not with my mind or my heart but with my whole
> being; that the existence of tens of thousands of such people in
> Moscow—while I and thousands of others over-eat ourselves

176

with beef-steaks and sturgeon and cover our horses and floors with cloth and carpets—no matter what all the learned men in the world may say about it necessity—is a crime, not committed once but constantly; and that I with my luxury not merely tolerate it but share in it.[4]

Tolstoy's passion was foreign to English readers, but there was only a difference of degree between it and what they would have felt at the smug complacency of the beadles and parish boards in *Oliver Twist*.

Between the benevolence of David Hume and Dickens's orphans, three things had occurred. The first was the Industrial Revolution and the rise of the urban slums that Engels and Disraeli had described. The second was the expansion of the reading public. By 1850, more than half of English adults were literate, and the figure approached 100 percent by the end of the century. They included the kind of people who saw how things had changed, close-up and not from a salon. There was also a remarkable increase in female literacy during the period, and women wrote some of the classic novels of the time, such as Elizabeth Gaskell's *North and South* (1855) and George Eliot's *Middlemarch* (1871). The third change was the religious awakening with which we associate the Victorian era. The Regency rakes retired to their clubs and a pious middle class worked to restore the church and the country to a very different kind of morality. "God Almighty has set before me two Great Objects," said William Wilberforce. "The suppression of the Slave Trade and the Reformation of Manners." The Clapham Sect of Evangelicals was the principal anti-slavery party in the eighteenth century and would go on to support nineteenth-century reform legislation.

The revolt against the ravages of the Industrial Revolution led in several directions, and one was backwards to the Middle Ages. In architecture, the Gothic style was revived as a rejection of the eighteenth century's neoclassical orderliness and regularity. In an essay on "The Nature of the Gothic" in *The Stones of Venice* (1851–53), John Ruskin said that the inventive and extravagant Gothic allowed for the artist's individuality and was therefore democratic. The Pre-Raphaelite Brotherhood, which Ruskin defended after Dickens had attacked it, portrayed scenes from chivalric romances, such as King Arthur at Avalon and the Quest for the Holy Grail. Writers such as Thomas Carlyle, John Ruskin, and William Morris wondered how people could be starving amid such prosperity and proposed a return to the guild socialism of a medieval community.

More practically, the Victorians adopted a series of reform measures. The 1832 Reform Act had expanded the franchise but stopped well short of giving everyone the vote. It was limited to male householders living in properties worth at least £10 a year, but as people became wealthier the property restriction became less of a barrier and the voting rolls increased. These were the people who elected governments that abolished slavery in the British Empire, passed the Factory Act, and enacted railway-safety laws. An 1848 statute was the first piece of legislation that attempted to deal with issues of public health. Trade unions were legalized, and, after the franchise was extended, the 1873 Judicature Act sought to cure the abuses that Dickens had satirized in *Bleak House*.

Dickens the reformer also inspired the era's philanthropic movements. Thousands of the abandoned children of *Oliver Twist* were taken in by the Barnardo's Homes established by Thomas Barnado (1845–1905). Sir George Williams created the YMCA in 1844 to promote Muscular Christianity. Florence Nightingale (1820–1910) invented the modern nursing profession and was one of Lytton Strachey's *Eminent Victorians*. William Booth (1829–1912) founded the Salvation Army and became its first General. Dickens himself partnered with Angela Burdett-Coutts (1814–1906) in housing projects for the East End poor.

In America, *Uncle Tom's Cabin* was, next to the Bible, the nineteenth century's best-selling book. Published in 1852, it was one of the reasons why nine years later the country went to war over slavery. Before 1850 escaped slaves could find their freedom by fleeing to a free state. Northerners might have hated slavery but could take comfort in the thought that it was happening elsewhere. But that changed with the 1850 Fugitive Slave Act, which required the citizens of free states to cooperate with slave catchers. Thereafter the terminus of the Underground Railway became Ontario and not New

York. Josiah Henson, the inspiration for Uncle Tom, became a Canadian citizen, as did Harriet Tubman and 40,000 more ex-slaves.

The Fugitive Slave Act didn't satisfy anyone. Northerners were no longer able to think themselves insulated from the moral stain of slavery, and William Lloyd Garrison burned a copy of the Constitution, calling it "a covenant with death, and an agreement with hell." The Southerners were also unhappy and complained that Northerners were unlawfully refusing to help capture the slaves. Whether Lincoln really told Harriet Beecher Stowe that she was "the little woman who wrote the book that started this great war" is unclear. But even if apocryphal, the idea took root because it wasn't entirely false.

The Narrative Turn

There are two kinds of stories. There are the ones we tell about us to ourselves, and all the other stories. When Joan Didion said that we tell ourselves stories in order to live, she was thinking about the first kind of stories. Without them we'd still live, breathe, eat, and so on, but we'd do it without a sense of personal identity.

John Locke thought that our identity is constituted by our memories of the past. Similarly, Charles Taylor writes that we understand our lives only by seeing them embedded in a narrative.[5] What makes me really me are the stories that connect me with things that happened when I was a child, a teenager, and a minute ago. Without long- and short-term memory, I would lack a sense of what makes me the same person over the passage of time.

Suppose that, because of retrograde amnesia, I couldn't remember anything prior to the 2000 election. I could remember what happened afterwards, but not before, not Watergate or the First Iraq War. People like that do exist. In an extreme case, HM (his name hidden to protect his privacy) lost his long-term memory after an operation. He could only remember things that happened a moment ago. If you chatted with him, you'd think he was an ordinary person, but if you returned a few minutes later he'd have no memory of having talked to you. "It's like waking up in a dream," he said.[6] The hero of the film *Memento* (2000) suffered from the same disorder, as did Rosencrantz and Guildenstern in the Tom Stoppard play of that name. In such cases, Locke and Taylor would question whether we'd be talking about the same person, over time. Things no longer remembered and impossible to retrieve from a mental trash folder belonged to another person, and Locke thought the memory-less man could not be blamed for what he had done.[7]

Happily, there are few people like HM. We'll remember things we've done, even if we see them through rose-tinted glasses. And as we do so, we'll find other people intruding, if only because we're curious about how we rank in the pecking order. Salieri was embittered when he recognized his inferiority to Mozart. When he was thirty-three, Julius Caesar wept because he was still a nobody, while at that age Alexander had conquered the world.

Apart from comparing ourselves with other people, we're simply curious about them. We're what Aristotle called a *zōon politikon*, a political or social animal, and we'll want to meet other people, to learn something from them, to be entertained by them. Contact with other people satisfies our need for solidarity, which is one of the most basic of human needs. If the other person is a friend, we'll want to know about his past. We'll especially want to know everything about people we love, what they were like as kids, what movies they enjoy, what music they like.

Because we're curious about other people, there will be a market for biographies and autobiographies. Sometimes that's nothing more than voyeurism, and we all have a taste for that. We've made stars of people such as Paris Hilton because we enjoy watching the bizarre and outrageous. Beyond accounts of real people, we'll also want to read novels, to delight in Hugo Rahner's magical play-world.[8] "O Jesu, this is excellent sport," we'll say, when Falstaff invites us to watch his play. We leave behind adulthood's grim moral life and let Falstaff pretend to be Prince Hal's father.

> FALSTAFF: Banish Harvey, banish Russell, banish Poins; but
> for sweet Jack Oldcastle, kind Jack Oldcastle, true
> Jack Falstaff, valiant Jack Oldcastle, and therefore
> more valiant being, as he is, old Jack Oldcastle,

> banish him not thy Harry's company: banish not
> him thy Harry's company. Banish plump Jack, and
> banish all the world.

But reality intrudes when Hal steps out from the play and says, "I do; I will."[9] *Henry V*, the story of how Prince Hal becomes the valiant King Henry, is also a tragedy that breaks Falstaff's heart.

If stories can mask reality, they also have the power to reveal truths hidden from the world. *Hamlet* is a story about stories, beginning with the ghost story told to Hamlet and Horatio. The shade of his father tells Hamlet how his stepfather killed him to become king. To exact his revenge Hamlet will employ another story, told in a play ("the play's the thing") that shows how his father was poisoned. From this the king realizes that Hamlet has become dangerous and arranges for Hamlet to play in a duel with Laertes, whose foils are secretly tipped with poison. All will die, but, before he does, Hamlet ensures that the play's secrets will be revealed when he asks Horatio "to tell my story."

The centrality of stories has led to a *narrative turn* in politics and social research, where the building blocks of reality are not facts or events so much as the stories we tell about them. Stories can be manipulative and can mislead, by presenting a narrative with little factual basis. Nevertheless, their emotional salience is needed when a normative response is required, as in Dickens's stories about people left behind. Facts and statistics might tell us how to promote the common good, but not why we should care to do so. We need a Dickens or Tolstoy for that.

MORAL LEARNING

Today we wouldn't say we need kindness. Justice has taken its place. But if kindness made us more liberal its abandonment has made us illiberal. As justice is defined today, it's encouraged the woke left to abandon free-speech principles and turn commonplace conservative ideas into thought crimes. Kindness itself is made a vice, if it offers forgiveness to the enemy.

Among the non-believing "nones," that was to be expected, for the Bible's narratives about forgiveness have been forgotten. The Jewish people stumble again and again, but the Covenant persists. God forgives them and never declares a breach of contract. In the Gospels, Christ never wrote anything down except once. The scribes and Pharisees had brought Him a woman taken in adultery and told Him that the law would have her stoned. Would he reject this? Instead, He wrote on the ground with His finger, and said that the first stone should be cast by a person without sin. After this, He wrote once more on the ground,[10] and the scribes and Pharisees left, without casting a stone. The focus had shifted from the woman's adultery to their own sins.

If Christ chose not to reveal what he had written, He had a reason. He taught through stories—parables—and not through rules. Saint Francis understood why He did so when he told his followers to "preach the Gospel at all times. If necessary, use words." While we don't know what Christ wrote, we do know that He thought that rules don't suffice unless tempered with self-awareness and mercy.

Christ had understood who the scribes and Pharisees really were. That's not the same thing as knowing someone. I know someone when I can recognize him in the street. I don't need a story for that. To understand his story, I must be able to see what motivates him and why he acted as he did. Before judging him, I must be able to sit in his shoes.

That is the job of the historian, said philosopher R. G. Collingwood. To understand who Washington or Lincoln were, the historian must be able to get into their minds and reenact their deeds as they themselves saw them.

> History is thus the self-knowledge of the living mind. For even when the events which the historian studies are events that happened in the distant past, the condition of their being historically known is that they should "vibrate in the historian's mind"; that is to say, that the evidence for them should be here and now before him and intelligible to him. For history is not contained in books or documents; it lives only, as a present interest and pursuit, in the mind of the historian when he criticizes and

interprets those documents, and by so doing relives for himself the states of mind into which he inquires.[11]

That makes the historian's task much like that of a novelist. Each tells a story that aims to present a coherent whole, one which reveals an integrated mind that meets every situation with the same desires and motivations. Whatever might happen, a character must act as he does and cannot act otherwise. In Anouilh's *Antigone* (1944), the chorus tells us, "Her name is Antigone, and she must play her role right to the end." The difference between the novelist and the historian is that the latter's story is meant to be true. The novelist might also be a moralist and, like Dickens, pass judgment on what he narrates.[12]

By asking us to understand fully an offender, moral learning is liberal. It inclines us to mildness in sentencing when the condemned is shown to have a good heart. *Tout comprendre c'est tout pardoner.* It's also liberal when it asks the hypocrite to lay down his stones. A book, ostensibly about other people, might turn out to be about ourselves if we recognize that we're guilty of the same faults. "When you meet such a character as Micawber in Dickens," observes Northrop Frye, "you feel that there's a bit of Micawber in almost everyone you know, including yourself.[13]

The moral lesson is cheapened, however, when it caters to our self-regard by inviting us to identify with the moral hero. Harper Lee's 1960 novel *To Kill a Mockingbird* is popular because it asks the reader to picture himself as the liberal Atticus Finch. In 2015 Lee published a sequel to her book, *Go Set a Watchman,* in which Finch was presented as something less than an anti-racist hero. The new book shocked its bien-pensant readers. It shouldn't have.

A less manipulative novel pierces through our self-love. In Albert Camus' 1956 novel *The Fall* (*La chute*),[14] a lawyer who preens in his imagined virtue discovers that he's not a moral hero when he abandons a woman who has thrown herself from a bridge. He might have saved her but instead walks away. Unless you recognize yourself in the lawyer, you'll have missed the point, said Camus. For each one of us there's a person whom we were meant to rescue and whom we failed to save.[15] "Nothing is so difficult as not deceiving oneself," wrote Ludwig Wittgenstein.[16]

In that sense, Harper Lee's feel-good *To Kill a Mockingbird* was a failure and her sequel a superior book. That was also why Flannery O'Connor's short story "Everything that Rises Must Converge" (1961) is so much better than both of them. Like Lee's novels, O'Connor's story is set in a state in the Deep South that is painfully emerging from its racist past, but O'Connor refuses to offer cheap grace to Julian, the ostensibly more liberal character. He is a spoiled boy who is deeply ashamed of his mother, a smug racist. "Everything that gave her pleasure was small and depressed him."[17] But when she dies at the end of the story, his liberalism is recognized as a mask he adopts to justify his hatred for the only person who will ever love him.

In sum, Trilling was right to link the narrative turn with liberalism. Not merely are American stories liberal in the sense that they're rooted in the moral sense of a liberal people, but by nature they incline us to liberalism. They awaken our sense of empathy for suffering people left behind, and they ask us to understand ourselves more closely. We become less ready to judge unfairly, lest we ourselves be judged.

17.

LIBERAL UNCERTANTIES

In societies that think self-esteem a positive good, uncertainty and self-doubt are regarded as psychic faults. Motivational speaker Tony Robbins thinks they're a kind of mental illness that holds people back. On his website, he contrasts self-doubters with the assertive, self-confident people who always seem to know the right thing to do. "When they enter a room, people notice. When they speak, people listen."

Robbins has a point. We naturally gravitate to people who seem wholly sure of themselves, who never betray a flicker of uncertainty. They seem to possess an inner strength that we can't help but admire. That's one reason why high-self-esteem psychopaths so easily prey upon self-doubters, and why we tend to elect narcissists who demand our trust and then betray it. It's also why there is such a thing as excessive self-confidence.

Overconfidence can be a fatal flaw. Varus thought the German tribes no match for his Roman legions. General Elphinstone felt a retreat from Kabul would bring his troops to safety, and General

Custer believed that Little Big Horn would be a routine policing action. Military blunders often begin with a leader's mistaken self-confidence.

As a moral question, excessive self-confidence may blind a person to his own faults and make him too quick to condemn others. That was the point of the story about the woman taken in adultery. It was also why Christ told his parable about the Pharisee and the publican. The Pharisee boasted that he tithed and fasted twice a week and gave thanks that he was better than the publican at the back of the temple. For his part, the publican looked down and said, "O God, be merciful to me a sinner." His prayer would be heard, said Christ, but not that of the Pharisee. The self-confident would be humbled, and the humble self-doubter would be exalted.[1]

Self-confidence about whether one will be "justified" and admitted to Heaven at death is condemned by the Church as the unforgiveable sin of presumption. It might be a theological error if it denies the indeterminacy of God's grace, and it's a moral fault if the presumptuous think that they're liberated from moral restraints because God will take care of them. They might see themselves as "Justified Sinners" and assured of Heaven even if they sin.

JUSTIFIED SINNERS

The permission slip to sin was the subject of James Hogg's 1824 gothic novel *The Private Memoirs and Confessions of a Justified Sinner*. The novel is divided between the delusional memoir of Robert Wringhim, the justified sinner, and an editor who recounts what really happened to him. As a child, Wringhim was raised in the strict Calvinist faith of Scottish Presbyterians who believed that some were predestined for Heaven and some for Hell and that nothing they could do would alter their fate. His minister, whom he called "Father" and who might have been his true father, persuaded him that he had been justified and chosen for salvation. His name had been written into the book of life, and nothing would change that. There are some sects in today's America who still think like that, who tell their members they can know whether they've been saved. For them, self-doubt reveals a lack of faith, if not greater sins.

In his memoir, Wringhim recounts how he fell in with a mysterious shapeshifter called Gil-Martin, who is really the devil in disguise. Gil-Martin becomes Wringhim's directing mind and persuades him to torment and kill his brother. He also kills his mother and a young woman whom he has seduced. The demonic possession is so thorough that he does all this without being conscious of his actions. His crimes begin to be observed, however, and he is driven from his home and made to become a vagabond, sleeping in barns and tormented by demons. In the end he hangs himself, knowing that this is the unforgiveable sin of despair and that his suicide will doom him to Hell.

Hogg's novel was a satire on an extreme form of Calvinism, but we don't have to look far to find the Justified Sinners of our day. They're the January 6 rioters who stormed the Capitol and the mobs that pillage and burn as they shout, "No Justice, No Peace." All are asserting the right to riot if they don't get their way because they serve a higher goal. The difference is that the motivation today is ideological rather than religious.

In Seattle, an Antifa group purported to secede from the city by creating a downtown Capitol Hill Autonomous Zone (CHAZ) and demanding that the police be defunded. Seattle Mayor Jenny Durkan welcomed the protests and compared the occupation to a "summer of love." She banned the use of tear gas to rein in the violence, and police abandoned a precinct station within the CHAZ. Predictably, chaos resulted. On June 20, 2020, two people were shot and one died. Another person was killed nine days later, and women were raped. First responders were denied access to the area. Buildings were trashed and burned, and people defecated in the streets. Crime in the area rose 525 percent over the same period in 2019. The press had written puff pieces about Antifa,[2] whose members thought themselves Justified Sinners.

The CHAZ protestors belonged to a lumpen underclass of jobless urban radicals. The students who protested a Federalist Society speaker at Stanford Law School in 2023 were from a wholly different class, an entitled group that had been admitted to one of the nation's leading law schools, and whose members could expect after graduation to be hired at a starting salary of more than $200,000 a year. In an aristocratic society, they are our princelings.

They have the strongest sense of entitlement. When they heard that Judge Kyle Duncan, a conservative, had been invited to speak at their school, they decided to take action. They shouted him down and screamed obscenities at his face. "Scumbag," they yelled. "You're a liar. We hate you." One student said she hoped Duncan's daughter would be raped. They were his intellectual and moral superiors, they told him. He had graduated from a lower-ranked school and wouldn't have been admitted to Stanford. The U.S. Marshals who were charged with protecting the judge concluded that he was in physical danger and escorted him out of the building.[3]

None of the students were punished for this. The law-school dean did send the judge a letter of apology, but then she ended up on the receiving end of a protest. Hundreds of masked, black-clad students hijacked her next class. Walking back to her office, she faced a gauntlet of hundreds of furious students. Afterwards, recognizing that they had harmed their job prospects, the protesters demanded that their names be hidden and their faces obscured on the videos. But their posters had plastered the names and faces of the Federalist Society members who had invited the judge.

Before the protesters could think themselves justified and excused from the duty to let the judge speak, they had to think his beliefs so hateful that ordinary moral requirements were suspended. *The Nation* magazine agrees with them,[4] and that is also how Antifa sees things. If, as they think, all their enemies are fascists and they're the antifascists, they can do whatever they want. When the enemy is Hitler, and the world is divided between Schmittian friends and enemies, everything is permitted.

Lionel Trilling called this the Angelic Fallacy, the idea that everything is forgiven when one is on the side of the angels. "How can we possibly be guilty when we have in mind the welfare of others, and of *so many* others."[5] In his 1947 novel, *The Middle of the Journey*, Trilling took on the excuses the Stalinists thought this had given them.

The book is set in the 1930s, when nearly every intellectual thought that the economic crisis could only be solved through communism. At the time, Trilling was one of them, and in the novel he appears as Arthur Croom, an academic who has joined a number of communist-front groups. By 1947, however, Trilling had repudiated communism and become a liberal, and, in the novel, he is portrayed as its principal character, John Laskell. Whittaker Chambers appears halfway through as Gifford Maxim and very nearly walks off with the book. Like Chambers, Maxim is a former Soviet agent who has become an anti-communist and now fears for his life. The repellent Nancy Croom, Arthur's wife, is what Chambers had been, a Marxist who had spied for the Soviet Union.

Maxim is the book's most arresting character. He has all the good lines, and it's a mark of Trilling's liberalism that Maxim is given the chance to present his case so forcefully. Trilling and Chambers knew each other, and while they weren't friends Trilling recognized Chambers' honesty and decency. When an Alger Hiss investigator asked Trilling to give him some dirt about Chambers, Trilling replied, "Whittaker Chambers is a man of honor." Writing twenty-seven years later, Trilling vividly recalled the investigator's outburst of contemptuous rage.[6]

That didn't mean that he agreed with Chambers, however. In the novel, Maxim tells Laskell, you have to choose between me and the Crooms. *No, I don't*, answers Laskell. *You're telling me that, if I reject communism, I have to become a right-wing reactionary like you. I don't buy it. I'll remain a liberal, while I expect you will turn illiberal.*

The novel was remarkably prescient and predicted how an anti-communism devoid of self-doubt might turn into right-wing McCarthyism. When the Hiss case broke out in 1948, many saw how the Crooms had resembled the Hisses, even as Maxim was clearly Whittaker Chambers. Trilling had never met Alger and Priscilla Hiss, but the parallels were so close that Trilling's novel became required reading for the FBI.

Liberal Skepticism

Trilling's self-doubt differed from the philosophical skepticism that denies we're entitled to believe any statement about the world. Like Descartes, the skeptic might fear that everything he sees is a dream and that what his senses report are illusions. Alternatively, the Pyrrhonian Skeptic might simply suspend judgment, choosing neither to believe nor not to believe. But Trilling's prudential skeptic was not a philosopher. His liberalism simply admitted the possibility of error, and he refused to believe the extreme ideologues who would impose a cruel illiberalism upon all of us.

E. M. Forster described liberalism's diffidence and murkiness in *Howards End* (1910) when he contrasted the morally thick, rule-bound Henry Wilcox with the more morally aware Margaret Schlegel. To moral questions, Wilcox brings a lawyer's clarity and also his limitations. By contrast, Margaret understands morality's necessary messiness:

> Life's very difficult and full of surprises. At all events I've got as far as that. To be humble, to be kind, to go straight ahead, to love people rather than pity them, to remember the submerged—well, one can't do all these things at once, worse luck, because they're so contradictory. It's then that proportion comes in—to live by proportion. Don't begin with proportion. Only prigs do that. (76)

The liberal self-doubter will share Margaret's openness to the importance of context and the sense that we're all connected to everyone else. He'll be suspicious of ideological shortcuts that ask us to ignore the broader consequences of a choice, and by instinct he'll shy away from the absolutist who would turn every moral question into an issue of rights. He might want to concede free-speech rights in nearly all cases and still wonder whether neo-Nazis should be permitted to march through Skokie.

Apart from extreme cases, he will agree with John Stuart Mill's prudential arguments in *On Liberty* against censoring people. He'll think that "settled science" is an oxymoron and that the badge of truth for a contested idea is its willingness to be challenged. Opinions that are censored might possibly be true, or if partly in error might yet contain a portion of the truth. In either case, he'll want to hear the other side. It's what they teach law students, at schools other than Stanford. *Audi alteram partem* was the motto inscribed on the building of my law school.

We're not to accept as true a claim just because a consensus of people believes it. Truth is not about counting numbers. The scientific method doesn't censor nonbelievers, and we've learned from experience that stories in partisan newspapers that begin with "experts believe" are often wrong. We've seen too many consensus claims about the origins of COVID and "Modern Monetary Theory" proven false.

Self-doubt was never so needed as it is today, when extreme partisans on both sides are so willing to believe that the country is only a short step away from tyranny. On the right, the 2016 "Flight 93 Election" essay likened America to the plane that crashed into Shanksville, PA on 9/11 after its passengers attacked the hijackers. The 2016 election gives you a choice, said the essay. Charge the cockpit or you die. You may die anyway. But if you don't try, death is certain, in the form of Hillary Clinton. It's like Russian Roulette, and with Trump, at least you can spin the cylinder and take your chances.

Flight 93 alarmists on the right are paid back with interest by Flight 93 scaremongers on the left, who think that Trump and his supporters are democracy-denying fascists. The f-word is casually tossed around by woke politicians to describe innocuous conservative policies, as though Hitler were just about to seize power. "When we talk about progressive values," says Rep. Alexandria Ocasio-Cortez (D-NY), "I can say what my progressive value is, and that is freedom over fascism."[7] And if you want to know where fascism comes from, *The Nation* magazine has the answer. It's the burbs, and all the little Hitlers with their leaf-blowers: "America's Suburbs Are Breeding Grounds for Fascism."[8]

Trilling didn't fall for this and traced the origins of liberalism back to the self-doubting Montaigne.[9] Maxim and the Crooms abounded with self-confidence. Not Laskell, which is why some readers thought that Maxim had had the better of the contest. But that was not what Trilling had meant to say. For him, self-doubt and diffidence were liberal virtues and a shield against the way in which overconfidence blinds one to the requirements of humanity.

The liberal possesses what John Keats called a "negative capability," the ability of coming to rest in doubt and uncertainty without reaching a too-hasty conclusion. The openness to a conflicting vision, the uncertainty about ultimate ends, can look like a weakness, a want of confidence, by people too full of themselves. It's more likely just the opposite, however, since it requires moral strength to resist the temptation to make a snap judgment. It doesn't take courage to go along with the crowd. It's the holdout who should be admired, and the fiercer the demand to conform, the more it should be resisted. The greatest of thinkers—Ludwig Wittgenstein, Richard Feynman—were people who kept on questioning and did not permit their minds to come to rest.

The self-doubter seeks wisdom from wherever he may get it, if not through his reasoning than through his emotions. Nancy Croom admires Duck Caldwell, a shiftless wastrel, because he fits her image of a proletarian, but Laskell's instinctive sense that the man has an evil heart turns out to be more accurate.

Our emotions, hunches, and instincts are coded with information that we ignore at our risk. That's an idea most closely associated with Edmund Burke and economist Friedrich Hayek. "Principles are often more effective guides for action," said Hayek, "when they appear as no more than an unreasoned prejudice, a general feeling that certain things simply 'are not done.'"[10] More recently, experimental psychologist Gerd Gigerenzer has shown that our instincts and hunches are smarter than we might think. They are "fast and frugal" and permit us to make quick decisions based on limited information, economizing on wasteful overthinking and over-searching. They can even lead us to more accurate decisions than pure ratiocination would give us.

Hayek ridiculed the hubris of economic planners who think they can cabin an economy into tight, little rules and set commodity prices in the illusion that that they know the worth of things. The regulator's fixed prices can never match the knowledge reflected in prices struck in open markets by millions of traders.[11] In time, even Soviet leaders became Hayekians. When all the world becomes communist, said Mikhail Gorbachev, we'll let New Zealand have an open economy to teach us how to set prices.

As a literary scholar and the author of a biography of Matthew Arnold, Trilling also believed in the lessons our aesthetic imagination might teach us. In *The Middle of the Journey*, the spokesperson for dated *Yellow Book* aestheticism is Duck's wife, Emily. Everyone views her ideas with condescension, but Laskell makes love to her, and she becomes the book's moral center, offering Laskell absolution for their affair and for his share of responsibility in the death of her daughter.

The self-doubter is also a Burkean who will reconsider his beliefs when they conflict with received beliefs. Even John Stuart Mill recognized the informational value of a settled tradition. In his essay on Coleridge, he wrote how the poet had understood that "the long duration of a belief . . . is at least proof of an adaptation in it to some portion or other of the human mind; and if, on digging down to the root, we do not find, as is generally the case, some truth, we shall find some natural want or requirement of human nature which the doctrine in question is fitted to satisfy."[12] Montaigne also agreed that radical reforms are ordinarily very imprudent. "To change the foundations of so great a structure, that is a job for those who wipe out a picture in order to clean it, who want to reform defects of detail by universal confusion and cure illness by death."[13]

There are no moral safe harbors, however, not in our emotions, traditions, or reasons. They might all be colored by prejudices and personal animus. Indeed, it's hard to believe that they're not. We might think that, through self-reflection, we can correct for this, but our conscience doesn't offer an inerrant touchstone. Even Aquinas thought that it might mislead us,[14] and Blaise Pascal wrote that men never do evil so completely and cheerfully as when they believe they are following their conscience.[15] I am quite willing to concede that the Antifa rioters believe in the rightness of their acts, but that doesn't excuse them.

Doubting everything, the prudential skeptic understands the cloudiness of many moral choices, and this offers a refuge from those who think the world neatly divides between us and them. In *The Middle of the Journey*, only the young give themselves over to murderous certainties. Self-doubt is the virtue of the older people, people like the middle-aged Laskell or the elderly Benjamin Franklin at the 1787 Constitutional Convention in Philadelphia.

At eighty-two, Franklin was the oldest delegate and often had to be carried to it in a litter. Too weak to stand, he asked others to read his speeches for him. This was his last act, and he knew it. He had been a chief player in every movement towards independence, from the 1754 Albany Plan on, and now with only a few years to live he wanted desperately for the Convention to succeed. He let others quarrel about the details, so long as the delegates agreed on a new constitution. With the benefit of hindsight, we'd like to think this a sure thing. It wasn't, however, and on the Convention's last day Franklin rose to address the delegates. Some of them had objected to parts of it. He also had his reservations. But as he grew older, he said, he became more likely to mistrust his judgment.

He made fun of the overconfident. He spoke of a French lady who had said that, while she didn't know how it happened, whenever she disagreed with anyone it was always she who was in the right. Don't be like that woman, he told the delegates. "On the whole, Sir, I cannot help expressing a wish that every member of the Convention who may still have objections to it, would with me, on this occasion doubt a little of his own infallibility."[16]

He then moved that the delegates sign the document, which all but three did. As they walked to the dais to put their names on it, he remarked on the chair at which George Washington had sat. It featured a sun over the ocean. He had often wondered, during the course of the Convention, whether it represented a rising or a setting sun. "But now at length I have the happiness to know that it is a rising and not a setting sun."[17] He had put away self-doubts about whether America would remain liberal.

18.

THE WANDERER

There are only two stories. A man goes on a journey. *The Odyssey.*
Or a stranger comes to town. *The Iliad.* They're really the same
story. In both there's a wanderer.

The Greek myths begin when someone decides to wander. Zeus
often descended to Earth, and his escapades were the scandal of
Olympus. Theseus took part in so many exploits that there was a
saying "nothing without Theseus."[1] It began when he left Troezen
for Athens, taking the dangerous land route and killing bandits and
villains along the way. But almost as soon as he reached Athens, he
left for Crete to confront and kill the Minotaur. He returned to become king of Athens, but, as he was never satisfied at home, he took
to the sea with Jason and the Argonauts, and that was how the story
of Phaedra and Hippolytus began.

Aeneas lingers in Carthage and spends a whole winter in happy
self-indulgence. But that was not his destiny. He was meant to be
the ruler of Italy and to bring the whole world under the rule of law.
When the gods remind him of this, he knows he must wander on,
even if he must leave the woman he loves and become the remote
cause of the Punic Wars.

The greatest of travels was to the underworld, which Orpheus visited to claim Eurydice, and where Odysseus met the companions who had fallen on his travels. Later Aeneas would find his father in the underworld, and modern literature began when Virgil conducted Dante through Hell. In most Christian denominations, the faithful are asked to believe that, in the words of the Apostle's Creed, Christ descended into Hell and rose again on the third day.

Religions get their start with travelers. In Judaism and Christianity, God tells Abraham, "Go from your country, your people and your father's household to the land I will show you."[2] The New Testament begins with a Joseph looking for a manger and with Christ leaving Nazareth for Galilee. Islam has its *hijra* from Mecca to Medina. Things need a wanderer to get going.

The hero announces his arrival by wandering into history. He is Caesar crossing the Rubicon, or Napoleon crossing the Alps. He is Richard the Lionheart embarked on the Third Crusade and Dwight Eisenhower leading what he called a *Crusade in Europe*. He is Galahad on a quest for the Holy Grail. He is Isaac Jogues, leaving France for the last time and knowing he will never see it again.

Travel alone doesn't make one a wanderer. The Crusader on his way to Jerusalem and the pilgrim on the road to Canterbury weren't really wanderers, since they had a destination in mind. Columbus had a goal. He wanted to get to China, but the New World got in his way. Like Moses, Abraham was bound for Canaan. Fugitive slaves also had a destination in mind, a place they called the Promised Land. Isaac Jogues traveled to seek martyrdom. They weren't wanderers.

The wanderer travels without a fixed goal in mind. The knight-errant's quest was a random walk into deep forests and down strange lanes. He took the unbeaten path where strange adventures and fabulous beasts might await him. On his way he might chance upon a *peregrinus* from a foreign land or one of the wandering scholars—the *vagrantes*—about whom the troubadours sang. None of them were lost. They simply didn't have a destination in mind. They were wanderers, and as J. R. R. Tolkien observed not all who wander are lost.

THE WANDERER

In *Moby-Dick*, Ishmael was a wanderer. He travels to the sea, but the sea is not a destination. Instead, the watery part of the world offered a rudderless escape from a soul-destroying life on shore.

> Whenever I find myself growing grim about the mouth; whenever it is a damp, drizzly November in my soul; whenever I find myself involuntarily pausing before coffin warehouses, and bringing up the rear of every funeral I meet; and especially whenever my hypos get such an upper hand of me, that it requires a strong moral principle to prevent me from deliberately stepping into the street, and methodically knocking people's hats off—then, I account it high time to get to sea as soon as I can.

Before there was liberalism, there was wandering. Before there was a destination in a Lockean state, there was someone who, like Chuck Berry, wandered about with no particular place to go. But while they didn't have a destination in mind, they'd likely end up as a liberal. That might happen in three ways. First, the wanderer was by disposition a liberal, someone open to new possibilities, a person without ties, a *voyageur sans bagage*. Like Jack Reacher, the wanderer carries nothing with him, except possibly a passport and a toothbrush. Second, his travels would bring him to rest at a place that suited him, and this would be a liberal society. Finally, the receiving state would recognize this and liberalize itself to attract him.

It's people whom the wanderer goes forth to meet. Not empty beaches. There's nothing more banal than a lonely stretch of sand. But add people tanning beside their cabanas or having a drink at the bar and you're drawn to the beach, since the friendliest of people await you there. The instinct of sociability brings them to the strand, and what is behind this is a sense of benevolence.

THE VOYAGEUR SANS BAGAGE

Not so long ago there was a cult of the wanderer. He might be a frat kid from *Animal House* on a road trip, or an ex-serviceman cruising

Route 66 in a top-down Corvette. He was the eighteen-year-old Paddy Leigh Fermor who walked from Holland to Constantinople after he was expelled from his public school.

Like Fermor, young people ought to wander. They're not to be yoked to a harness and ordered what to do. There is no set of rules to tell them what to make of their lives. They'll have to find out for themselves, and that means wandering from idea to idea, cause to cause, and job to job, like the heroes of a *Bildungsroman*. They should be encouraged to follow where their curiosity leads, and that was the theme of many of our folktales. They told kids it was OK to trade the cow for the magic beanstalk. Go off and seek your fortune, they told Jack. Be a giant-killer. They became folktales because they were repeated, and they were repeated because they offered good advice.

Famously, the wanderer was Jack Kerouac who traveled *On the Road* because "the only people for me are the mad ones, the ones who are mad to live, mad to talk, mad to be saved, desirous of everything at the same time, the ones who never yawn or say a commonplace thing, but burn, burn, burn like fabulous yellow roman candles exploding like spiders across the stars and in the middle you see the blue centerlight pop and everybody goes 'Awww.'"[3] In the placid and happy 1950s, we yearned for the open road because we knew we were born to wander. Homelife is sweet, but *prends garde à la douceur des choses*, warned Paul-Jean Toulet. Beware of the sweetness of things.

Kerouac told his readers about a forbidden life of sex, drugs, and jazz. There's a pearl waiting for you somewhere, and to find it all you need do is walk to the edge of town and hitch a ride. That was something I did in boarding school when I was fifteen. I'd say I was going home, but what I really did was head down the highway and hold out my thumb. Like Kerouac, I learned how to talk to the drivers and let them know they didn't make a mistake in picking me up. It's not done anymore, and I can't imagine how I got along without email or cell phones, except that there was a confraternity of the road, and wherever you ended up you'd find people who seemed to be waiting for you and who understood why you were there, even if you didn't.

In Germany, it was called wanderlust and associated with the Romantic cult of nameless longing. The wanderer travels through both the world and his own psyche. Wandering brings self-understanding, and when the traveler looks ahead to the path it stares back at him, like the *Wanderer above the Sea of Fog* by Caspar David Friedrich (1774–1840).

The wanderer is on the side of exploration and novelty, and by nature is a liberal. The stay-at-homes who find the psychic cost of leaving unbearable are conservatives. The liberal might feel a bit of that too, but this is exceeded by the psychic cost of staying home. He possesses an openness and curiosity, a willingness to shake things up that is always on the side of liberalism.

Louis Hartz traced the origins of American liberalism to wanderers from Old Europe. "It is one thing to stay at home and fight the 'canon and feudal law,' and it is another to leave it far behind."[4] By crossing the ocean, America's wanderers had become liberals and escaped Europe's social revolutions. The Europeans had their Reign of Terror, while we had the 1787 Constitutional Convention.

Many of America's wanderers came from England, and, in *The Origins of English Individualism* (1978), Alan Macfarlane argues that that country owes its liberal traditions to its relative mobility. As early as the thirteenth century, land was frequently bought and sold, and many of these transactions were between non-kin. One study found that few of the names in a 1367 registry were to be found in the same village seventy-six years later.[5] Much earlier than the French, the English had wandered to the city and to a freer society, and Macfarlane said that this was the origin of English individualism. Seven hundred years ago, Englishmen were highly mobile both geographically and socially, market-oriented and acquisitive—moderns in short.

If the wanderer left his farms and followed Dick Whittington to London,[6] that also helped explain why liberalism took root in England. City air makes you free, it was said, since it offers anonymity and an escape from prying eyes. Where one does not know the neighbors, the social stigma of promise-breaking is weak. That's why the divorce and bankruptcy rates are higher in the more mobile parts of America.[7]

Historically, the most liberal cities were seaports, like Pericles' Athens. They attracted the restless Ishmaels whose wanderlust wasn't satisfied by the road, and who wanted to ship out to someplace more exotic. Coastal cities were also more likely to have foreign-born residents, wanderers from other countries who brought with them new ideas, customs, and religions, like *Moby-Dick*'s Queequeg. Even if he had no desire to travel, the urban resident in a port city was perforce a wanderer.

Cities offered something else to the wanderer. Hunter-gatherers like the Hurons that Isaac Jogues sought to convert, or herders like Cain, had to perform all the tasks necessary to keep body and soul together. They couldn't rely on others to perform them. That changed when people moved to cities like Siena and became good at a single task. For other things they'd trade with the butcher, the baker, and the potter, who themselves were skilled in their trades. People learned to depend upon others and to get along with them, and this fostered Montesquieu's *doux commerce* and was a source of liberalism.

Since the wanderer shakes things up, some conservatives will want to keep him out and oppose immigration. Open borders alarm them, especially the mass immigration portrayed in Jean Raspail's *The Camp of the Saints* (1973), in which Western civilization is threatened by mass immigration from the Third World. Similarly, Michel Houellebecq's *Submission* (2015) described an Islamic takeover in France, which soft-hearted and cynical Western liberals contrive to permit, even though the introduction of sharia law in France would prove fatal to liberalism. In the end, suggested Houellebecq, it was really the illiberal conservative who would welcome Islamic illiberalism. The true liberal will welcome immigration, but only a liberty-preserving liberalism, and the example of Canada shows this can be done through immigration policies that don't discriminate based on race or religion and which attract liberals from abroad.

The Wanderer Comes Home to Rest

While the road might beckon you, what if you could never leave it? In that case it would be more like a punishment than a pearl. You'd be like the Flying Dutchman or the Ghost Rider in the Sky. You'd be like Cain, whom God condemns to wander for his sin. "I shall be a restless wanderer on the earth and whoever finds me will kill me."[8]

You'd be like the sea-weary *Seafarer* in the Anglo-Saxon poem, or the *Wanderer* (the *eardstapa*, from *eard* or earth, and *steppan* to step) who longs for the happier time before he left home. You'd be a man without a country and condemned to travel the seas forever, like Philip Nolan in Edward Everett Hale's story. You'd be like Satan, going to and fro in the earth and walking up and down in it.[9]

Like Odysseus, the wanderer must come at last to rest, home from the sea and the road. And the journey itself will have led him to a liberal country, even if he didn't begin his travels in search of it. He'll simply stop where he feels comfortable, and that's more likely to be America than Iran. He'll end his wandering at a place where there are plenty of opportunities to flourish, a place like Athens, where people are content to leave him alone if he's not bothering anyone. All the better if he's permitted to voice his opinions and participate in the democratic process.

When I was a child, there was a cheap little toy that came as a gift in a Cracker Jack box. It was a piece of cardboard covered in plastic, and in it were little steel balls. You were supposed to shake it so that each of the balls would come to rest in the cardboard holes. That's what our migration patterns are like. Half of us were born in a state or country other than the state in which we now live. We were shaken up and ended up in a state that suited us, and it would be liberal. We're a country of wanderers, and that has made America liberal.

In economics there's a name for this. It's called Tiebout sorting, from an article by Charles Tiebout on how mobile people sort themselves out by where they end up.[10] If they don't like where they are, they can "vote with their feet." Were moving costless, we'd all end up in a community that perfectly matched our preferences about things like schools, taxes, and crime. Of course, moving isn't costless, but half of us are like the little balls in the Cracker Jack game. We're going to be shaken up and we'll move, and the only question is where we'll go. Some will find themselves settling in California, some in Texas, but we'll all end up in liberal America and not Iran.

JURISDICTIONAL COMPETITION

The 1893 Columbian Exposition was held to commemorate the four-hundredth anniversary of Columbus's discovery of the Americas (they were off by a year). Harry Houdini was on hand to perform his magic acts, and Little Egypt danced the hoochie coochie. Cracker Jacks, Juicy Fruit gum, and Aunt Jemima pancake mix were first introduced to the public, and a little-known history professor read a paper that revolutionized historiography and invented public choice economics. His name was Fredrick Jackson Turner, and he was only thirty-one years of age.

American history was shaped by the frontier, said Turner, the border of settlement that from our earliest days was ever shifting westward. Eastern states were corrupt, undemocratic, and immobile, while Western states were the repository of republican virtue, democratic, and mobile. The East was illiberal, and the West was liberal. The East was the Court Party, the West was the Country Party.

The wanderer was more likely to be liberal, and so the Western states liberalized to attract him. They might hold a fair, as Chicago did in 1893 or St. Louis in 1904, or they might tailor their laws to appeal to him. They needed settlers and competed for people by offering them fresh starts, free land, and egalitarianism. They gave women the franchise, enacted initiative and referendum laws, and supported the popular election of senators under the Seventeenth Amendment.[11] They were liberals.

All this came to define the American Dream, the idea that there were boundless possibilities of self-improvement in this country. In time, the Eastern states that were losing people to the West began to compete for people by liberalizing themselves. Even Old Europe was swept into this, to retain people who would otherwise move to North America. Liberalism was the driving force of history, said Turner, and it all came from wanderers and the frontier.

Turner presented his essay "The Significance of the Frontier in American History" three years after the American census reported the disappearance of the frontier. Until then, there had always been an unmapped and unsettled wilderness, but by 1890 this had all been tamed. There's even less of a frontier today when every square foot in America can be viewed on Google Maps. But the idea of jurisdictional competition, the notion that states and cities compete for residents through their legal regime and public goods, is as powerful as ever and a core insight of public choice economics. It explains why cities have a stake in the quality of their schools and the integrity of their public officials. Bad schools lower housing values, and ordinary citizens will pay for public corruption when markets discount the municipal bonds of corrupt cities and states.[12]

Turner's Frontier Thesis has not fared as well among historians. It supplanted a racial "Germ" theory, which had held that liberty and democracy had originated with Germanic tribes, and which conservative restrictionists employed as a justification for limiting immigration from Eastern and Southern Europe. By contrast, the Frontier Thesis was liberal and racially neutral, and that is why illiberal and race-conscious modern historians have come full circle and rejected it. Nevertheless, the Frontier Thesis continues to explain how the demand for wanderers has helped make America liberal.

19.

LIBERAL FEMINISM

The wanderer is a liberal hero. But wanderers don't build civilizations without women. Frederick Jackson Turner's frontier was wonderfully entrepreneurial, but it was entirely masculine. For the most part, there weren't churches, either. Natty Bumppo was unmarried and unchurched.

In a study of pew rents, Roger Finke and Rodney Stark found that religious membership in America had always increased over time. Only 17 percent of Americans were members of a church in 1776, compared to 62 percent in 1980.[1] Women had made the difference. The two authors reported that church membership grew as the frontier receded and the percentage of women increased.

That shouldn't surprise anyone. Religion restrained male aggressiveness, and the origins of feminism can be traced to the Judeo-Christian tradition, to the matriarchs in the Jewish Bible and Christianity's female saints. Where you'll find a true patriarchy is in the pre-Christian family-based religions of Greece and Rome, where men headed the household and women were given away in marriage.

First-wave Feminism

Since conservatives prize religion, the link between women and churches should have made them sympathetic to feminism, at least in its first iteration as liberal feminism. The 1848 Seneca Falls Declaration, drafted by Elizabeth Cady Stanton, modeled itself on the Declaration of Independence. "We hold these truths to be self-evident," it said, "that all men and women are created equal." It asked that women be given the vote, that they should have full property rights and equal access to education. Men slowly came to agree, and it was progressive Republicans who provided the crucial congressional support for the Nineteenth Amendment's extension of the franchise. The Amendment came into effect in August 1920, and that November women cast their ballots for Warren G. Harding.

What followed in the subsequent decades was a social revolution in which glass ceilings were slowly shattered in law, business, and politics. In the 1950s, when Sandra Day O'Connor attended Stanford Law School, only 10 percent of U.S. law students were women, and good jobs eluded them after they graduated. O'Connor herself was forced to take a position as an unpaid deputy county attorney. Today, however, a majority of law students are women. There are more women than men in the workforce, and most managers are women too. Conservative feminists, such as Christina Hoff Sommers, the author of *The War Against Boys* (2000) and *Who Stole Feminism* (1994), argue that the battle for feminism is essentially over in America. The women have won.

No father will wish to limit his daughter's career options. Should she want to stay at home or work outside, the choice is hers, and both parents will wholly support her. Some conservatives might be sorry that we've moved on from an older America in which men were breadwinners and women stayed home. However, even they will recognize that two-income families are largely a consequence of something that can't be changed: a welfare state that requires high marginal income rates to support it.

A number of federal laws protect women in the workforce. Title VII of the Civil Rights Act prohibits discrimination on the basis of sex, and, under the 1978 Pregnancy Discrimination Act of 1978, this includes decisions based on pregnancy. The Family and Medical Leave Act of 1993 requires twelve weeks of unpaid maternity leave for mothers if they work for a company with fifty or more employees. These laws are consistent with a liberal feminism which recognizes that, in the early days of the sexual revolution, working women faced unfair cultural barriers. Such laws are often supplemented by provisions in company employment handbooks, which were added to attract women as employees. The ungentlemanly sexual advances that were not uncommon in the 1950s will result in a painful visit from Human Resources today.

Illiberal Feminism

As Christina Hoff Sommers has argued, we've reached the limit of what liberal feminism might offer in the form of legislative rights. Were more demanded, it might be self-defeating since it's hard to disaggregate women from the general population. We're all interconnected. Married women have husbands, sisters have brothers, and mothers have sons. When the Title IX evidentiary standards for sexual assault were lowered to a "preponderance of the evidence," and the campus judicial processes were heavily biased in favor of female accusers, mothers banded together to defend their sons.

Despite this, a newer generation of left-wing gender feminists has abandoned liberalism, which had allied them to things they hated such as a free-market economy. They blamed capitalism for the lingering barriers women face, and argued that all our institutions, state and private, perpetuate male dominance. In the absence of evidence, sad-girl narratives took the place of truth and invited free-floating anger against men and boys. What is especially poisonous are the gender-studies programs at universities, taught by some of the most privileged people on earth (white, Western, wealthy women). If marriage and natality rates decline drastically in the next decade, toxic feminism will bear part of the blame.

There's no basis for the resentment. There is a wage gap between men and women, but it's a consequence of the employment choices women have made and can't be blamed on a patriarchal labor system. Women get equal pay for equal work, but they tend to work at different jobs. They'll work in relatively low-paying positions, and also trade off their employment prospects to raise children. When they work at the same jobs, or don't have children, the pay gap essentially disappears.[2]

In the Me Too era, attention has focused on a report that nearly one in five women has been a victim of rape or attempted rape. Those figures, from the Centers for Disease Control, have been challenged, however. While the CDC estimates that nearly two million women were raped in 2011, the National Crime Victimization Survey puts the number at 238,000 rapes and sexual assaults, and it's been argued that the CDC's methodology is flawed and its numbers misleading. The CDC didn't get a reputation for being data-driven during the COVID pandemic and now encourages biological males to "chestfeed" infants. In any event, the left normalizes rape when the victim is the daughter of a conservative judge or the perp belongs to Hamas.

That's not to excuse real rapes. However, gender feminists have spread false stories about male violence, which the media has accepted uncritically. It's not the case that domestic violence spikes on Super Bowl Sunday, even if all the press bought into the story. Claims about the number of women who are victims of domestic violence have also been challenged.[3]

Complaints about how the patriarchy has suppressed female authors, composers, and artists are fanciful. There have been extraordinarily talented female novelists such as Jane Austen, and they haven't been hidden from view. Philosopher Gilbert Ryle is said to have answered, when asked if he ever had read a novel, "Oh yes. All six of them. Every year." Other complaints, such as a musicologist's claim that Beethoven's Ninth Symphony reveals the "throttling, murderous rage of a rapist incapable of attaining release," might win their author a MacArthur Genius award but reveal a seriously disturbed mind.[4]

Nineteenth-century feminists had a valid complaint about being denied proper educational opportunities, but that's not the case today. As recently as 1970, college graduates were 60–40 male to female, but those figures have been reversed and now it's 60–40 women to men. College-admissions officers have even begun to worry about a tipping point, where the student body is so heavily female that no one, male or female, will want to go there. Looking at the numbers, the left-of-center Brookings Institution calls this a "male college crisis."[5]

The American Association of University Women still speaks of a harmful gender gap in education. In fact, women are highly overrepresented in psychology and the healing professions, while men gravitate to STEM programs in science, technology, and engineering. That makes the AAUW upset, but it's what one would have expected after reading Carol Gilligan's *In a Different Voice* (1982). Gilligan reported that women place greater emphasis than men on care for others and interpersonal relationships, while men are more rule-oriented. Gilligan did not take a position on whether this was due to biology or upbringing, but the differences she described were so fundamental that it would seem hard to reject nature out of hand. If so, the AAUW's battle against biology will be an uphill one, as it would be if it sought gender equality for bricklayers (99 percent male).

If we're trying to keep score about gender differences, it's not a story about uniquely male privilege. Men are twice as likely to be homeless as women, three times more likely to die of a drug overdose, four times more likely to commit suicide, and fifteen times more likely to be incarcerated. They're also forty times more likely to die in combat, not that we'd want to change that, any more than we'd want to reduce the female life expectancy rates from seventy-nine years to match the male rate of seventy-three.

In sum, feminist complaints about oppression are absurdly overstated. In reality, American women are almost the most privileged class in world history. They control a third of the country's household financial assets and are expected to hold two-thirds of U.S. private wealth by 2030. Some of this is a result of their entry into the workforce and the shattering of glass ceilings. It's also money they have inherited from husbands whom they have outlived, as women do on average. They will be the beneficiaries of 70 percent of the $41 trillion that will be inherited over the next two generations, in what is anticipated will be the largest intergenerational wealth transfer in history.

With their pussy hats, Handmaid costumes, and infinite capacity for self-pity, illiberal feminists are now getting some pushback, and there's some fraying at the intersectional edges. White feminists are mocked as Karens ("Can I speak to the manager?") by people of color, who reasonably think that they have greater cause for complaint. In what might be a sign that gender feminists have overplayed their hand, they've begun to ally themselves with the transgendered, always a safe thing to do on the left.

Liberal feminists will also sympathize with the transgendered. Up to a point. They'll see no reason to scorn a sincere person who so describes himself. As for using a person's preferred pronouns, that's ordinarily simply a matter of politeness, unless the request comes from a nasty person who is primed to denounce you. Otherwise, it is brutish to cause offense where it's so easy to accede to a request.

That's not an argument for legislating politeness, when this threatens to be more of a sword to be used against conservatives than a shield that protects the transgendered. It opens up the possibility of politicized witch hunts by partisan prosecutors against political enemies. The gay or transgendered person who brings a complaint against a conservative for a want of respect when he might so easily have walked away is not to be pitied. Instead, he's better seen as a bully, triumphally enforcing his legal privileges and preening in his victim status.

In the *Masterpiece Cakeshop* series of cases, the LGBTQ community took it upon itself to persecute Jack Phillips, a skilled baker. When he was asked to bake cakes celebrating same-sex marriages and transgender operations, he refused because he thought his religious beliefs barred him from doing so. He'd sell a plain cake, but not one on which he used his artistic tools to design a customized cake for the wedding.

In the first case, dating from 2012, the gay couple could have gone elsewhere and in fact did so for the wedding cake they wanted. They weren't really inconvenienced but nevertheless brought a complaint before the Colorado Civil Rights Commission to punish the owner. The Commission ruled in favor of the couple, and this was upheld by the Colorado Court of Appeals, which managed to distinguish a case in which three bakeries refused to make a cake with the message "Homosexuality is a detestable sin. Leviticus 18:22." That was a constitutionally protected exercise of free speech rights, but not the refusal to make a cake for the gay couple. The decision was reversed by the Supreme Court in 2018 because of the Commission's overtly anti-religious bias.[6] A member of the Commission had said that "freedom of religion and religion has been used to justify all kinds of discrimination throughout history, whether it be slavery, whether it be the Holocaust."

If Jack Phillips thought that he could now go about his business, the LGBTQ community made sure he had another thing coming. On the same day that the U.S. Supreme Court agreed to hear Phillips's challenge to the Colorado Civil Rights Commission, Autumn Scardina asked him to bake a cake celebrating her gender transition. This went to trial, and the court's fine of $500 was affirmed by the Colorado Court of Appeal in 2023. The fine wasn't great, but when you're dragged into court for more than a decade, the process is the punishment, and the LGBTQ community knows this. After the 2023 Supreme Court decision in *303 Creative v. Elenis*, which held that a Christian designer's free-speech rights permitted her to decline to provide her services to celebrate a gay wedding, one might think that we'll hear no more of such cases, but sadly that would shortchange the grim determination of the LGBTQ community and its creative lawyers to punish dissenters.

The left regards gays and the transgendered as an oppressed class in need of the state's protection, in the form of civil-rights commissions like that of Colorado. The Supreme Court has agreed with this, in a 2020 decision written by Justice Gorsuch which held that the 1964 Civil Rights Act's protections against discriminating on the basis of sex extend to gays and the transgendered.[7] After that decision, the idea that an employer today would fire a person for being gay is fanciful.

What can get you fired, and this with the backing of federal courts, is opposition to the gay-rights agenda. The Second Circuit Court of Appeals has ruled that an employer was permitted to fire an employee who skipped LGBTQ training on religious grounds.[8] In Britain, this turned into a Lord of the Flies moment at a girls school when a female teacher was forced to apologize and fired for saying "good afternoon, girls" to her class.[9] The students held a protest and made signs saying, "Trans Lives Matter." The children were eleven years of age and students at a girls school, so the teacher couldn't have thought that any of them thought they were boys.

Illiberal feminists who support the transgender movement sadly ignore how it is anti-feminist when it demands that women compete against transgendered male athletes. Before she transitioned, Lia Thomas ranked 554th in the 200 freestyle, sixty-fifth in the 500 freestyle, and thirty-second in the 1650 freestyle. When competing as a woman, she beat Olympic silver medalist Emma Weyant. That was in swimming. In Mixed Martial Artist boxing, there are apparently audiences who pay to see physical males beat up women, and transgender MMA fighter Fallon Fox gave her female opponent a broken skull. The round had lasted only two minutes. Afterwards Fox claimed that she was the real victim. "The scope of vitriol and anger was mind-blowing."[10] Feminists who think there are only two genders are labeled TERFs, or trans-exclusionary radical feminists, and Fox has boasted that she holds the record for punching TERFS. Evidently, the instincts of chivalry didn't survive the gender transition.[11]

Liberal feminists will think this madness, and they'll also object to the transgender wars that bring drag queens into the elementary-school classroom and give nine-year-olds puberty blockers without their parents' consent. You can have your drag-queen show, says the liberal, but please tell me why you might want to do so in front of children? Worse still, a proposed law in Oregon would allow children beginning at age fifteen to obtain gender-reassignment surgery without notifying their parents.[12] Children under twenty-one are not permitted to buy cigarettes in the state, but they would be able to make life-changing decisions about their sexual identities.

20.

LAUGHTER

Laughter is liberal in spirit since illiberalism is naturally comic. Few things gall more than being ridiculed, and our laughter urges illiberals to mend their ways. No wonder that they hate laughter, then.

THE SUPERIORITY THESIS

The leading explanation of why we laugh is the superiority thesis, under which we signal that we're better than a butt by laughing at him. We've always known that, when we laugh, we laugh *at* someone, and the superiority thesis has a long history. In the *Philebus*, Plato argued that the pleasure derived from comedy was based on our enjoyment of another's misfortune. Aristotle proposed a similar explanation, defining the risible as a mistake or deficiency. However, the idea that laughter reveals a sense of superiority is most closely identified with Thomas Hobbes.

We seek power over other people, said Hobbes, and we laugh when we're struck with the realization that we enjoy that power. Our laughter is a cry of triumph and a "sudden glory."[1] Relative to the wit, the butt is degraded; relative to the butt, the wit moves up a notch. The butt knows this, of course, which is why he resents the joke. Speaking for butts everywhere, Hazlitt said that our humiliation is their triumph.[2] And while some have objected that our laughter is too innocent to convey a message of superiority, I'm more inclined to agree with Baudelaire that laughter is man's way of biting.[3]

Laughter contains a coded message about how we should live and tells the butt to mend his ways. That's how satire has always seen itself. In the Preface to *Absalom and Achitophel* (1681), Dryden announced that "the true end of Satyre is the amendment of Vices by correction. And he who writes Honestly, is no more an Enemy to the Offendour, than the Physician to the Patient, when he prescribes harsh remedies to an inveterate Disease." Later, in his rules for satire, Dryden said that "the Poet is bound, and that *ex Officio*, to give his Reader some one precept of moral virtue; and to caution him against some one particular vice or folly.[4]

There's a morality of laughter that identifies comic vices to be avoided. Our laughter also identifies comic virtues, the qualities of the superior people who laugh but aren't laughed at. They are agile, lighthearted, and possess a special grace. We sense that they understand what life asks of us in order to extract all the good it offers, and naturally seek to emulate them. They are liberals.

There would be little point to laughter's signal of superiority if the comic vice were not correctable. Ordinarily, the butt is unaware that he's ridiculous until this is pointed out to him, and after this he can mend his ways. We don't laugh when the defect can't be corrected, however. It's not funny when the blind or lame stumble. What Swift said of his satire is true of all laughter.

> His Satyr points at no Defect,
> But what all Mortals may correct; . . .
> He spar'd a Hump or crooked Nose,
> Whose Owners set not up for Beaux
> True genuine Dulness mov'd his Pity
> Unless it offer'd to be witty.
> (*Verses on the Death of Dr. Swift*)

It's also not funny when the signal of superiority communicates bitterness or contempt. This is the bitter satire of Juvenal, and the laughter of most late-night talk shows. It asks the audience to revel in its hatred and thinks it funny merely to mention the name of a despised conservative. This is laughter, to be sure, but it's like the laughter of boors who guffaw when they see a person sucker punched.

What's missing from such laughter is the necessary element of playfulness. We laugh when we're "in play." Robertson Davies recalled a reading by Stephen Leacock during which the audience laughed throughout, after jokes, during them, and before they were told.[5] They had come expecting to laugh and weren't going to be disappointed. Jack Benny had the same gift. He'd put his hand to his cheek and say "Well!" and we'd be off.

Other explanations of laughter have been proffered. J. Y. T Greig counted eighty-eight of them. All seem wanting to me, however. Some have suggested that what's needed is surprise, and that is indeed a necessary condition for laughter. John Cleese explained how it matters when he told me about the crucial importance of timing. Think of the Biggus Dickus scene in Monty Python's *Life of Brian* (1979). We're led to expect that something wicked will come our way, and, after the scene is prolonged to just the right moment, the emotional tension is punctured. Then we explode in laughter. Surprise isn't a sufficient condition, however. Thunderclaps aren't funny, and no one ever laughed at Haydn's Surprise Symphony.

Kant's notion that we laugh when we recognize an incongruity is also unconvincing.[6] To illustrate his thesis, Kant wrote jokes and unsurprisingly they're not funny. There are also incongruities in mathematics, and they're not funny either. Puns rely on incongruities, but that's notoriously the lowest form of humor, and in any event signal the punster's superiority over the less witty.

Comic Illiberalism

The leading modern statement of the superiority thesis is Henri Bergson's *Le Rire* (1900), which defined the risible as a rigidity (*raideur*) of body or character. The more someone resembles a machine, the more he's funny, said Bergson. He becomes a machine-man when he takes a single principle and absurdly extends it beyond its reasonable scope, where erudition turns into pedantry, prudence into avarice, and liberalism into illiberalism.

Legal rules become risible when they resemble machine law, the product of a demented robot that has no understanding of humanity, of what it means to live well and of the common good. Bergson gave an example of this in the customs inspector who sees a boat foundering and narrowly saves a shipwrecked passenger. Then, when they're both lying exhausted on shore, the inspector asks him if he has anything to declare. In the same way, rules are laughable when they're divorced from common sense.

Machine law transcends political labels and comes in both right- and left-wing varieties. A good example of the former is an article law professor and Judge Richard Posner cowrote about baby-selling.[7] In the law-and-economics literature that Posner helped pioneer, sales are efficient because they transfer ownership from lower- to higher-valued users. You'll buy a television set from Best Buy because you value it more than the store, and it values the money more than you do. Baby selling is no different, said Posner. You'll buy the child because you value it more than the seller. The buyer wouldn't throw the TV set out the window, and for the same reason you'd not expect him to mistreat the child. The article was pure machine law by an academic who was a prisoner of his free-market ideology, and happily served to prevent Posner from being appointed to the Supreme Court.

The Onion, a humor magazine that slants mildly left, took on free-market absolutists with a story entitled "Libertarian Reluctantly Calls Fire Department."

> CHEYENNE, WY—After attempting to contain a living-room blaze started by a cigarette, card-carrying Libertarian Trent Jacobs reluctantly called the Cheyenne Fire Department Monday. "Although the community would do better to rely on an efficient, free-market fire-fighting service, the fact is that expensive, unnecessary public fire departments do exist," Jacobs said. "Also, my house was burning down."

Machine law is primarily the province of the left, however. If they didn't impose such an enormous cost on the American economy, progressive licensing requirements would be a wonderful source of humor. They're usually backed by a cartel of insiders, as well as a class of regulators on autopilot who think that every business needs a burdensome set of rules. Occasionally, the absurdity is recognized, as happened when Virginia proposed to license yoga studios. That's basic consumer protection, it was argued, for just think how the unlicensed yogi might harm her students when (without touching them) she confuses the *sahasrara* (crown) with the *svadhishthana* (sacrum). That's got to hurt.

The proposal would have sent applicants loads of paperwork to fill out and imposed a $2,500 application fee. The state licensing body was the State Council for Higher Education for Virginia (SCHEV), which normally concerns itself with university affairs. It wasn't clear how the expertise SCHEV had gained from overseeing law schools was going to help it evaluate downward-dog poses, however, and the proposal was laughed away.[8] But despite the odd setback, licensing requirements have become ubiquitous. The libertarian Institute for Justice, which litigates to set them aside, reports that today one in three U.S. workers requires a license, up from one in twenty sixty years ago.[9] That has wastefully locked people in to jobs for which they're licensed in one state, and made it harder to move to another state with its separate licensing requirements.

The administrative state and its wasteful, job-destroying regulations impose an enormous burden on our economy and turn ordinary Americans into criminals. Consider the following, unintentionally funny federal crimes that FreedomWorks has uncovered:

1 USC §461 & 9 CFR §381.171(d) make it a crime to sell "Turkey Ham" as "Ham Turkey" or with the words "Turkey" and "Ham" in different fonts.

18 U.S.C. §1865 & 36 C.F.R. §2.15(a)(4) make it a crime to let your pet make a noise that scares the wildlife in a national park.

27 USC §§205, 207 & 27 CFR §4.64(a)(8) make it a crime to advertise wine in a manner that suggests it has intoxicating qualities.

Such rules are anti-human and amount to machine law. They shouldn't have survived the laugh test. They're also illiberal insofar as they subject individuals to liberticide restrictions. They're a barrier to entry by the New Man and entrench an anti-competitive cartel of big businesses whose compliance experts are skilled in working around the rules, and this poisons the American Dream by turning us into an immobile aristocracy.

Bergson recognized the connection between laughter and liberty. Anticipating Sir Karl Popper, he celebrated the freedom of what he called an open society in *Two Sources of Morality and Religion* (1932). An open society is mobile, organic, and fluid, while a closed society is unchanging, mechanical, and stratified, like an ant colony. Open societies do not impose top-down order; instead, they let the individual choose his best life-plan. Closed societies demand an unthinking allegiance and unalterable duties. They are shot through with mechanistic rules that leave little room for private choices and invite our laughter.

The *piagnoni* on the left recognize we're laughing at them, and they hate it. Under a consent decree, the Portland, OR police department was required to undergo LGBTQ training. To determine someone's identity, the directive said that officers should respectfully ask for the person's pronouns, and if that didn't work they should use gender-neutral pronouns such as "they" or "them." When some cops thought this funny, their trainers said that their laughter "was indicative of racism, ableism and white supremacy." Clearly, more DEI training would be needed.[10]

The hilarious comedies of times past, *Blazing Saddles* (1974), *Animal House* (1978), and *Airplane* (1980), could not be made today. "Joey, do you like movies about gladiators?" *Airplane*'s Captain Rex asks a five-year-old, as if there were anything wrong with pedophilia. Some things are sacred, after all. We're not permitted to laugh when, in *Life of Brian*, Stan says he wanted to be a woman. "From now on I want you all to call me Loretta. I want to have babies." At the time this was hilarious, but this explains why the movie has disappeared. John Cleese has been told that the movie could be turned into a play, but only if the Loretta joke goes. As for "The Lumberjack Song," what is that but a slur on the transgendered?

Major comedians such as Jerry Seinfeld say that they no longer want to play on college campuses. The audience isn't there to laugh, but to display its outrage at offenses against wokeness. That has made us lonely, since shared joke-telling is one of the strongest ways in which people bond with each other. We've learned to mistrust people we had thought our friends, since a crack we had thought innocent can now get us fired. And then we're surprised to learn that we're in a loneliness epidemic that amounts to a public-health crisis.[11]

Hollywood's efforts at comedy with a leftward slant are preachy and unfunny. From *The Chair* (2021) we learned that the proper way to begin a meeting with a stranger is by exchanging preferred pronouns. The person in front of you might look like a birthing person, and indeed might resemble Margot Robbie, but then you can't be sure until she says, "she, her." That kills laughter, since no one finds a political sermon funny. Shows like that really aren't trying to entertain us. Instead, the point is to kick down at an inferior set of deplorables who aren't familiar with the latest set of cultural signifiers.

Laughter remains, however. It's simply gone underground and become what the Russian critic Mikhail Bakhtin called carnival laughter. This is the transgressive laughter of Mardi Gras, the Feast of Fools, and the charivari. It kicks up against an overlord class of woke CEOs, academic deans, and the media and offers relief from oppressive, illiberal social norms.

Some of the funniest comedy comes from parodies of woke culture. Titania McGrath (real name: Andrew Doyle) mocks leftish lunacy and succeeds by expressing the ideas of a non-binary ecosexual who supports armed peaceful protest. "Why do bigots find gender identity so confusing?" she asks. "It simply means the immutable yet fluid feeling that one is male or female or neither or both based on conceptions of masculinity and femininity that are innate but also social constructs that don't exist. This really isn't hard." Or "by removing blue checks from important left-wing celebrities, Elon Musk is literally erasing their existence and committing digital genocide. This is a second Rwanda." In defense of a rapist's right to be housed in a female prison, she writes, "just because Isla has a penis, testicles and a track record of sexual assault doesn't make her any less of a lady." In pre-Musk days, Twitter suspended her four times for hate speech.

Then there's the *Babylon Bee*, which was also blocked by Twitter before Musk took it over. The *Bee*, a parody site with a religious edge, reported that Planned Parenthood warns us that making Down Syndrome Barbies could teach young girls to value human life. "Our eugenics program could be in jeopardy if kids start to see Down Syndrome kids as precious gifts worthy of love. We can't allow that to happen." The *Bee* also makes fun of the pratfalls of an aging President Biden, something on which the liberal media keeps a tight lid. "Biden Assures Nation We Have Nothing To Worry About Thanks To This Cool New Padded Helmet He's Wearing." Labeling itself as "false news you can trust," the site was fact-checked by humorless leftists, and, when it wrote that CNN was using an industrial-sized washing machine to spin the news, Snopes rated the article false.

In the battle against woke illiberalism, the liberal's strongest weapon is laughter.

21.

THE VIRTUES OF LIBERALISM

We've examined the roots of liberalism without bothering to define it. I did not try to describe its essence and still less to offer a one-sentence definition for all the things it might mean. But if it doesn't rise to the level of a concrete idea, no matter, said Goethe:

> When I hear people speak of liberal ideas, it is always a wonder
> to me that men are so readily put off with empty verbiage. An
> idea cannot be liberal; but it may be potent, vigorous, exclusive,
> to fulfill its mission of being productive. Still less can a con-
> cept be liberal; for a concept has quite another mission. Where,
> however, we must look for liberality, is in the sentiments; and
> the sentiments are the inner man as he lives and moves.[1]

Liberalism is not without content, however, and I've made its virtues the subject of this book. There has been a turn to the virtues in philosophy, but for the most part this has meant the ethics of philosophers and theologians. I, more humbly, have examined the very different way in which laymen were taught their liberalism. When

John Maynard Keynes said that ordinary people are the slaves of defunct thinkers, he was referring to economists, not philosophers.

Liberalism is not an abstract theory, but a tradition of virtues and customs embedded in our culture. We learned magnanimity from the Code of Chivalry and were taught that brutishness is illiberal from the Code of the Gentleman. Through the stories of Hans Christian Andersen and the novels of Charles Dickens, kindness became a liberal virtue. The Republican Virtue of the Founders can be traced back to twelfth-century Sienese merchants. Liberalism was born of the virtues and thus does not threaten them.

Liberalism arises from a sense of benevolence and generosity. It delights in gift-giving, and a liberal would think it shameful to pass an injured person by without helping him. The illiberal who faults liberalism for selfish individualism and an unconcern for the common good misses his mark. He takes aim at the abstract rights of libertarians and natural lawyers, but ignores the virtues of liberalism and its essential altruism.

A state that has fallen into illiberalism is not made liberal through a thicker set of rights or a better set of economic incentives. Liberalism arose from the virtues, and when weakened only they can revive it. The selfish state is not reformed except through benevolence and fraternity. The heartless woke republic is not healed except through humility and self-understanding. All politics is virtue politics.

Liberal virtues are a subset of virtues generally. They are social, concerned with our relations with others, and don't speak to the virtue of piety and our duties to God. They're also narrower than the Aristotelian idea of virtue as the pursuit of human excellence. They don't tell us what the best life for an individual might be, except for that part which concerns his role as a member of society. Provided we practice the virtues of benevolence and good citizenship, liberalism need not assume that there is a special end for which we should strive. What that end might be, if it exists, is of the greatest importance, but it makes little sense to charge liberalism for that which it was never meant to do.

Let me summarize what an examination of the roots of liberalism has taught us. The virtues of liberalism consist of a minimal set of requirements. Liberals are (1) egalitarians, (2) who seek the common good and oppose corruption, (3) are willing to live with uncertainty, (4) value autonomy, and (5) practice a *vita activa* that defends what is right.

As *egalitarians*, liberals believe, with Jeremy Bentham, that everyone counts as one and no one counts as more than one. They might disagree about how gains are to be divided and costs allocated, and they'll likely adopt a form of prioritarianism in which tax burdens and welfare benefits effect a wealth transfer from rich to poor. This will be done, however, in the belief that gains to the winner exceed losses to the losers, because $100 in the hands of a poor person will be valued more than the same amount in the pocket of Elon Musk.

What they'll not do is discount the interest of a fellow citizen down to zero, as the extreme prioritarianism of Rawls's *Theory of Justice* would do in ignoring everyone save the very poorest. Nor would they seek to stir up racial hatred, as *Radio Mille Collines* did in urging Hutus to kill Tutsis, or as CRT provocateurs do in the United States. Instead, they'd honor those who, like General Dallaire or the Jesuit missionaries, demonstrated their egalitarianism, the more so if they had to expand the borders of liberalism to do so.

Liberals will oppose an aristocracy that artificially locks children into the same social and economic classes as their parents. To the extent that immobility is genetically based, some degree of immobility is to be expected, but the fact that other societies are much more mobile than we are suggests that the barriers in America are legally constructed, and that the complacency of America's left- and right-wing elites about the rise of aristocracy is a moral wrong.

As egalitarians, liberals will identify the *common good* as the touchstone by which to judge public policies. That will call for something more than the rational egoist's self-interest. Liberalism requires the benevolence that is willing to sacrifice where there's no expected payoff, neither now nor in the future. It's not self-interest that funds a welfare system or leads one to volunteer in wartime. The benevolence might be general, or it might take the form of the nationalist's sense of fraternity for his fellow citizens.

The common good excludes the racial and gender preferences in which only the favored class matters. To correct historical patterns of injustice, or to remedy existing forms of prejudice, the liberal might permit special preferences to be granted to a disfavored class, but this cuts against the grain and requires an explanation for why this is consistent with the common good. Granting an absolute priority to one race, gender, or class and ignoring everyone else reveals a palsied moral imagination. As Stuart Hampshire noted, "there is no consideration of any kind that overrides all other considerations in all conceivable circumstances."[2]

In seeking the common good, the liberal will condemn as corruption the favors granted to those with special access to justice. He'll be suspicious of the way in which interest-group competition has served to benefit concentrated groups at the expense of dispersed ones. The liberal will recognize that different groups do compete for advantage, but unlike James Madison he'll not assume that the common good will emerge from interest-group bargaining. Had Madison been correct, we'd not have ended up with the lobbyists of K Street, the self-seeking political donors, and what J. G. A. Pocock regarded as "the greatest empire of patronage and influence the world has known."[3]

Corruption may take the form of self-deception, where we favor ourselves unduly in asserting our rights or entitlements. A more encompassing moral vision would be willing to recognize and yield to the superior claims of other people, and to recognize the *uncertainty* of many moral questions. When so many people think themselves justified sinners, a measure of self-doubt is a liberal virtue.

Liberals will also think that one of the elements of the common good is personal *autonomy*. The right to choose *x* has moral significance and not just because *x* was a good thing to do. It might be good, but it also matters how we get to it. By taking control of our lives, we make them *our* lives and no one else's. In addition, we're more likely to know our own good than the paternalist who wants to choose for us. Our desire for autonomy will also express itself in the manner in which we prize individuality by permitting people to go their own way when no one is harmed, and in which we respect their privacy.

224

Finally, a virtuous liberalism imposes the affirmative duties of a *vita activa*, with all the fortitude this might require. The liberal is not a desert monk who lives a contemplative life. Like the wanderer, he'll possess the get-up-and-go of those who need to move on, and like a knight he'll feel obliged to right injustices and save those who would perish without him. In the Rwandan genocide, the true liberal was Roméo Dallaire. Bill Clinton and Boutros Boutros-Ghali had subscribed to all the correct liberal doctrines, but their nonfeasance was shameful.

These are the virtues of the Western tradition. They are not self-justifying. They are embedded in our culture, but it does not follow that they're to be followed for that reason. That would offend the No-Ought-From-Is principle we saw in Chapter Two. And as they are rooted in contingent, historical experience, they invite a charge of moral relativism.

Nevertheless, the liberal who identifies himself as a member of a Western culture may rationally adhere to it. These are my values, he says, and I'm proud of them. I know I've been born into a particular culture and am aware of the happenstance of the circumstances of my beliefs, but nevertheless I feel an allegiance to them. They have served me well and I will pause before I jettison them for a rival system of untried beliefs. As Richard Rorty argued, "a belief can still regulate action, can still be thought worthy dying for, among people who are quite aware that this belief is caused by nothing deeper than contingent historical circumstances."[4]

The objection from historicism will also fall flat with those who insist that their principles are universally valid. If you tell them that other codes permit infanticide, they'll still think it wrong. An acknowledgement of the historical roots of Western liberalism does not entail moral relativism.

One might therefore pay the woke left and the right-wing Integralist the compliment of examining their presuppositions and comparing them to the virtues of liberalism. It's possible to weigh each tradition against our Moral Sense, while recognizing its contingency and possible incompleteness. Moral claims are not true or false, but they may still be subjected to reasoned debate. They might be accepted if they are seen to deal fairly with everyone or rejected when they impose unjust burdens on an individual or group.

We can't prove who is right, nor can we explain why illiberals or virtue-skeptics are wrong. But if proof eludes us, why is that so bad? If the principles were demonstrably true, there would be no room for political disagreement, any more than there is for the temperature at which water boils. Since that's not the case, one must make an election, for or against liberalism, and accept the moral responsibility of the choice. And it's the possibility of choice that gives liberalism its nobility.

What happens next? We're about to choose a new president, and no one would confuse either candidate with Dwight Eisenhower or Adlai Stevenson. And yet neither poses a serious threat to the country's liberalism. When leftists complain that Trump will jail his enemies, fetter their free-speech rights, and spread misinformation, it's well to remember that these are things of which they themselves might be accused, and that their hypocrisy is justly rebuked by liberals.

Prediction is a mug's game, but of one thing I am confident. The dour and barbarian cult of wokeness is unlikely to survive beyond the current generation. It demands that we live in what C. S. Lewis described as Hell, a society where everyone is perpetually concerned with his own dignity, a society shot through with envy and self-importance.[5] It offers a creed of sin without absolution, of guilt without soul-easing joys, of frowns without laughter. In place of justice it offers cringy pandering, and in place of kindness it preaches resentment. It muffles our moral sense and encourages moral neuters to take pleasure in the vilest of emotions. It rejects the West's high culture, its art, music, and literature, and offers nothing in its place. In place of this nullity, without gentleness, artistry, learning, enterprise, or heroes, its emptiness will be seen by all.

Herb Stein said that "things that can't go on forever . . . stop." The enemies of liberalism have made us lonely and unhappy. They have ravaged our cities, wrecked our educational system, and told us to loathe fellow Americans. This can't go on forever, and it won't.

Change won't come from a "Madisonian Constitution," whose checks and balances have not made America free or saved it from corruption. Nor will it come from a nihilistic political class, left and right, that defines itself by its hatred of its opponents, or from clever theorists who proffer a new definition of liberalism that aligns with their politics. Instead it must come bottom up, like the cord in Lorenzetti's Allegory of Good Government, from ordinary people who thrill to tales of faithful knights, who sorrow for the Little Match Girl, and who embrace the virtues and greatness of liberalism.

ACKNOWLEDGMENTS

I am most grateful to the many people who've helped me: Brian Bix, Dan Bonevac, Deal Hudson, Rob Koons, Joyce Malcolm, and especially Jim Bowman. In addition, I owe a debt to friends who by their example instructed me in the nobility of liberalism: Bill Allen, Joe Bast, David Cheshin, Alex Colville, Irwin Cotler, Adrian Duplantier, Rick Hart, Alan Kors, Michael Novak, Jeff Sessions, Roger Shattuck, and Jim Wooton. A special thanks goes to Bob Tyrrell, who reminded me that liberalism is on the side of laughter.

I also thank George Mason's Scalia Law School for its generous support, Peter Vay at the Scalia Law Library, Jane Barton for secretarial help, and José Coradin for tech support.

My heartfelt thanks to everyone at Encounter Books: to the production team of Nola Tully, Elizabeth Bachmann, Analisa Gomez, and Matt Purple; the book editor, Benjamin Riley; the marketing team of Sam Schneider and Lauren Miklos; and especially to Roger Kimball.

Finally, as always, my most heartfelt thanks go to my wife, Esther Goldberg.

April 5, 2024

BIBLIOGRAPHY

This biography doesn't include articles from scholarly journals and news sources, but where necessary these can be found in the endnotes.

A Complete Collection of State Trials. London: J. Walthoe, 1730.

Abramoff, Jack. *Capitol Punishment: The Hard Truth about Washington Corruption from America's Most Notorious Lobbyist.* Chicago: WND, 2011.

Adams, Henry. *Adams.* New York: Library of America, 1983.

Adams, John. *Revolutionary Writings.* New York: Library of America, 1983.

Adams, John. *The Selected Writings of John and John Quincy Adams.* New York: Knopf, 1946.

African Rights. *Rwanda: Death, Despair and Defiance.* London: African Rights, 1994.

Alcoholics Anonymous: The Story of the Many Thousands of Men and Women Who Have Recovered from Alcoholism. 4th ed. New York: Alcoholics Anonymous World Services, 2001.

Aquinas. *On Kingship.* Trans. Gerald B. Phelan. Westport: Hyperion, 1979.

Aquinas, Thomas. *On Law, Morality, and Politics.* Trans. Richard J. Regan. Indianapolis: Hackett, 2002.

Anderson, Benedict. *Imagined Communities.* London: Verso, 1983.

Angier, Tom, ed. *The Cambridge Companion to Natural Law Ethics.* Cambridge: Cambridge University Press, 2019.

Anscombe, G. E. M. *Collected Philosophical Papers.* Minneapolis: University of Minnesota Press, 1958.

Arendt, Hannah. *Eichmann in Jerusalem: A Report on the Banality of Evil.* New York: Viking, 1963.

Arendt, Hannah. *The Human Condition.* 2d ed. Chicago: Chicago University Press, 1998.

Arieli, Yehoshua. *Individualism and Nationalism in American Ideology.* Cambridge: Harvard University Press, 1966.

Aristotle. *Nicomachean Ethics*. Trans. H. Rackham. Cambridge: Loeb Classical Library, 1939.

Arnold, Matthew. *A French Eton: Middle Class Education and the State*. London: Macmillan, 1864.

Atkinson James B. and David Sices, trans. and ed. *Machiavelli and His Friends: Their Personal Correspondence*. DeKalb: Northern Illinois University Press, 1996.

Axelrod, Robert. *The Evolution of Cooperation*. New York: Basic Books, 1984.

Bacon, Francis. *Works of Francis Bacon*. London: J. Johnson, 1803.

Bailyn, Bernard. *The Ideological Origins of the American Revolution*. Cambridge: Harvard University Press, 1967.

Bakhtin, Mikhail. *Rabelais and his World*. Trans. Hélène Iswolsky. Bloomington: Indiana University Press, 1984.

Balakrishnan, Gopal. *The Enemy: An Intellectual Portrait of Carl Schmitt*. London: Verso, 2000.

Bancroft, George. *History of the United States from the Discovery of the American Continent*. Boston: Little, Brown & Co., 1843.

Banfield, Edward C. *The Moral Basis of a Backward Society*, Glencoe: Free Press, 1958.

Banfield, Edward C. *The Unheavenly City*. Boston: Little, Brown, 1968.

Baron, Hans. *In Search of Florentine Civic Humanism: Essays on the Transition from Medieval to Modern Thought*. Princeton: Princeton University Press, 1988.

Baron-Cohen, Simon. *Autism and Asperger Syndrome*. Oxford: Oxford University Press, 2008.

Baron-Cohen, Simon. *The Science of Evil: On Empathy and the Origins of Cruelty*. New York: Basic Books, 2011.

Baudelaire, Charles. *Œuvres Complètes*. Paris: Pléiade, 1976.

Becker, Carl Lotus. *The Declaration of Independence: A Study on the History of Political Ideas*. New York: Vintage, 1922.

Beiser, Frederick C. *The Romantic Imperative: The Concept of Early German Romanticism*. Cambridge: Harvard University Press, 2003.

Bell, Daniel. *The End of Ideology: On the Exhaustion of Political*

Ideals in the 1950s. Cambridge: Harvard University Press, 1960.

Benedict, Ruth. *Patterns of Culture.* Boston: Houghton Mifflin, 1934.

Berger, Joseph, Morris Zelditch, and Bo Anderson, eds. *Sociological Theories in Progress.* New York: Houghton, Mifflin, 1966.

Bergson, Henri. *Laughter.* Trans. Cloudesley Brereton and Fred Rothwell. Los Angeles: Green Integer, 1999.

Bergson, Henri. *Two Sources of Morality and Religion.* Notre Dame: University of Notre Dame Press, 1977.

Berlin, Isaiah. *Four Essays on Liberty.* Oxford: Oxford University Press, 1969.

Berlin, Isaiah. *The Crooked Timber of Humanity.* Princeton: Princeton University Press, 1990.

Berman, Harold J. *Law and Revolution: The Formation of the Western Legal Tradition.* Cambridge: Harvard University Press, 1983.

Berry, Charlotte. *The Margins of Late Medieval London, 1430–1540.* London: University of London Press, 2022.

Blackburn, Carol. *Harvest of Souls: The Jesuit Missions and Colonialism in North America, 1632–1650,* Montreal: McGill-Queens University Press, 2000.

Blackburn, Simon. *Ruling Passions: A Theory of Practical Reasoning.* Oxford: Clarendon, 1998.

Blackstone, William. *Commentaries on the Laws of England.* Oxford: Oxford University Press, 2016.

Bloch, Marc. *Feudal Society.* Trans. L. A. Manyon. London: Routledge, 1962.

Blumenson, Martin. *The Patton Papers 1885–1940.* New York: Houghton Mifflin, 1972.

Bock, Gisela, Quentin Skinner and Maurizio Viroli, eds. *Machiavelli and Republicanism.* Cambridge: Cambridge University Press, 1990.

Bonner, Michael Brem and Fritz Hamer, eds. *South Carolina in the Civil War and Reconstruction Eras: Essays from the Proceedings of the South Carolina Historical Association.* Columbia: South Carolina University Press, 2007.

Borjas, George J. *Heaven's Door: Immigration Policy and the American Economy.* Princeton: Princeton University Press, 1999.

Bowles, Samuel, Herbert Gintis and Melissa Osborne Groves, eds. *Unequal Chances: Family Background and Economic Success.* Princeton: Princeton University Press, 2005.

Bowsky, William A. *A Medieval Italian Commune: Siena under the Nine.* Berkeley: California University Press, 1981.

Bradley, F. H. *Ethical Studies.* Oxford: Oxford University Press, 2d ed. 1927.

Brooks, Peter. *Seduced by Story: The Use and Abuse of Narrative.* New York: New York Review Books, 2022.

Brumwell, Stephen. *Paths of Glory: The Life and Death of General James Wolfe,* Montreal: McGill-Queen's University Press, 2006.

Buckley, F. H. *Fair Governance: Paternalism and Perfectionism.* Oxford: Oxford University Press, 2009.

Buckley, F. H. *Just Exchange: A Theory of Contract.* London: Routledge, 2004.

Buckley, F. H. *The Morality of Laughter.* Ann Arbor: Michigan University Press, 2003.

Buckley, F. H. *The Once and Future King: The Fall and Rise of Crown Government.* New York: Encounter, 2014.

Buckley, F. H. *The Republic of Virtue: How We Tried to Ban Corruption, Failed, and What We Can Do About It.* New York: Encounter, 2017.

Buckley, F. H. *The Way Back: Restoring the Promise of America.* New York: Encounter, 2016.

Budziszewski, J. *Written on the Heart: The Case for Natural Law.* Downers Grove: IVP, 1997.

Burke, Edmund. *The Writings and Speeches of Edmund Burke.* Oxford: Oxford University Press, 1989.

Burns, J. H. and Mark Goldie, eds. *The Cambridge History of Political Thought 1450–1700.* Cambridge: Cambridge University Press, 1991.

Butler, Joseph. *Six Sermons.* Indianapolis: Hackett, 1983.

Cacioppo, John T. and William Patrick. *Loneliness.* New York: Norton, 2008.

Campbell, Joseph. *Romance of the Grail: The Magic and Mystery of Arthurian Myth.* Novato: New World Library, 2015.

SELECTED BIBLIOGRAPHY

Camus, Albert. *Carnets*. Paris: Gallimard, 1962.

Camus, Albert. *Théâtre, recits, nouvelles*. Paris: Gallimard, 1962.

Capellanus, Andreas. *The Art of Courtly Love*. Trans. John Jay Parry. New York: Columbia University Press, 1960.

Caraman, Philip. *The Lost Paradise: The Jesuit Republic in South America*. New York: Seabury, 1976.

Carlyle, Thomas. *Past and Present*. New York: New York University Press, 1965.

Carrier, Roch. *Montcalm and Wolfe*. Toronto: HarperCollins, 2014.

Casgrain, H. R. *Wolfe and Montcalm*. Toronto: Toronto University Press, 1964.

Cassirer, Ernst. *The Philosophy of the Enlightenment*. Princeton: Princeton University Press, 1951.

Castonguay, Jacques. *Les casques bleus au Rwanda*. Paris: L'Harmattan, 1998.

Chang, Ruth ed., *Incommensurability, Incomparability and Practical Reason*. Cambridge: Harvard University Press, 1997.

Cicero. *On Duties*. Trans. Walter Miller. London: Loeb, 1913.

Cicero. *On Ends*. Trans. H. Rackham. London: Loeb, 1931.

Clark, Kenneth. *Civilisation*. New York: Harper & Row, 1969.

Coccia, Emanuele. *The Life of Plants: A Metaphysics of Mixture*. Trans. Dylan J. Montanari. London: Polity, 2018.

Cohen, Joshua, ed. *For Love of Country: Debating the Limits of Patriotism*. Boston: Beacon, 1996.

Coke, Edward. *Selected Writings and Speeches*. Indianapolis: Liberty Fund, 2003.

Colbourn, Trevor, ed. *Fame and the Founding Fathers: Essays by Douglas Adair*. Indianapolis: Liberty Fund, 1998.

Colish, Marcia L. *Medieval Foundations of the Western Intellectual Tradition, 400–1100*. New Haven: Yale University Press, 1997.

Collingwood, R. G. *The Idea of History*. Oxford: Oxford University Press, 1946.

Coplan, Amy and Peter Goldie, eds. *Empathy: Philosophical and Psychological Perspectives*, Cambridge: Cambridge University Press, 2011.

Cortés, Juan Donoso. *Essays on Catholicism, Liberalism, and*

Socialism: Considered in Their Fundamental Principles. Trans. Rev. William McDonald. Dublin: M. H. Gill, 1879.

Coulanges, Numa Fustel de. *The Ancient City: A Study of the Religion, Laws, and Institutions of Greece and Rome.* Trans. Willard Small. Mineola: Dover, 2006.

Coulanges, Numa Fustel de. *Questions historiques.* Camille Jullian, ed. Paris: Hachette, 1893.

Crisp, Roger, ed. *How Should One Live: Essays on the Virtues.* Oxford: Oxford University Press, 1996.

Dallaire, Roméo. *Shake Hands with the Devil: The Failure of Humanity in Rwanda.* New York: Carol & Graf, 2003.

Dante. *Monarchy.* Trans. Prue Shaw. Cambridge: Cambridge University Press, 1996.

d'Aurevilly, Barbey. *The Anatomy of Dandyism.* Trans. D. B. Wyndham Lewis. London: Peter Davies, 1928.

Dawkins, Richard. *The Selfish Gene.* Oxford: Oxford University Press, 2006.

Deneen, Patrick. *Why Liberalism Failed.* New Haven: Yale University Press, 2019.

Des Forges, Alison. *"Leave None to Tell the Story": Genocide in Rwanda.* New York: Human Rights Watch, 1999.

Digby, Kenelm Henry. *The Broad-Stone of Honour.* London: Rivington, 1823.

Digby, Kenelm Henry. *The Broad-Stone of Honour: Godefridus.* London: Rivington, 1823.

Disraeli, Benjamin. *Sybil, or the Two Nations.* London: Longmans, Green, 1871.

Douglas, Robert Langdon. *A History of Siena.* London: John Murray, 1902.

Dryden, John. *Essays,* volume 2. W. P. Ker, ed. New York: Russell & Russell, 1961.

Dugakin, Lee. *The Altruism Equation: Seven Scientists Search for the Origins of Goodness.* Princeton: Princeton University Press, 2006.

Dunkelman, Marc J. *The Vanishing Neighbor: The Transformation of American Community.* New York: Norton, 2014.

Dworkin, Ronald. *Sovereign Virtue.* Cambridge: Harvard University

Press, 2000.

Eagleton, Terry. *Reason, Faith, and Revolution: Reflections on the God Debate*. New Haven: Yale University Press, 2009.

Edmonds, David. *Parfit: A Philosopher and his Mission to Save Morality*. Princeton: Princeton University Press, 2023.

Farrand, Max, ed. *The Records of the Federal Convention of 1787*. Rev. ed. New Haven: Yale University Press, 1937.

Fingarette, Herbert. *Self-Deception*. Berkeley: California University Press, 2000.

Finke, Roger and Rodney Stark. *The Churching of America, 1776–2005: Winners and Losers in Our Religious Economy*. 2d ed. Piscataway: Rutgers University Press, 2005.

Finnis, John. *Aquinas*. Oxford: Oxford University Press, 1998.

Finnis, John. *Natural Law and Natural Rights*. 2d ed. Oxford: Oxford University Press, 2011.

Finnis, John. *Religion & Public Reason*. Oxford: Oxford University Press, 2011.

Fisher, David Hackett. *Champlain's Dream*. New York: Simon & Schuster, 2008.

Fisher, Roger and William Ury. *Getting to Yes: Negotiating Agreement without Giving In*. Boston: Houghton Mifflin, 1981.

Fitzhugh, George. *Cannibals All! Or Slaves without Masters*. Cambridge: Harvard University Press, 1988.

Fitzhugh, George. *Sociology for the South, or The Failure of the Free Society*. Richmond: A. Morris, 1854.

Fitzpatrick, John C., ed. *The Writings of George Washington*. Washington: U.S. Government Printing Office, 1939.

Foot, Philippa. *Natural Goodness*. Oxford: Oxford University Press, 2001.

Foot, Philippa. *Virtues and Vices and Other Essays in Moral Philosophy*. Oxford: University Press, 2002.

Forster, E. M. *Howards End*. New York: Knopf, 1991.

Fortescue, John. *De Laudibus Legum Angliae*. Trans. Francis Gregor. Cincinnati: Robert Clarke, 1874.

Franzero, Carlo Maria. *Beau Brummell: His Life and Times*. New York: John Day, 1958.

Froissart, Jean. *Chronicles*. Trans. Geoffrey Brereton. London: Penguin, 1968.

Frye, Northrop. *The Educated Imagination*. Bloomington: Indiana University Press, 1964.

Fukuyama, Francis. *Liberalism and its Discontents*. New York: Farrar, Straus and Giroux, 2022.

Galston, William A. *Liberal Purposes: Goods, Virtues, and Diversity in the Liberal State*. Cambridge: Cambridge University Press, 1991.

Gauthier, David. *Morals by Agreement*. Oxford: Oxford University Press, 1986.

Gautier, Léon. *Chivalry*. Trans. Henry Frithz. New York: Routledge, 1891.

Gellner, Ernest. *Nationalism*. New York: New York University Press, 1997.

Gellner, Ernest. *Nations and Nationalism*. Ithaca: Cornell University Press, 1983.

Gemes, Ken and John Richardson, eds. *Oxford Handbook of Nietzsche*. Oxford: Oxford University Press, 2013.

George, Robert P. *In Defense of Natural Law*. Oxford: Oxford University Press, 1999.

George, Robert P. *Making Men Moral: Civil Liberties and Public Morality*. Oxford: Oxford University Press, 1993.

George, Robert P. *Natural Law and Moral Inquiry: Ethics, Metaphysics, and Politics, in the Work of Germain Grisez*. Washington: Georgetown University Press, 1998.

Gibbard, Allan. *Meaning and Normativity*. Oxford: Oxford University Press, 2012.

Gibbon, Edward. *The Decline and Fall of the Roman Empire*. Chicago: University of Chicago Press, 1952.

Gide, André. *Journal 1926–1950*. Paris: Gallimard, 1997.

Gigerenzer, Gerd. *Gut Feelings: The Intelligence of the Unconscious*. New York, Penguin, 2008.

Gilder, George. *Wealth and Poverty*. San Francisco: ICS, 1993.

Gilligan, Carol. *In a Different Voice: Psychological Theory and Women's Development*. Cambridge: Harvard University Press, 1982.

Gilmore, Grant. *The Ages of American Law*. New Haven: Yale

University Press, 1977.

Girard, René. *I See Satan Fall Like Lightning.* Trans. James C. Williams. New York: Orbis Books, 2001.

Girouard, Mark. *The Return to Camelot: Chivalry and the English Gentleman.* New Haven: Yale University Press, 1982.

Glaeser, Edward L. *Triumph of the City.* New York: Penguin, 2011.

Glendon, Mary Ann. *Rights Talk: The Impoverishment of Political Discourse.* New York: Free Press, 1991.

Godwin, William. *An Enquiry Concerning Political Justice.* Oxford: Oxford University Press, 2013.

Goethe, Johann Wolfgang von. *The Maxims and Reflections of Goethe.* Trans. Bailey Saunders. London: Macmillan, 1906.

Goodin, Robert E., Philip Pettit, and Thomas W. Pogge, eds. *A Companion to Contemporary Political Philosophy.* Oxford: Blackwell, 1993.

Gourevitch, Philip. *We Wish to Inform You That Tomorrow We Will be Killed with Our Families: Stories from Rwanda.* New York: Farrar, Straus and Giroux, 1998.

Graham, R. B. Cunninghame. *A Vanished Arcadia: Being some Account of the Jesuits in Paraguay 1607 to 1767.* New York: Haskell House, 1968.

Gray, Francine du Plessix. *Simone Weil.* New York: Penguin, 2001.

Gray, John. *Post-Liberalism: Studies in Political Thought.* London: Routledge, 1993.

Greenfeld, Liah. *Nationalism: Five Roads to Modernity.* Cambridge: Harvard University Press, 1992.

Greer, Allan, ed. *The Jesuit Relations: Natives and Missionaries in Seventeenth Century North America.* Boston: Bedford/St. Martin's, 2000.

Greig, J. Y. T. *The Psychology of Laughter and Comedy.* New York: Cooper Square, 1923.

Grisez, Germain. *Contraception and the Natural Law.* Milwaukee: Bruce, 1964.

Grisez, Germain. *The Way of the Lord Jesus: Christian Moral Principles.* Chicago: Franciscan Herald Press, 1983.

Gronow, R. H. *The Reminiscences and Recollections of Captain*

Gronow. New York: Viking, 1964.

Haakonssen, Knud. *The Cambridge Companion to Adam Smith.* Cambridge: Cambridge University Press, 2006.

Habermas, Jürgen. *The Philosophic Discourse of Morality.* Trans. Frederick G. Lawrence. Cambridge: MIT Press, 1990.

Hagel, John H. and Alvin E. Roth. *The Handbook of Experimental Economics.* Princeton: Princeton University Press, 1995.

Hague, William. *William Wilberforce: The Life of the Great Anti-Slave Trade Campaigner.* Orlando: Harcourt, 2007.

Hamilton, Alexander. *The Papers of Alexander Hamilton.* Harold C. Syrett and Jacob E. Cooke, eds., New York: Columbia University Press, 1962.

Hamilton, Edith. *Mythology.* Boston: Little Brown, 1942.

Hamilton, J. S., ed. *Fourteenth Century England, volume VIII.* Woodbridge UK: Boydell Press, 2014.

Hamilton, W. D. *Narrow Roads of Gene Land.* Oxford: W. H. Freeman, 1996.

Hampshire, Stuart. *Innocence and Experience.* Cambridge: Harvard University Press, 1989.

Hankins, James, *Political Meritocracy in Renaissance Italy: The Virtuous Republic of Francesco Patrizi of Siena.* Cambridge: Harvard University Press, 2023.

Hankins, James, ed. *Renaissance Civic Humanism: Reappraisals and Reflections.* Cambridge: Cambridge University Press, 2000.

Hankins, James. *Virtue Politics: Soulcraft and Statecraft in Renaissance Italy.* Cambridge: Harvard University Press, 2020.

Hardin, Russell. *Morality within the Limits of Reason.* Chicago: University of Chicago Press, 1988.

Hare, R. M. *Moral Thinking,* Oxford: Oxford University Press, 1981.

Hare, R. M. *The Language of Morals.* Oxford: Oxford University Press, 1964.

Harman, Oren. *The Price of Altruism.* New York: Norton, 2010.

Hartz, Louis. *The Liberal Tradition in America.* Orlando: Harcourt, 1991.

Hayek, F. A. *Law, Legislation, and Liberty.* Chicago: University of Chicago Press, 2022.

Hazlitt, William. *Lectures on the English Comic Writers*. London: Oxford, 1907.

Himmelfarb, Gertrude. *Victorian Minds: A Study of Intellectuals in Crisis and Ideologies in Transition*. Chicago: Ivan R. Dee, 1995.

Hirschman, Albert O. *The Passions and the Interests*. Princeton: Princeton University Press, 2013.

Hirst, Paul Q. *The Pluralist Theory of the State: Selected Writings of G. D. H. Cole, J. N. Figgis and H. J. Laski*. London: Routledge, 2016.

Hobbes, Thomas. *Leviathan*. London: Penguin, 1968.

Hobson, Theo. *God Created Humanism: The Christian Basis of Secular Values*. London: Society for Promoting Christian Knowledge, 2017.

Hogg, James. *The Private Memoirs and Confessions of a Justified Sinner*. Edinburgh: Edinburgh University Press, 2002.

Holmes, Oliver Wendell Jr. *The Essential Holmes: Selections from the Letters, Speeches, Judicial Opinions, and Other Writings of Oliver Wendell Holmes, Jr*. Richard Posner, ed. Chicago: University of Chicago Press, 1992.

Holmes, Stephen. *The Anatomy of Antiliberalism*. Cambridge: Harvard University Press, 1993.

Hook, Sidney. *The Hero in History*. New York: Cosmo, 2008.

Howard, Michael, George J. Andreopoulis, and Mark R. Shulman, eds. *The Laws of War: Constraints on Warfare in the Western World*. New Haven, Yale University Press, 1994.

Howard, Philip. *The Death of Common Sense: How Law Is Suffocating America*. New York: Random House, 1994.

Howe, Mark de Wolfe. *Touched with Fire: Civil War Letters and Diary of Oliver Wendell Holmes, Jr*. New York: Fordham University Press, 2000.

Huizinga, John. *Homo Ludens: A Study of the Play Element in Culture*. Boston: Beacon, 1950.

Hume, David. *A Treatise of Human Nature*. L. A. Selby-Bigge, ed. Oxford: Oxford University Press, 1967.

Hume, David. *Enquiries*. 2d ed. L. A. Selby-Bigge, ed. Oxford: Oxford University Press, 1962.

Hume, David. *Hume: Political Essays*. Cambridge University

Press, 1994.

Hutcheson, Francis. *An Inquiry into the Original of Our Ideas of Beauty and Virtue.* Indianapolis: Liberty Fund, 2004.

Hyde, Lewis. *The Gift: Imagination and the Erotic Life of Property.* New York: Vintage, 1983.

Ignatieff, Michael. *The Warrior's Honor: Ethnic War and the Modern Conscience.* New York: Henry Holt, 1997.

Imbruglia, Girolamo. *The Jesuit Missions of Paraguay and a Cultural History of Utopia.* Trans. Mark Weyr. Leiden: Brill, 2017.

Jefferson, Thomas. *The Papers of Thomas Jefferson.* Julian P. Boyd, ed. Princeton: Princeton University Press, 1954.

Jefferson, Thomas. *Writings.* New York: Library of America, 1984.

Joinville, Jean de. *Joinville and Villehardoin: Chronicles of the Crusades.* London: Penguin, 2009.

Jones, Maldwyn. *American Immigration.* Chicago: University of Chicago Press, 1992.

Jones, Michael. *The Black Prince: England's Greatest Medieval Warrior.* New York: Pegasus, 2018.

Jones, Robert W. and Peter Coss, eds. *A Companion to Chivalry.* Woodbridge: Boydell, 2019.

Kaeuper, Richard W. *Holy Warriors: The Religious Ideology of Chivalry.* Philadelphia: Pennsylvania University Press, 2009.

Kant, Immanuel. *Critique of Practical Reason.* Trans. Lewis White Beck. Indianapolis: Bobbs-Merrill, 1956.

Kant, Immanuel. *Groundwork for the Metaphysics of Morals.* Rev. ed. Trans. Mary Gregor and Jens Timmermann. Cambridge: Cambridge University Press, 2012.

Kant, Immanuel. *Religion within the Boundaries of Mere Reason.* Trans. Allen Wood and George Di Giovani. Cambridge: Cambridge University Press, 1998.

Keen, Maurice. *Chivalry.* New Haven: Yale University Press, 1984.

Kekes, John. *Against Liberalism.* Ithaca: Cornell University Press, 1997.

Kenny, Anthony, ed. *Aquinas: A Collection of Critical Essays.* Notre Dame: Notre Dame University Press, 1969.

Kenton, Edna, ed. *The Jesuit Relations and Allied Documents.* New

York: Boni, 1925.

Keown, John and Robert P. George, eds. *Reason, Morality and Law: The Philosophy of John Finnis*. Oxford: Oxford University Press, 2013.

Kerouac, Jack. *On the Road*. New York: Library of America, 2007.

Kimmage, Michael. *The Conservative Turn: Lionel Trilling, Whittaker Chambers, and the Lessons of Liberal Anti-Communism*. Cambridge: Harvard University Press, 2009.

Koch, Adrienne and William Peden, eds. *The Selected Writings of John and John Quincy Adams*. New York: Knopf, 1946.

Kohn, Hans. *American Nationalism: An Interpretive Essay*. New York: Macmillan, 1957.

Kołakowski, Leszek. *God Owes Us Nothing*. Chicago: University of Chicago Press, 1998.

Kotkin, Joel. *The City: A Global History*. New York: Modern Library, 2006.

Knox, Bernard M. W. *The Heroic Temper: Studies in Sophoclean Tragedy*. Berkeley: California University Press, 1964.

Kraut, Richard. *Aristotle on the Human Good*. Princeton: Princeton University Press, 1989.

Kraye. Jill, ed. *The Cambridge Companion to Renaissance Humanism*. Cambridge: Cambridge University Press, 1996.

Ladurie, Emmanuel le Roy. *Love, Death and Money in the Pays d'Oc*. Trans. Alan Sheridan. New York: George Braziller, 1982.

Larmore, Charles. *The Morals of Modernity*. Cambridge: Cambridge University Press, 1996.

Lasch, Christopher. *The Revolt of the Elites and the Betrayal of Democracy*. New York: Norton, 1995.

Lewis, C. S. *The Screwtape Letters*. London: Macmillan, 1960.

Lévi-Strauss, Claude. *The Elementary Structures of Kinship*. Trans. James Harle Bell and John Von Sturmer. Boston: Beacon Press, 1969.

Lincoln, Abraham. *Lincoln: Speeches and Writings 1832–1858*. New York: Library of America, 2008.

Lincoln, Abraham. *Lincoln: Speeches and Writings 1859–1865*. New York: Library of America, 2009.

Lind, E. A. and Tom R. Tyler. *The Social Psychology of Procedural Justice*. New York: Plenum, 1988.

Liptay, John and Christopher Tollefson, eds. *Natural Law Ethics in Theory & Practice: A Joseph Boyle Reader*. Washington: Catholic University Press, 2020.

Llull, Raymond. *The Book of the Order of Chivalry*. Trans. Noel Fallows. Woodbridge: Boydell, 2013.

Locke, John. *A Letter Concerning Toleration and Other Writings*. Indianapolis: Liberty Fund, 2010.

Locke, John. *Questions Concerning the Law of Nature*. Ithaca: Cornell University Press, 1990.

Locke, John. *The Reasonableness of Christianity*. Stanford: Stanford University Press, 1958.

Locke, John. *Two Treatises of Government*. Student ed. Cambridge: Cambridge University Press, 1988.

Lowell, James Russell. *Political Essays*. Boston: Houghton Mifflin Company, 1888.

Loyola, Ignatius. *The Autobiography of St. Ignatius of Loyola*. New York: Harper, 1974.

Lutz, Donald. *The Origins of American Constitutionalism*. Baton Rouge, Louisiana State University Press, 1988.

Machiavelli, Niccolò. *Discourses on Livy*. Trans. Harvey C. Mansfield and Nathan Tarcov. Chicago: University of Chicago Press, 1996.

Machiavelli, Niccolò. *The Prince*. 2d ed. Quentin Skinner and Russell Price, eds. Cambridge: Cambridge University Press, 2019.

Macedo, Stephen. *Liberal Virtues: Citizenship, Virtue, and Community in Liberal Constitutionalism*. Oxford: Oxford University Press, 1991.

Malory, Sir Thomas. *Le Morte d'Arthur*. London: Macmillan, 1900.

MacIntyre, Alasdair. *After Virtue*. 2d ed. Notre Dame: Notre Dame University Press, 1984.

MacIntyre, Alasdair. *Is Patriotism a Virtue?* (The Lindley Lecture). Lawrence: Kansas University Press, 1984.

MacIntyre, Alasdair. *Three Rival Versions of Moral Inquiry*. Notre Dame: Notre Dame University Press, 1991.

MacIntyre, Alasdair. *Whose Justice? Which Rationality?* Notre Dame:

Notre Dame University Press, 1988.

Macfarlane, Alan. *The Origins of English Individualism: The Family Property and Social Transition.* Oxford: Blackwell, 1988.

Mackie, John. *Ethics: Inventing Right and Wrong.* London: Penguin, 1977.

Macpherson, C. B. *The Political Theory of Possessive Individualism: Hobbes to Locke.* Oxford: Oxford University Press, 1964.

Madison, James. *The Papers of James Madison.* Robert A. Rutland et al., ed. Chicago: University of Chicago Press, 1962.

Maier, Pauline. *American Scripture: Making the Declaration of Independence.* New York: Vintage, 1997.

Manent, Pierre. *An Intellectual History of Liberalism.* Trans. Rebecca Balinski. Princeton: Princeton University Press, 1994.

Mansfield, Harvey C. *Machiavelli's Effective Truth: Creating the Modern World.* Cambridge: Harvard University Press, 2023.

Mansfield, Harvey C. *Machiavelli's Virtue.* Chicago. University of Chicago Press, 1966.

Marilley, Suzanne M. *Women Suffrage and the Origins of Liberal Feminism in the United States, 1820–1920.* Cambridge: Harvard University Press, 1996.

Maritain, Jacques. *Man and the State.* Washington: Catholic University of America Press, 1998.

Markus, Friedrich. *The Jesuits: A History.* Trans. John Noël Dillon. Princeton: Princeton University Press, 2022.

Marsilius of Padua. *The Defender of the Peace.* Trans. Annabel Brett, Cambridge: Cambridge University Press, 2005.

Martin, Mike W. *Self-Deception and Morality.* Lawrence: Kansas University Press, 1986.

Mauss, Marcel, *The Gift: Forms and Functions of Exchange in Archaic Societies.* Trans. Ian Cunnison, New York: Norton, 1967.

McCormick, John P. *Carl Schmitt's Critique of Liberalism.* Cambridge: Cambridge University Press, 1997.

McCormick, John P. *Machiavellian Democracy.* Cambridge: Cambridge University Press, 2011.

McDonald, Forest. *Novus Ordo Seclorum: The Intellectual Origins of the Constitution.* Lawrence: Kansas University Press, 1985.

McKim, Robert and Jeff McMahan, eds. *The Morality of Nationalism*. Oxford: Oxford University Press, 1997.

Macneil, Ian. *The New Social Contract: An Inquiry into Modern Contractual Relations*. New Haven: Yale University Press, 1980.

McWhorter, John. *Woke Racism: How a New Religion Has Betrayed Black America*. New York: Portfolio/Penguin, 2021.

Mele, Alfred R. *Self-Deception Unmasked*. Princeton: Princeton University Press, 2001.

Merrill, Walter M. *Against Wind and Tide: A Biography of Wm. Lloyd Garrison*. Cambridge: Harvard University Press, 1963.

Milgram, Stanley. *Obedience to Authority: An Experimental View*. New York: Harper & Row, 1974.

Mill, John Stuart. *Collected Works*. Indianapolis: Liberty Fund, 2006.

Mill, John Stuart. *On Liberty*. London: Penguin, 1985.

Mill, John Stuart. *Three Essays on Religion*. New York: Henry Holt, 1879.

Milligan, Burton A., ed. *Three Renaissance Classics*, New York: Scribner's, 1953.

Milton, John, *Areopagitica and Other Writings*. London: Penguin, 2014.

Miner, Brad. *The Complete Gentleman: The Modern Man's Guide to Chivalry*. Rev. ed. Washington: Regnery, 2021.

Moore, G. E. *Principia Ethica*. Rev. ed. Cambridge: Cambridge University Press, 1993.

Montaigne. *The Complete Essays*. Trans. Donald M. Frame. Stanford: Stanford University Press, 1958.

Montesquieu, Charles-Louis de Secondat. *The Spirit of the Laws*. Trans. Anne M. Cohler, Basia Carolyn Miller, and Harold Samuel Stone. Cambridge: Cambridge University Press, 1989.

Murdoch, Iris, *The Sovereignty of Good*. London: Routledge, 2001.

Murphy, Mark C. *Natural Law and Practical Rationality*. Cambridge: Cambridge University Press, 2001.

Murray, Venetia. *An Elegant Madness: High Society in Regency England*. New York: Viking, 1999.

Nagel, Thomas. *The Possibility of Altruism*. Princeton: Princeton University Press, 1970.

Nagel, Thomas. *The View from Nowhere.* Oxford: Oxford University Press, 1986.

Namier, Lewis. *The Structure of Politics at the Accession of George III.* 2d ed. London: Macmillan, 1957.

Nauert, Charles G. *Humanism and the Culture of Renaissance Europe.* Cambridge: Cambridge University Press, 1995.

Nelson, Eric. *The Theology of Liberalism: Political Philosophy and the Justice of God,* Cambridge: Harvard University Press, 2019.

Newman, John Henry Cardinal. *The Idea of a University.* London: Longmans, Green, 1907.

Nicolson, Harold. *Diaries and Letters: The War Years 1939–1945.* New York: Atheneum, 1967.

Nowak, Martin A. *Super Cooperators: Altruism, Evolution, and Why We Need Each Other to Succeed.* New York: Free Press, 2011.

Nozick, Robert. *Anarchy, State, and Utopia.* New York: Basic Books, 1974.

Oakeshott, Michael. *Rationalism in Politics and Other Essays.* London: Methuen, 1962.

Oakeshott, Michael. *The Voice of Liberal Learning.* Indianapolis: Liberty Fund, 2001.

O'Connor, Flannery. *Collected Works.* New York: Library of America, 1988.

Off, Carol. *The Lion, the Fox, & the Eagle: A Story of Generals and Justice in Rwanda and Yugoslavia,* Toronto: Random House Canada, 2000.

Olson, Mancur. *Power and Prosperity: Outgrowing Communist and Capitalist Dictatorships.* New York: Basic Books, 2000.

Olson, Mancur. *The Logic of Collective Action: Public Goods and the Theory of Groups.* 2d ed. Cambridge: Harvard University Press, 1971.

Ortega y Gasset, José. *Meditations on Quixote.* Trans. Evelyn Rugg & Diego Marín. New York: Norton, 1961.

Orwell, George. *My Country Right or Left.* New York: Harcourt, Brace, and World, 1968.

Orwell, George. *The Penguin Essays of George Orwell.* London: Penguin Books, 1984.

Painter, Sidney. *French Chivalry: Chivalric Ideas and Practices in Medieval France*. Ithaca: Cornell University Press, 1940.

Pangle, Lorraine. *Aristotle and the Philosophy of Friendship*, Cambridge: Cambridge University Press, 2008.

Parfit, Derek. *Equality or Priority* (The Lindley Lecture). Lawrence: University of Kansas Press, 1991.

Parfit, Derek. *On What Matters 1*. Oxford: Oxford University Press, 2011.

Parfit, Derek. *On What Matters 2*. Oxford: Oxford University Press, 2011.

Parfit, Derek. *On What Matters 3*, Oxford: Oxford University Press, 2017.

Parfit, Derek. *Reasons and Persons*. Oxford: Oxford University Press, 1986.

Parkman, Francis. *France and England in North America: Pioneers of France in the New World*. New York: Library of America, 1983.

Pascal, Blaise. *Œuvres*. Paris: Gallimard, 1987.

Pascal, Blaise. *Œuvres Complètes*, volume 2. Paris: Gallimard, 2000.

Paul, Ellen Frankel, Fred D. Miller, and Jeffrey Paul, eds. *Human Flourishing*. Cambridge: Cambridge University Press, 1999.

Paul, Ellen Frankel, Fred D. Miller, and Jeffrey Paul, eds. *Natural Law and Modern Moral Philosophy*. Cambridge: Cambridge University Press, 2001.

Perreau-Saussine, Émile. *Alasdair MacIntyre: An Intellectual Biography*. Trans. Nathan J. Pinkoski. Notre Dame: University of Notre Dame Press, 2022.

Perreau-Saussine, Emile. *Catholicism and Democracy: An Essay in the History of Political Thought*. Princeton: Princeton University Press, 2012.

Pettit, Philip. *Republicanism: A Theory of Freedom and Government*. Oxford: Oxford University Press, 1997.

Pigden, Charles, ed. *Hume on Is and Ought: New Essays*. London: Palgrave-Macmillan, 2010.

Pisan, Christine de. *The Book of Deeds of Arms and of Chivalry*. Trans. Tracy Adams. University Park: Pennsylvania State University Press, 1999.

Plato. *The Collected Dialogues*. Trans. Paul Shorey. New York: Pantheon, 1961.

Pocock, J. G. A. *The Machiavellian Moment: Florentine Political Thought and the Atlantic Republican Tradition*. Princeton: Princeton University Press, 2003.

Pocock, J. G. A. *Virtue, Commerce, and History: Essays on Political Thought and History, Chiefly in the Eighteenth Century*. Cambridge: Cambridge University Press, 1985.

Polyani, Karl. *The Great Transformation: The Political and Economic Origins of our Time*. 2d ed. Boston: Beacon Press, 2001.

Popper, K. R. *The Open Society and its Enemies*. London: Routledge, 1945.

Poser, Norman S. *Lord Mansfield: Justice in the Age of Reason*. Montreal: McGill-Queen's University Press, 2013.

Posner, Eric and Alan O. Sykes. *Economic Foundations of International Law*. Cambridge: Harvard University Press, 2013.

Potts, Timothy C. *Conscience in Medieval Philosophy*. Cambridge, Cambridge University Press, 1980.

Prunier, Gérard. *The Rwanda Crisis: History of a Genocide*. New York: Columbia University Press, 1995.

Pullen, H. F. *The Shannon and the Chesapeake*. Toronto: McClelland and Stewart, 1970.

Putnam, Robert. *Bowling Alone: The Collapse and Revival of American Community*. New York: Simon & Schuster, 2000.

Rahner, Hugo. *Man at Play*. London: Burns & Oates, 1965.

Rawls, John. *A Brief Inquiry into the Meaning of Sin and Faith*. Cambridge: Harvard University Press, 2010.

Rawls, John. *A Theory of Justice*, Cambridge: Harvard University Press, 1971.

Rawls, John. *Justice as Fairness: A Restatement*. Cambridge: Harvard University Press, 2001.

Raz, Joseph. *The Morality of Freedom*. Oxford: Oxford University Press, 1986.

Reeves, Richard V. *Of Boys and Men: Why the Modern Male is Struggling, Why it Matters, and What to Do About It*. Washington: Brookings, 2022.

Reid, Herbert. *The Sense of Glory*. Cambridge: Cambridge University Press, 1933.

Reid, Thomas. *An Inquiry into the Human Mind on the Principles of Common Sense*. Derek R. Brookes, ed. University Park: Pennsylvania State University Press, 1997.

Renan, Ernest. *Qu'est-ce qu'une nation?* Paris: Presses-Pocket, 1992.

Rhees, Rush. *Discussions of Simone Weil*. Albany: SUNY Press, 2000.

Ridley, Matt. *The Origins of Virtue*. London: Penguin, 1997.

Roché, Henri-Pierre. *Jules et Jim*. Paris: Folio, 1979.

Rorty, Richard. *Contingency, Irony, and Solidarity*. New York: Cambridge University Press, 1989.

Rosen, Jeffrey. *The Pursuit of Happiness: How Classical Writers on Virtue Inspired the Lives of the Founders and Defined America*. New York: Simon & Shuster, 2024.

Rossiter, Clinton. *Conservatism in America*. Cambridge: Harvard University Press, 1982.

Roth, Alvin E., ed. *Game-Theoretic Models of Bargaining*. Cambridge: Cambridge University Press, 1985.

Ruskin, John. *The Stones of Venice*. Sunnyside: George Allen, 1886.

Russell, Daniel C., ed. *The Cambridge Companion to Virtue Ethics*. Cambridge: Cambridge University Press, 2013.

Sahlins, Marshall. *Stone Age Economics*. Chicago: Aldine-Atherton, 1972.

Sandel, Michael. *Liberalism and the Limits of Justice*. Cambridge: Cambridge University Press, 1982.

Sanders, Barry. *Sudden Glory: Laughter as Subversive History*. Boston: Beacon, 1995.

Sandoz, Ellis, ed. *Political Sermons of the American Founding Era 1730–1805*. 2d ed. Indianapolis: Liberty Fund, 1998.

Sandoz, Ellis, ed. *The Roots of Liberty: Magna Carta, Ancient Constitution, and the Anglo-American Tradition of Rule of Law*. Indianapolis: Liberty Fund, 1993.

Santayana, George. *Character and Opinion in the United States*. New York: Scribner's, 1924.

Sarreal, Julia J. S. *The Guaraní and their Missions: A Socioeconomic History*. Stanford: Stanford University Press, 2014.

Sattin, Anthony. *Nomads: The Wanderers who Shaped our World.* New York: Norton, 2022.

Saul, Nigel. *Chivalry in Medieval England.* Cambridge: Harvard University Press, 2011.

Scanlon, T. M. *Being Realistic about Reasons.* Oxford: Oxford University Press, 2014.

Scanlon, T. M. *What We Owe Each Other.* Cambridge: Harvard University Press, 1998.

Scanlon, T. M. *Why Does Inequality Matter?* Oxford: Oxford University Press, 2018.

Schama, Simon. *Dead Certainties (Unwarranted Speculations).* New York: Knopf, 1991.

Schmitt, Carl. *Political Theology. Four Chapters on the Concept of Sovereignty.* Trans. George Schwab. Chicago: Chicago University Press, 2005.

Schmitt, Carl. *The Concept of the Political.* Trans. George Schwab. Chicago: University of Chicago Press, 1995.

Schumpeter, Joseph A. *Capitalism, Socialism and Democracy.* London: Routledge, 1942.

Sedgwick, Henry Dwight. *In Praise of Gentlemen.* Boston: Little, Brown, 1935.

Segal, Robert A., ed. *In Quest of the Hero.* Princeton: Princeton University Press, 1990.

Sesardic, Neven. *Making Sense of Heritability.* Cambridge: Cambridge University Press, 2005.

Shaftesbury, Earl of. *Characteristics of Men, Manners, Opinions, Times.* Cambridge: Cambridge University Press, 1999.

Siedentop, Larry. *Inventing the Individual: The Origins of Western Liberalism.* Cambridge: Harvard University Press, 2014.

Silverglate, Harvey A. *Three Felonies a Day: How the Feds Target the Innocent.* New York: Encounter Books, 2009.

Simmons, A. John. *On the Edge of Anarchy: Locke, Consent, and the Limits of Society.* Princeton: Princeton University Press, 1993.

Simmons, A. John. *The Lockean Theory of Rights.* Princeton: Princeton University Press, 1992.

Singer, Peter, ed. *A Companion to Ethics.* Oxford: Blackwell, 1991.

Sitwell, Edith. *English Eccentrics.* London: Folio Society, 1994.

Skinner, Quentin, *The Foundations of Modern Political Thought,* Cambridge: Cambridge University Press, 1978.

Skinner, Quentin. *The Renaissance.* Cambridge: Cambridge University Press, 1998.

Skinner, Quentin. *Visions of Politics: Renaissance Virtues.* Cambridge: Cambridge University Press, 2002.

Smith, Adam. *An Inquiry into the Nature and Causes of the Wealth of Nations.* Indianapolis: Liberty Fund, 1981.

Smith, Adam. *The Theory of Moral Sentiments.* D. D. Raphael and A. L. MacFie, eds. Indianapolis: Liberty Fund, 1982.

Smith, Tara. *Ayn Rand's Normative Ethics: The Virtuous Egoist.* Cambridge University Press, 2006.

Sober, Elliot and David Sloan Wilson, *Unto Others: The Evolution and Psychology of Unselfish Behavior.* Cambridge: Harvard University Press, 1998.

Solomon, Robert C. *The Passions: Emotions and the Meaning of Life.* Indianapolis: Hackett, 1993.

Solomon, Robert C., ed. *Thinking about Feeling: Contemporary Philosophers on Emotions.* Oxford: Oxford University Press, 2004.

Sommers, Christina Hoff. *The War Against Boys: How Misguided Policies are Harming our Young Men.* New York: Simon & Shuster, 2013.

Sommers, Christina Hoff. *Who Stole Feminism: How Women Have Betrayed Women.* New York: Simon & Shuster, 1994.

Stacey, C. P. *Quebec, 1759.* Toronto: Macmillan, 1959.

Stark, Rodney. *For the Glory of God: How Monotheism Led to Reformations, Science, Witch-hunts, and the End of Slavery.* Princeton: Princeton University Press, 2003.

Stark, Rodney. *The Rise of Christianity.* San Francisco: HarperSanFrancisco, 1997.

Stark, Rodney. *The Victory of Reason: How Christianity Led to Freedom, Capitalism, and Western Success,* New York: Random House, 2005.

Starn, Randolph. *Ambrogio Lorenzetti: The Palazzo Publico, Siena.* New York: George Braziller, 1994.

Stendhal. *Le Rouge et le Noir*, in I *Œuvres romanesques complètes.* Paris: Gallimard, 2005.

Stephen, James Fitzjames. *Liberty, Equality, Fraternity.* 2d ed. New York: Holt & Williams, 1874.

Stevenson, C. L. *Facts and Values: Studies in Ethical Analysis.* New Haven: Yale University Press, 1963.

Stocker, Michael and Elizabeth Hegeman. *Valuing Emotions.* Cambridge: Cambridge University Press, 1996.

Stoner, James. *Common Law and Liberal Theory: Coke, Hobbes, and the Origins of American Constitutionalism.* Lawrence: University of Kansas Press, 1992.

Strachey, Lytton. *Eminent Victorians.* New York: G. P. Putnam, 1918.

Strauss, Leo. *Liberalism Ancient and Modern.* Chicago: Chicago University Press, 1968.

Strauss, Leo. *Thoughts on Machiavelli.* Chicago: Chicago University Press, 1958.

Sykes, Charles J. *A Nation of Victims: The Decay of the American Character.* New York: St. Martin's Press, 1992.

Tamir, Yael. *Liberal Nationalism.* Princeton: Princeton University Press, 1993.

Taylor, Charles. *Sources of the Self: Making of the Modern Identity.* Cambridge: Harvard University Press, 1989.

Taylor, Charles. *The Ethics of Authenticity.* Cambridge: Harvard University Press, 1992.

Taylor, Charles. *The Language Animal: The Full Shape of the Human Linguistic Capacity.* Cambridge: Harvard University Press, 2016.

Thiele, Leslie Paul. *Friedrich Nietzsche and the Politics of the Soul: A Study in Heroic Individualism.* Princeton: Princeton University Press, 1990.

Thompson, Richard F. and Stephen A. Madigan. *Memory: The Key to Consciousness.* Washington: Joseph Henry, 2005.

Thwaites, Reuben Gold, ed. *The Jesuit Relations and Allied Documents.* Cleveland: Burrows, 1896–1900.

Timbs, John. *English Eccentrics and Eccentricities.* Detroit: Singing Tree, 1969.

Titmuss, Richard M. *The Gift Relationship: From Human Blood to Social Policy.* New York: Pantheon, 1971.

Tocqueville, Alexis de. *Democracy in America.* Trans. Harvey C. Mansfield and Delba Winthrop. Chicago: Chicago University Press, 2000.

Toll, Ian W. *Six Frigates: The Epic History of the Founding of the U.S. Navy.* New York: Norton, 2006.

Tolstoy, Leo. *What Then Must We Do?* Trans. Aylmer Maude. London: World's Classics, 1925.

Toulmin, Stephen. *An Examination of the Place of Reason in Ethics.* Cambridge: Cambridge University Press, 1964.

Trevelyan, G. M. *England Under the Stuarts.* London: Folio, 1996.

Trilling, Diana. *The Beginning of the Journey.* New York: Harcourt, Brace, 1993.

Trilling, Lionel. *The Liberal Imagination.* New York: New York Review Books, 2008.

Trilling, Lionel. *The Middle of the Journey.* New York: New York Review Books, 2008.

Trinkhaus, Charles. *In our Image and Likeness: Humanity and Divinity in Italian Humanist Thought.* Notre Dame: Notre Dame University Press, 1995.

Troyes, Chrétian de. *Arthurian Romances.* London: Penguin, 1991.

Tuck, Richard. *Natural Rights Theories: Their Origin and Development.* Cambridge: Cambridge University Press, 1979.

Turner, Frederick Jackson. *The Frontier in American History.* Mineola: Dover, 1996.

Unger, Roberto. *The Critical Legal Studies Movement.* Cambridge: Harvard University Press, 1983.

Veatch, Henry B. *For an Ontology of Morals.* Chicago: Northwestern University Press, 1971.

Veblen, Thorstein. *The Theory of the Leisure Class: An Economic Study of Institutions.* New York: Macmillan, 1899.

Viroli, Maurizio. *Machiavelli's God.* Trans. Antony Shugaar, Princeton: Princeton University Press, 2010.

Vries, Hent De and Lawrence E. Sullivan, eds. *Political Theologies, Public Religions in a Post-Secular World.* New York: Fordham

University Press, 2006.

Waddell, Helen. *The Wandering Scholars*. Boston: Houghton, Mifflin, 1927.

Waldron, Jeremy. *God, Locke, and Equality: Christian Foundations in Locke's Political Thought*. Cambridge: Cambridge University Press, 2002.

Waldron, Jeremy. *One Another's Equals: The Basis of Human Equality*. Cambridge: Harvard University Press, 2017.

Walzer, Michael. *The Struggle for a Decent Politics: On "Liberal" as an Adjective*. New Haven: Yale University Press, 2023.

Warren, Robert Penn, *The Legacy of the Civil War: Meditations on the Centennial*. New York: Random House, 1961.

Washington, Booker T. *My Larger Education, Being Chapters from my Experience*. Garden City: Doubleday Page, 1911.

Washington, George. *Writings*. New York: Library of America, 1997.

Weber, Max. *The Protestant Ethic and the Spirit of Capitalism*, London: Routledge, 2001.

Weil, Simone. *L'Enracinement*. Paris: Gallimard, 1949.

Whelan, Edward. *The Union of the British Provinces*. Charlottetown: Haszard, 1865.

Williams, George C. *Adaptation and Natural Selection: A Critique of Some Current Evolutionary Thought*, Princeton: Princeton University Press, 1966.

Williams, George C., ed. *Group Selection*. New Brunswick: Aldine, 2008.

Wills, Garry. *Inventing America: Jefferson's Declaration of Independence*. Garden City: Doubleday, 1978.

Wilson, A. N. *The Victorians*. New York: Norton, 2003.

Wilson, E. O. *On Human Nature*. Cambridge: Harvard University Press, 1978.

Wilson, E. O. *Sociobiology: The New Synthesis*. Cambridge: Harvard University Press, 1975.

Wilson, James Q. *Moral Judgment*. New York: Basic, 1997.

Wilson, James Q. *The Moral Sense*. New York: Free Press, 1993.

Wilson, Woodrow. *Congressional Government: A Study in American Politics*. Mineola: Dover, 2006.

Wise, Steven M. *Though the Heavens May Fall: The Landmark Trial that Led to the End of Human Slavery*. New York: Perseus, 2005.

Witte, John. *The Blessings of Liberty: Human Rights and Religious Freedom in the Western Legal Tradition*. Cambridge: Cambridge University Press, 2021.

Wittgenstein, Ludwig. *Culture and Value*. Trans. Peter Winch, Chicago: Chicago University Press, 1980.

Wollheim, Richard. *On the Emotions*. New Haven: Yale University Press, 1999.

Wood, Gordon S. *The Creation of the American Republic, 1776–1787*. Chapel Hill: North Carolina University Press, 1998.

Wood, Gordon S. *The Radicalism of the American Revolution*. New York: Vintage, 1993.

Yolton, J. W. *John Locke: Problems and Perspectives*. Cambridge: Cambridge University Press, 1969.

Zahavi, Amotz and Avishag Zahavi. *The Handicap Principle: A Missing Piece of Darwin's Puzzle*. Oxford: Oxford University Press, 1997.

ENDNOTES

CHAPTER 1

1   Schmitt, *Concept of the Political*, 26, 51.
2   Id., 40–45, 79.
3   *Schmitt, Political Theology*, 5.
4   Cortés, *Essays on Catholicism*, 42.
5   Rossiter, *Conservatism in America*, 71.
6   Trilling, *The Liberal Imagination*, xv.
7   Gide, *Journal*, 715 (July 16, 1940); 722 (July 28, 1940).
8   Id., 702, 705, 837 (June 21, 1940); (June 26, 1940); (Oct. 10, 1942).
9   Quoted in Hirst, *The Pluralist Theory of the State*, 116.
10 Mill, *On Liberty*, 151.
11 Parfit, *Reasons and Persons*, 46.
12 Larmore, *The Morals of Modernity*, 152–67.
13 So are many Integralists. They admire Notre Dame's John Finnis, who thinks we're presented with a list of incommensurable goods, such as friendship, knowledge, play, and religion, and that there is no single measure of value or objective way to say which is best. Finnis, *Natural Law*, 93; John Finnis, "Commensuration and Public Reason," in Chang, *Incommensurability, Incomparability and Practical Reason*, 215.

CHAPTER 2

1   Hume, *Treatise*, 516; John Rawls, "Two Concepts of Rules," *Philosophical Review* 64 (1955): 3.

2   David Hume, "Of the Original Contract," in *Hume: Political Essays*, 186, 193; Simmons, *On the Edge of Anarchy*, 215; Ronald Dworkin, *The Original Position*, in Daniels, *Readings Rawls*, 18; Buckley, *Just Exchange*, 26–27.

3   Rawls, *A Theory of Justice*, 343.

4   Gauthier, *Morals by Agreement*, 4; Smith, *Ayn Rand's Normative Ethics*, 17.

5   Montesquieu, *The Spirit of the Laws*, 389–90 at xxi.20, quoted in Hirschman, xxii.

6   Gauthier, *Morals by Agreement*, 268; Hume, *Enquiries: The Principles of Morals*, 190–91.

7   Blackburn, *Ruling Passions*, 137–44; Finnis, *Natural Law*, 142–44; Finnis, *Aquinas*, 113–16.

8   Aristotle, *Nichomachean Ethics*, 1088 at 1169b7. Pangle, *Aristotle and the Philosophy of Friendship*, 152–54.

9   See Parfit, *Equality or Priority*, 19 ff.

10 John C. Harsanyi, "Can the Maximin Principle Serve as a Basis for Morality? A Critique of John Rawls's Theory," *American Political Science Review* 69 (1975): 594.

11 Rawls, *A Theory of Justice*, 15.

12 In *Justice as Fairness*, Rawls amended his theory of justice to incorporate a requirement of fair equality of opportunity, as well as policies to curb excessive wealth concentration. Id., 43–44.

13 Pascal, *Œuvres*, volume 2, 754 at *Pensée* 483.

14 *Hume, Treatise*, 469–70; Hare, *The Language of Morals*, 28–31, 82, 92–93.

15 Grisez, *Christian Moral Principles*, 105.

16 S.T. I-II, q.94, a.2–3. See also Finnis, *Natural Law*, 36; Finnis, *Aquinas*, 102; George, *In Defense of Natural Law*, 37.

17 Grisez, *Contraception*, 62. F. H. Buckley, "Contra Naturam," *Northern Illinois University Law Review* 43 (2022): 98.

18 Moore, *Principia Ethica*, 118.

19 Taylor, *Sources of the Self*, 77–78.

CHAPTER 3

1 Becker, *The Declaration of Independence*, 27. See also Hartz, *The Liberal Tradition in America*, 78.

2 John Dunn, "The Politics of Locke in England and America in the Eighteenth Century," in Yolton, *John Locke*, 67.

3 Taylor, *Sources of the Self*, 261.

4 Jefferson, *Papers*, volume 10, 443–455 (22 June–31 December 1786).

5 Hutcheson, *Inquiry into the Original*, 93–103.

6 Cicero, *On Duties*, 23–25 at I.vii.22.

7 Plato, *Protagoras*, 352c–d, 357c–358d. Socrates makes the same argument in the *Meno*, 77b–78b.

8 Nestar Russell and John Picard, Book Review, *Journal of the History of the Behavioral Sciences* 49 (2013): 221.

CHAPTER 4

1 Smith, *Moral Sentiments*, 9.

2 Hume, *Enquiries*, 169 at I.i.

3 Jesse Prinz, "Is Empathy Necessary for Morality?" in Coplan, *Empathy*, 211; Stephan Darwall, "Empathy, Sympathy, Care," *Philosophical Studies* 89 (1998): 261.

4 Onora O'Neill, "Kant's Virtues," in Crisp, *How Should One Live*, 77.

5 Thompson and Madigan, *Memory*, 61; Wilson, *Moral Sense*, 123–24.

6 Alvin E. Roth, "Laboratory Experimentation in Economics: A Methodological Overview," The Economic Journal 98 (1988): 979–83.

7 Alvin E. Roth and Michael Malouf, "Game-theoretic Models and the Role of Information in Bargaining," *Psychological Review* 86 (1979): 574.

8 Daniel Kahneman, Jack L. Knetsch, and Richard Thaler, "Fairness and the Assumptions of Economics," *The Journal of Business* 59 (1986): S285; Werner Guth, Rolf Schmittberger, and Bernd Schwarze, "An Experimental Analysis of Ultimatum Bargaining," *Journal of Economic Behavior & Organization* 3 (1982): 367.

9   See Olmstead and Rhode, "Rationing Without Government: The West Coast Gas Famine of 1920," *The American Economic Review* 75 (1985): 1044, 1052–53; Frank, *Passions Within Reason*, 177–78.

10 Robert Trivers, "The Evolution of Reciprocal Altruism," *The Quarterly Review of Biology* 46 (1971): 35–57.

11 Wilson, *Sociobiology*, ch. 27.

12 Sober, *Unto Others*, 301–02.

13 Wilson, *On Human Nature*, 19, 153.

CHAPTER 5

1   Whelan, *Union of the British Provinces*, 9.

2   Loyola, *Autobiography*, 21.

3   Blackburn, *Harvest of Souls*, 59.

4   Thwaites, *Jesuit Relations*, volume 5, 211. The *Relations* were published in the 1890s as a seventy-three-volume compilation edited by Reuben Gold Thwaites (hereafter *JR*).

5   *JR*, volume 12, 117–19.

6   *JR*, volume 6, 229.

7   Id.

8   *JR*, volume 10, 211–215.

9   Blackburn, *Harvest of Souls*, 39.

10 *JR*, volume 10, 89.

11 *JR*, volume 10, 91.

12 Bancroft, *History of the United States*, 122.

13 *JR*, volume 31, 16–69.

14 Parkman, *France and England in North America*, volume 1, 566.

15 Michel Riquet, "Jesuites fondateurs de Republics II," *Revue des Deux Mondes* (février 1987): 291.

16 Caraman, *Lost Paradise*, 64, 116–18.

17 Caraman, *Lost Paradise*, 157–58; Sarreal, *Guaraní and their Missions*, 53–64; Imbruglia, *Jesuit Missions of Paraguay*, 15–19.

18 *JR*, volume 5, 247–53.

19 Smith, *Wealth of Nations*, volume 1, ii.2.

20 See Pratap Bhanu Mehta, "Self-interest and Other Interests," in

Haakonssen, *The Cambridge Companion to Adam Smith*, 246; Alexander Broadie, "Sympathy and the Impartial Spectator," in Haakonsen, 158.

21 Gilder, *Wealth and Poverty*, 21.

22 Alvin Roth, "Toward a Focal Point Theory of Bargaining," in Roth, *Game-Theoretic Models*, 259, 265–67; Macneil, 44–47.

23 Fisher and Ury, *Getting to Yes*; David Luban, "Bargaining and Compromise: Recent Work on Negotiation and Informal Justice," *Philosophy & Public Affairs* 14 (1985): 397, 399.

24 Macneil, 44-47; Stewart Macaulay, "Non-Contractual Relations in Business: A Preliminary Study," *American Sociological Review* 28 (1963): 55, 61.

25 Weber, *The Protestant Ethic*, 57.

26 *Merchant of Venice*, IV.i.197–98.

27 Hyde, *The Gift*, 25; Unger, *The Critical Legal Studies Movement*, 64.

28 *Merchant of Venice*, I.i.132, I.iii.93.

29 Mauss, *The Gift*, 10–11.

30 Miller McPherson, Lynn Smith-Lovin and Matthew E. Brashears, "Social Isolation in America: Changes in Core Discussion Networks over Two Decades," *American Sociological Review* 71 (2006): 353.

31 Mauss, *The Gift*, 11.

32 Matthew 10:8. *Alcoholics Anonymous*, 110.

33 Lévi-Strauss, *Elementary Structures of Kinship*, 115.

34 Sahlins, *Stone Age Economics*, 194.

35 Plato, *Apology*, 22c1–2.

36 Plato, *Apology* 31d2–3; Plato, *Phaedrus* 242b8–c2.

37 John 3:16.

38 Colossians 3:15.

39 Carlyle, *Past and Present*, 148.

40 Huizinga, *Homo Ludens*, 58–62; Franz Boas, "The Indians of British Columbia," *Popular Science Monthly* 32, March 1888: 631; Franz Boas, "The Social Organization and the Secret Societies of the Kwakiutl Indians." U.S. National Museum Annual Report for 1885, 342–43, Washington, DC: Smithsonian Institution, 1897.

41 Benedict, *Patterns of Culture*, 188.

42 Zahavi and Zahavi, *The Handicap Principle*. On spite, see Stuart A.

West and Andy Gardner, "Altruism, Spite, and Greenbeards," *Science* 327 (2010): 1341.

43 Ewen Callaway, "Size doesn't always matter for peacocks," *Nature*, April 18, 2011.

44 Amotz Zahavi recognized this as a costly signaling strategy, one which had earlier been identified by economist Michael Spence in "Job Market Signaling," *The Quarterly Journal of Economics* 87 (1973) 355.

45 *Complete Collection of State Trials*, volume 1, 353–65; "Passages in Parliament against Francis, Viscount St. Alban," in Bacon, Works, volume 4, 526.

46 558 U.S. 310, 360 (2010).

47 134 S. Ct. 1434 (2014).

Chapter 6

1 Talmon Joseph Smith, "The Greatest Wealth Transfer in History Is Here, With Familiar (Rich) Winners," *The New York Times*, May 14, 2023.

2 Laurence J. Kotlikoff and Lawrence H. Summers, "The Role of Intergenerational Transfers in Aggregate Capital Accumulation," *Journal of Political Economy* 89 (1981): 706.

3 Burke, *Reflections on the Revolution in France*, volume 8, 102.

4 Hamilton's breakthrough articles on inclusive fitness may be found in Chapter 2 of volume 1 of his collected essays, *Narrow Roads of Gene Land*. For a more extensive version of Hamilton's Law, in the statistical form proposed by George Price, see W. D. Hamilton, "Selfish and Spiteful Behavior in an Evolutionary Model," *Nature* 228 (1970): 1218, in *Narrow Roads of Gene Land*, 177–82.

5 Raj Chetty et al., Mobility Report Cards: The Role of Colleges in Intergenerational Mobility, NBER Working Paper 23618 (2017).

6 Lincoln, *Speeches and Writings, 1859–1865*, 85.

7 Fitzhugh, *Sociology for the South*, 248.

8 Wood, *The Radicalism of the American Revolution*, 71.

9 Raj Chetty et al., "The Fading American Dream: Trends in Absolute

Income Mobility Since 1940," *Science* 356 (2017): 398.

10 Bhashkar Mazumder, "The Apple Falls Even Closer to the Tree than We Thought: New and Revised Estimates of the Intergenerational Inheritance of Earnings," in Bowles, *Unequal Chances*, 80.

Chapter 7

1 Edmonds, *Parfit*, 160.

2 Kant, *Groundwork*, 23 at 4.408. However, Kant had to postulate the existence of God to show that the moral life would be a happy one. Kant, *Critique of Practical Reason*, 128–30 at II.ii.5.

3 Lutz, *The Origins of American Constitutionalism*, 140–41.

4 Matthew 12:48–50.

5 Virgil, *Aeneid*, vi.314.

6 Pascal, *Pensée* 211.

7 S.T. II, q.66, a.1–2.

8 Siedentop, *Inventing the Individual*, 337.

9 Dworkin, *Sovereign Virtue*, Part I. See also Raz, *Morality of Freedom*, ch. 9.

10 Maritain, *Man and the State*, 77.

11 Rawls, *Brief Inquiry*, 5; Paul Weithman, "On John Rawls's 'A Brief Inquiry into the Meaning of Sin and Faith,'" *Journal of Religious Ethics* 40 (2012): 557.

12 *Dred Scot v. Sandford*, 60 U.S. 393, 350 (1856) (McLean J., dissenting).

13 Vries, *Political Theologies*; see also Eagleton, *Reason, Faith, and Revolution.*

14 Berman, *Law and Revolution*, 85–199.

15 *Pierce v. Society of Sisters*, 268 U.S. 510 (1925).

16 Larmore, *Morals of Modernity*, 42.

17 Aquinas, *On Kingship*, 27 [49].

Chapter 8

1   Roland G. Usher, "James I and Sir Edward Coke," *The English Historical Review* 19 (1903), 664.

2   Fortescue, *De Laudibus Legum Angliae*, 148–49 at ch. 37.

3   Trevelyan, *England Under the Stuarts*, 105.

4   Julie R. O'Sullivan, "The Federal Criminal 'Code' Is a Disgrace: Obstruction Statutes as a Case Study," *Journal of Criminal Law and Criminology* 96 (2006): 643.

5   William Stuntz, "The Pathological Politics of Criminal Law," *Michigan Law Review* 100 (2001): 506, 511.

6   Gilmore, *Ages of American Law*, 111.

7   *Somerset v. Stewart*, 98 E.R. 499 (1772). William R. Cotter, "The Somerset Case and the Abolition of Slavery in England," *History* 79 (1994): 31. For a more cautious view of the case, see Poser, *Lord Mansfield*, 286 ff. Seven years before, William Blackstone had argued that slavery was illegal in England. Blackstone, *Commentaries*, 273 at volume 1, ch. 14. William M. Wiecek, "Somerset: Lord Mansfield and the Legitimacy of Slavery in the Anglo-American World," *University of Chicago Law Review* 42 (1974): 86, 98–99.

8   347 U.S. 483 (1954).

9   *Plessy v. Ferguson*, 163 U.S. 537 (1896).

10 319 U.S. 624 (1943).

11 319 U.S. 624, 642 (1943).

12 491 U.S. 397 (1989).

Chapter 9

1   Parkman, *France and England*, volume 2, 1392.

2   Schama, *Dead Certainties*, 17.

3   Dallaire, *Shake Hands with the Devil*, 42.

4   Id., 144.

5   Interview: General Romeo Dallaire, *Frontline WGBH*, April 1, 2004 (https://www.pbs.org/wgbh/pages/frontline/shows/ghosts/interviews/dallaire.html).

6   Holmes, *Essential Holmes*, 86, 82.

7   Milton, *Areopagitica*, 111.

8   Toll, *Six Frigates*, 411.

9   Arendt, *The Human Condition*, 176.

10 Froissart, *Chronicles*, 144.

11 Id., 178; Jones, 367–73, 405–08.

12 Llull, *Order of Chivalry*, 46.

13 Ortega y Gasset, *Meditations on Quixote*, 152.

14 Gautier, *Chivalry*, 2.

15 Llull, *Order of Chivalry*, 44.

16 Troyes, *Arthurian Romances*, 387.

17 Malory, *Le Morte d'Arthur*, volume 2, 106 at 10.56.

18 Gaston Paris, "Etudes sur les romans de la Table Ronde. Lancelot du Lac, II: La conte de la Charette," *Romania* 12 (1883): 519.

19 Oriel Feldman Hall et al., "Moral Chivalry: Gender and Harm Sensitivity Predict Costly Altruism," *Social Psychological & Personality Science* 7 (2016): 542.

20 Kathleen Daly, "Discrimination in the Criminal Courts: Family, Gender, and the Problem of Equal Treatment," *Social Forces* 66 (1989): 152; Darrell Steffensmeier and Stephen Demuth, "Does Gender Modify the Effects of Race-ethnicity on Criminal Sanctioning? Sentences for Male and Female White, Black, and Hispanic Defendants," *Journal of Quantitative Criminology* 22 (2006): 241.

CHAPTER 10

1   Girouard, *Return to Camelot*, 92–110.

2   Digby, *The Broad-Stone of Honour: Godefridus*, 130.

3   Nicolson, *Diaries and Letters*, 171.

4   Quoted in Blumenson, Patton Papers, 723.

5   Eric de Saint-Denis, "Fontenoy: Une bataille, un homme, un dialogue," *Histoire, Économie et Société* 4 (1985): 479. Hay recalled something rather different. He said he had pulled out a bottle and told the French he hoped they would not run away.

6 Arnold, *A French Eton*, 117.

7 Washington, *My Larger Education*, 70.

8 Newman, *The Idea of a University*, 208–09.

9 Id., 120–21

10 Sedgwick, *In Praise of Gentlemen*, 6–7.

11 Washington, *Writings*, 3–10.

12 Sedgwick, *In Praise of Gentlemen*, ix.

13 Malory, *Le Morte d'Arthur*, volume 2, 404–05 at 18.25.

Chapter 11

1 *Henry V*, IV.1.

2 10 U.S.C. § 933.

3 *Parker v. Levy*, 417 U.S. 733 (1974).

4 U.S. Ct. App. Armed Forces, 18-0372, June 27, 2019.

5 67 M.J. 127 (CAAF, 2009).

6 *United States v. Schumacher*, 11 M.J. 612 (A.C.M.R. 1981) (public drunkenness); *U.S. v. Frazier*, 34 M.J. 194 (C.M.A. 1992); *U.S. v. Orellana*, 62 M.J. 595 (C.C.A. 2005) (adultery).

7 148 U.S. 84 (1893).

8 John Barry, "The Day We Stopped the War," *Newsweek*, January 20, 1992.

9 Saul, *Chivalry in Medieval England*, 8.

10 Posner and Sykes, *Economic Foundations of International Law*, 190–97.

11 Rasul v. Bush, 542 U.S. 466 (2004).

12 542 U.S. 507 (2004).

13 548 U.S. 557 (2006).

14 553 U.S. 723 (2008).

15 Quoted in Ignatieff, *The Warrior's Honor*, 118.

Chapter 12

1   Hankins, *Political Meritocracy*, 93.

2   Dante, *Monarchy*, 8 at I.iv. Marsilius, *Defender of the Peace*, 12–13 at I.2, 127 at I.19.

3   Montesquieu, *Spirit of the Laws*, 157 at 11.6.

4   Nicolai Rubinstein, "Political Ideas in Sienese Art: The Frescoes by Ambrogio Lorenzetti and Taddeo di Bartolo in the Palazzo Pubblico," *Journal of the Warburg and Courtauld Institutes* 61 (1958): 179.

5   Cicero, *On Duties*, 23–25 at I.vii.22. Skinner, *Visions of Politics: Renaissance Virtues*, 46–47; Hankins, *Virtue Politics*, 45.

6   Marsilius, *Defender of the Peace*, 71 at I.12.8.

7   Baron, *In Search of Florentine Civic Humanism*, volume 1, 52.

8   Machiavelli, *The Prince*, 54.

9   Id., 60 at 18; Pocock, *The Machiavellian Moment*, 166, 177; Hankins, *Virtue Politics*, 463–75; Skinner, *The Renaissance*, 128–38.

10 Strauss, *Machiavelli*, 9.

11 Machiavelli, *Discourses*, 131.

12 Viroli, *Machiavelli's God*, 27.

13 Quentin Skinner, "Pre-humanist origins of republican ideas," in Bock, Skinner, and Viroli, *Machiavelli and Republicanism*, 121, 139–41. See also Baron, *In Search of Florentine Civic Humanism*, volume 2, 116; Nicolai Rubenstein, "Italian Political Thought 1450–1530," in Burns and Goldie, *Cambridge History of Political Thought*, 30, 46.

14 Elena Fasano Guarini, "Machiavelli and the Crisis of the Italian Republics," in Bock, Skinner, and Viroli, *In Search of Florentine Civic Humanism*, 17, 29–30.

15 Machiavelli, *Discourses*, 237–38 at III.8.

16 Id., 90 at I.lii.

17 Id., 110 at I.lv.

18 Samuel McClintock, "A Sermon on Occasion of the Commencement of the New-Hampshire Constitution," in Sandoz, *Political Sermons*, volume 1, 789.

19 John Adams to Mercy Otis Warren, April 16, 1776, in Koch and Peden, 57.

20 Washington to the Marquis de Lafayette, February 7, 1788, in Fitzpatrick, *Writings of George Washington*, volume 29, 410.

21 John Adams, Novanglus no. 2, in Adams, *Revolutionary Writings*, 406–07; Wood, *The Creation of the American Republic*, 32.

22 H. Trevor Colbourn and Richard Peters, "A Pennsylvania Farmer at the Court of King George: John Dickinson's London Letters, 1754–1756," *Pennsylvania Magazine of History and Biography* 86 (1962): 241, 286; Bailyn, *Ideological Origins*, 83–92.

23 Namier, *Structure of Politics*, 2.

24 Madison, *Papers*, volume 9, 348.

25 David Hume, "Idea of a Perfect Commonwealth," in Hume, *Political Essays*, 221; Douglas Adair, "That Politics May Be Reduced to a Science: David Hume, James Madison, and the Tenth Federalist," in Colbourn, *Fame and the Founding Fathers*, 132.

26 Farrand, *Records of the Federal Convention*, volume 1, 50. Other delegates subscribed to the filtration theory: James Wilson at Farrand, *Records of the Federal Convention*, volume 1, 133: John Dickinson at Farrand, *Records of the Federal Convention*, volume 1, 136; Elbridge Gerry at Farrand, *Records of the Federal Convention*, volume 1, 152; Gouverneur Morris at Farrand, *Records of the Federal Convention*, volume 2, 54. Hamilton subsequently endorsed filtration in the New York ratifying debates. Hamilton, *Papers*, volume 5, 41 (June 21, 1788).

27 Gordon S. Wood, "A Note on Mobs in the American Revolution," *William & Mary Quarterly* 23 (1966): 635; Pauline Maier, "Popular Uprisings," *William & Mary Quarterly* (third series) 27 (1970): 29, 33–34.

28 Farrand, *Records of the Federal Convention*, volume 1, 288 (June 18).

29 Farrand, *Records of the Federal Convention*, volume 1, at 242 n. (June 15).

30 Farrand, *Records of the Federal Convention*, volume 2, 19–20 (July 17).

31 He wrote despairingly to Jefferson that "the plan . . . will neither effectually answer its national object, nor prevent the local mischiefs which everywhere excite disgust agst. the State Governments." Farrand, *Records of the Federal Convention*, volume 3, 77 (italics in

original) (Sept. 6).

32 Buckley, *The Once and Future King*, 52–57.

33 Skinner, *The Renaissance*, 44–45; Nicolai Rubenstein, "Italian Political Thought 1450–1530," in Burns and Goldie, *Cambridge History of Political Thought*, 51.

34 In a regression analysis, presidential governments have been found to be more corrupt than parliamentary ones that lack a separation of powers. Buckley, *The Republic of Virtue*, Appendix A.

35 Abramoff, *Capitol Punishment*, 198.

36 Wilson, *Congressional Government*, 318.

37 Buckley, *The Way Back*, 281–86.

38 Buckley, *The Once and Future King*, Appendix B.

Chapter 13

1 Atkinson and Sices, *Machiavelli and His Friends*, 416 (to Francesco Vettori, April 16, 1527).

2 Machiavelli, *The Prince*, 26 at 85–86.

3 Id., 26 at 89, quoting Petrarch's *Italia mia*.

4 Polyani, *The Great Transformation*, 35.

5 Gellner, *Nationalism*, 74.

6 Goodin, *Companion to Contemporary Political Philosophy*, 3.

7 Godwin, *Enquiry Concerning Political Justice*, 53–54.

8 Berlin, *The Crooked Timber of Humanity*, 245. John M. Taurek, "Should the Numbers Count?" *Philosophy & Public Affairs* 6 (1977): 293.

9 Robert Frost, "The Death of the Hired Man."

10 Popper, *The Open Society and its Enemies*, volume 2, 47–49.

11 Orwell, *Penguin Essays*, 196 ("Wells, Hitler and the World State").

12 Warren, *Legacy of the Civil War*, 78.

13 Lincoln, *Speeches and Writings 1832–1858*, 456.

14 Renan, *Qu'est-ce qu'une nation?*, 13.

15 Fustel de Coulanges, *Questions historiques*, 6.

16 Rorty, *Contingency, Irony, and Solidarity*, 191.

Chapter 14

1   Mill, *On Liberty*, 31.
2   Roché, *Jules et Jim*, 161.
3   Mill, *On Liberty*, 34.
4   Id., 53.
5   Berlin, *Four Essays on Liberty*, 178.
6   S.T. II.ii, q.47, a.4.
7   Stendhal, *Le Rouge et le Noir*, 702.
8   Tocqueville, *Spirit of the Laws*, 244 at I.ii.7.
9   Santayana, *Character and Opinion*, 210.
10 James Surowiecki, "How Mozilla Lost its CEO," *The New Yorker*, April 4, 2014.
11 Joshua T. Katz, "The Culture of the Canceled," *Sapir* 7 (August 2022).

Chapter 15

1   George Orwell, *My Country Right or Left*, 59.
2   Leah Litman and Laurence H. Tribe, "It's Hard to Overstate How Awful the Latest Injunction Against the Biden Administration Is," *Slate*, July 5, 2023.
3   Dustin Volz, "GOP Lawmaker says FBI Inappropriately Searched his Name in Spying Database," *The Wall Street Journal*, March 9, 2023.
4   Lee Brown and Tamar Lapin, "Letter to WH suggests dad of 'sexually assaulted' girl a 'domestic terrorist,'" *New York Post*, October 13, 2021.
5   Tyler Pager, "Biden's stark warning: The U.S. is threatened by its own citizens," *The Washington Post*, September 3, 2022.
6   "The Right to Privacy," *Harvard Law Review* 4 (1890): 193.
7   *Griswold*, 410 U.S. 113 (1983); *Lawrence*, 539 U.S. 558 (2003).
8   Peter Roff, "How Long Before Harassment of Trump Officials Gets Out of Hand?," *Newsweek*, July 11, 2018.
9   Coke, *Selected Writings*, 137 (Semayne's Case).
10 *The Washington Post*, April 19, 2022.

CHAPTER 16

1   Trilling, *The Liberal Imagination*, 282. See Michael Knox Beran, "Liberal Humanism's Lost World," *City Journal*, January 2023.

2   Polyani, *The Great Transformation*, 136.

3   Clark, *Civilisation*, 329.

4   Tolstoy, 17.

5   Taylor, *Sources of the Self*, 47.

6   Thompson and Madigan, *Memory*, 2–3.

7   Locke, *Essay*, 289 at II.xxvii.

8   Rahner, *Man at Play*, 65–66.

9   *I Henry IV*, II.iv.393–486.

10 John 8:3-11.

11 Collingwood, *The Idea of History*, 202.

12 Ladurie, *Love, Death and Money*, 148.

13 Frye, *The Educated Imagination*, 64.

14 Camus, *Théâtre, recits, nouvelles*, 1518.

15 Camus, *Carnets*, volume 3, 240–41.

16 Wittgenstein, *Culture and Value*, 34.

17 O'Connor, *Collected Works*, 485.

CHAPTER 17

1   John 18:10–14.

2   See, e.g., Margaret Sullivan, "Quick to vilify antifa, but slow to explain it," *The Washington Post*, September 4, 2017; Carlos Lozada, "How antifa justifies stifling speech, clobbering supremacists," *The Washington Post*, September 3, 2017; Mark Bray, "What the 'alt-left' antifa activists actually believe," *The Washington Post*, August 20, 2017; Perry Stein, "What draws Americans to anarchy? It's more than just smashing windows," *The Washington Post*, August 10, 2017.

3   Stuart Kyle Duncan, "My Struggle Session at Stanford Law School," *The Wall Street Journal*, March 17, 2023.

4   Elie Mystal, "Protesting an Anti-Trans Trump Judge Isn't Disrespectful, It's American," *The Nation*, March 15, 2023.

5   Trilling, *The Middle of the Journey*, 256.

6   Id., xix.

7   Josh Christenson and Caitlin Doombos, "House GOP Passes Parents' Rights School Bill, after AOC, Dems cry 'Fascism,'" *New York Post*, March 24, 2023.

8   P. E. Moskowitz, "America's Suburbs are breeding Grounds for Fascism," *The Nation*, June 8, 2023.

9   Kimmage, *The Conservative Turn*, 185.

10 Hayek, *Law, Legislation, and Liberty*, 85.

11 Friedrich Hayek, "The Use of Knowledge in Society," *The American Economic Review* 35 (1945): 519.

12 Mill, *Collected Works*, volume 10, 120.

13 Montaigne, *Complete Essays*, 731 at iii.9.

14 S.T. I-II, q.94, a.5–6.

15 Pascal, *Œuvres complètes*, volume 2, 817 at *Pensée* 667.

16 Farrand, *Records of the Federal Convention*, volume 2, 643 (Sept. 17, 1787).

17 Id., 648.

CHAPTER 18

1   Hamilton, *Mythology*, 209.

2   Genesis 12:1.

3   Kerouac, *On the Road*, 7.

4   Hartz, *The Liberal Tradition*, 64–65.

5   Macfarlane, *Origins*, 153.

6   Berry, *The Margins of Late Medieval London*, 93–136.

7   Margaret F. Brinig & F. H. Buckley, "No-Fault Laws and At-Fault People," *International Review Of Law & Economics* 18 (1998): 325; F. H. Buckley & Margaret F. Brinig, "The Bankruptcy Puzzle," *The Journal of Legal Studies* 27 (1998): 187.

8   Genesis 4:14.

9   Job 1:7.

10 Charles M. Tiebout, "A Pure Theory of Local Expenditures," *Journal of Political Economy* 64 (1956): 416.

11 See Theodore Roosevelt, "Nationalism and Popular Rule," *The Outlook*, January 21, 1911.

12 Barry Weingast, "The Economic Role of Political Institutions: Market-Preserving Federalism and Economic Development," *Journal of Law, Economics & Organization* 11 (1995): 1.

Chapter 19

1 Finke and Stark, *The Churching of America*. The figure reached 70 percent in 1999 but Gallup reports that, with the rise of the "nones," it has now declined to 47 percent.

2 Reeves, *Of Boys and Men*, 24–29.

3 Sommers, *Who Stole Feminism*, 194–98.

4 Quoted in Sommers, *Who Stole Feminism*, 28.

5 Richard V. Reeves and Ember Smith, "The Male College Crisis is not just in Enrollment, but Completion," Brookings, October 8, 2021.

6 *Masterpiece Cakeshop v. Colorado Civil Rights Commission*, 584 U.S. ___ (2018).

7 *Bostock v. Clayton County*, 590 U.S. ___ (2020).

8 *Zdunski v. Erie 2-Chautauqua-Cattaraugus BOCES*, 2022 U.S. Dist. LEXIS 51575

9 Jeffrey Clark, "Female teacher fired, forced to apologize after saying 'good afternoon, girls' to students: Report," Fox News, April 17, 2023.

10 Jos Truitt, "Fallon Fox on Life as a Trans Athlete," *The Guardian*, February 16, 2015.

11 Denycia Thompson, "Retired Trans MMA Fighter Fallon Fox Boasts Punching TERFS on Twitter," *MMA News*, April 15, 2022.

12 Wesley J. Smith, "Oregon Legislation Would Allow Children to Decide About Abortion/Transgenderism Without Parental Consent," *National Review*, March 25, 2023.

Chapter 20

1 Hobbes, 125.
2 Hazlitt, *Lectures*, 7.
3 Baudelaire, *De l'essence du rire*, in *Œuvres Complètes*, 525–28.
4 Dryden, *Original and Progress of Satire*, in *Essays*, volume 2, 15, 104.
5 Robertson Davies, *Afterword*, in Leacock, *Literary Lapses*, 156.
6 Kant, 54 at I.1.
7 Elisabeth M. Landes and Richard A. Posner, "The Economics of the Baby Shortage," *The Journal of Legal Studies* 7 (1978): 323.
8 A. G. Sulzberger, "Yoga Faces Regulation, and Firmly Pushes Back," *The New York Times*, July 10, 2009.
9 Dick M. Carpenter and Lisa Knepper, "License to Work: A National Study—Burdens from Occupational Licensing," Institute for Justice, 2012.
10 Maxime Bernstein, "Some Portland officers responded to LGBTQ+ training with racist feedback, report says," *The Oregonian*, April 18, 2023.
11 Fenit Nirappil, "Loneliness poses profound public health threat, surgeon general says," *The Washington Post*, May 2, 2023.

Chapter 21

1 Goethe, *Maxims*, 96 at Maxim 174.
2 Hampshire, *Innocence and Experience*, 172.
3 Pocock, Virtue, *Commerce, and History*, 87–88.
4 Rorty, *Contingency, Irony, and Solidarity*, 189.
5 C. S. Lewis, *The Screwtape Letters*, ix.

INDEX